W9-DGT-850

JEWISH AND CHRISTIAN TEXTS
IN CONTEXTS AND RELATED STUDIES

Executive Editor
James H. Charlesworth

A HISTORY OF THE HASMONEAN STATE

Josephus and Beyond

Kenneth Atkinson

Bloomsbury T&T Clark
An imprint of Bloomsbury Publishing Plc

B L O O M S B U R Y
LONDON · OXFORD · NEW YORK · NEW DELHI · SYDNEY

Bloomsbury T&T Clark

An imprint of Bloomsbury Publishing Plc

Imprint previously known as T&T Clark

50 Bedford Square	1385 Broadway
London	New York
WC1B 3DP	NY 10018
UK	USA

www.bloomsbury.com

BLOOMSBURY, T&T CLARK and the Diana logo are trademarks of Bloomsbury Publishing Plc

First published 2016

British Library Cataloguing-in-Publication Data

A catalogue record for this book is available from the British Library.

ISBN:	HB:	978-0-56766-902-5
	ePDF:	978-0-56766-903-2
	ePub:	978-0-56766-904-9

Library of Congress Cataloging-in-Publication Data

A catalog record for this book is available from the Library of Congress.

Series: Jewish and Christian Texts, volume 23

Typeset by Forthcoming Publications (www.forthpub.com)
Printed and bound in Great Britain

To the faculty and staff in the Department of History
at the University of Northern Iowa
for providing me with a nurturing and supportive scholarly environment

CONTENTS

ACKNOWLEDGEMENTS

I am grateful to James H. Charlesworth for accepting this book for publication, and for several valuable conversations on the topic. His wisdom greatly enhanced my research. I am thankful to Dominic Mattos, publisher at Bloomsbury T&T Clark and Bloomsbury Academic, and Miriam Cantwell at Bloomsbury, for guiding me through the publication process. Duncan Burns prepared the indexes, and greatly improved the book through his careful reading of my manuscript for consistency of style. I am especially indebted to the following for supplying me with articles that helped me write this book and for sharing their wisdom: E. Dąbrowa, Z. J. Kapera, D. Syon, and L. T. Zollschan. I am grateful to the University of Northern Iowa Graduate College for awarding me a Professional Development Assignment research leave to write this book.

ABBREVIATIONS

CIJ   Jean-Baptiste Frey, ed. *Corpus inscriptionum Iudaicarum*. Rome: Pontifical Biblical Institute, 1936–52

CIL   *Corpus inscriptionum latinarum*

FGrH Felix Jacoby, ed. *Die Fragmente der griechischen Historiker*. Leiden: Brill, 1954–64

FHG   Karl Müller, ed. *Fragmenta Historicorum Graecorum*. 4 vols. Cambridge: Cambridge University Press, 1841–51

LXX   Septuagint

PG   J.-P. Migne, ed. *Patrologia cursus completa...Series graeca*. 166 vols. Paris: Petit Montrouge, 1857–83

PL   J.-P. Migne (ed.), *Patrologia cursus completes Series prima [latina]*. 221 vols. Paris: J. P. Migne, 1844–65

S.E.   Seleucid Era

Abbreviations for classical sources follow Simon Hornblower and Antony Spawforth, *The Oxford Classical Dictionary*, 3rd ed. (Oxford: Oxford University Press, 2003). Lesser known abbreviations for selected primary editions are listed above. Ancient sources, both Jewish and Classical, generally follow the texts in the Loeb Classical Library series. Other critical editions are listed in the references section. Dead Sea Scrolls are cited according to the numbering and editions listed under references and the notes to the individual chapters. Unless indicated, all translations are mine.

Chapter 1

INTRODUCTION

The history of the nine decades when the Hasmonean dynasty ruled Judea (152–63 B.C.E.) is the tale of a family whose zeal for their ancestral faith helped them survive a turbulent period in the Middle East, and create an independent state surrounded by hostile powers. This book seeks to tell this exciting story by going beyond the accounts of the Hasmoneans in Josephus to bring together new evidence to reconstruct how the Hasmonean family transformed their kingdom into a nation that lasted until the arrival of the Romans. It also explores Josephus, whose life is intertwined with the Hasmoneans through a common ancestry and his historical accounts of their rule. This book has three basic goals:

- To compare Josephus's accounts of the Hasmonean state with archaeological findings, numismatics, literary works, and all relevant inscriptions.
- To show the interconnectedness between the Hasmonean state and the neighboring empires.
- To demonstrate the extent to which non-literary evidence can alter our reading of the literary records pertaining to the Hasmonean state.

This study differs from all previous books on the Hasmonean period because it is the only work to integrate the full array of extant data to reconstruct the relationships between the Hasmonean state and the rulers of the Seleucid and the Ptolemaic Empires, the Itureans, the Nabateans, the Parthians, the Armenians, and the Roman Republic. It accomplishes this by including a variety of previously unused sources, including papyrological documentation, inscriptions, archaeological evidence, numismatics, Dead Sea Scrolls, pseudepigrapha, and texts from the Hellenistic to the Byzantine periods.[1] This book includes reconstructions of several previously unknown

---

1. For the importance of integrating textual and archaeological evidence to reconstruct the history of the Hasmonean state, see H. Eshel 2008, vii–ix; Popović 2011, esp. 4–17.

historical events that shaped the reigns of the Hasmoneans and their faith, and which helped them create an independent state. It also explores how Josephus's political and social situation in Flavian Rome affected his accounts of the Hasmoneans and why any investigation of the Hasmonean state must go beyond Josephus to gain a full appreciation of this unique historical period that shaped Second Temple Judaism, and created the conditions for the rise of the Herodian dynasty and the emergence of Christianity.

Preceding Studies

The majority of studies devoted to Hasmonean history typically focus on Mattathias's rebellion to liberate Judea from Seleucid rule, following the oppressive decree of Antiochus IV Epiphanes (169–67 B.C.E.) that prohibited the practice of Judaism, and often end with Simon's establishment of an independent state. The cleansing of the temple by Judas and the impact of Hellenization in Judea are typically the major topics covered by these books.[2] Unfortunately, the later Hellenistic period when the Hasmonean family ruled a state and their relationships with their neighbors have not received as much attention. However, several new books on the Hasmonean period have departed from the traditional focus on the family's struggle for independence, often referred to as the Maccabean Revolt, to explore the development of the Hasmonean high priesthood.[3] Other recent works devoted to Second Temple Jewish religious practices contain valuable discussions concerning the relationship between the Hasmonean rulers and the major forms of Jewish sectarianism, namely the Pharisees, the Sadducees, the Essenes, and the Qumran community.[4] Several studies on Josephus that explore his importance as the chief chronicler for much of Jewish history contain important discussions of his presentations of the Hasmonean dynasty and its religious practices.[5] All these works are useful for understanding the history of the Hasmonean family and their creation of a state. However, despite their different subjects and methodological perspectives, these books largely adopt the outdated chronology and historical reconstructions of the Hasmonean state found in the revised

---

2. For influential examples, see Bar-Kochva 1989; Bickerman 1937; Bringmann 1983; Harrington 1988; Hengel 1974; Sievers 1990; Tcherikover 1959.

3. See Babota 2014; Brutti 2006; Hunt 2006; Rooke 2000; Seeman 2013.

4. See esp. Baumgarten 1997; Klawans 2012.

5. S. Cohen 1979; Gruen 2016; Rajak 1983; S. Schwartz 1990b; 2001; Thackeray 1929.

edition of Emil Schürer's classic multi-volume work on the late Second Temple Period and early Christianity.[6]

It is only recently that scholars have begun to depart from Schürer's presentation of Second Temple history to offer new reconstructions of selected aspects of the Hasmonean period. Edward Dąbrowa's study of the Hasmonean state focuses on ideology and institutions, such as the priesthood, kingship, court, capital, finances, and the military.[7] Eyal Regev has written a similar publication that explores the Hasmonean family's control of the Temple cult, the government, and the kingship.[8] Despite their many new insights, both authors primarily rely on Josephus to recount the major events of the Hasmonean state.

The Dead Sea Scrolls are the focus of several important books that deal extensively with the Hasmonean state, and which contain new historical information derived from the Qumran texts. One, the proceedings of the fourth international symposium of the Orion Center for the Study of the Dead Sea Scrolls, contains several essays that explore Jewish history and the religion of the Hasmonean period in light of the Qumran documents.[9] Hanan Eshel's book on the Hasmonean state is the first monograph dedicated solely to the question how we can learn political history from the Dead Sea Scrolls. However, he acknowledges his great dependence on the works of Josephus since the Dead Sea Scrolls lack narrative accounts of the Hasmoneans.[10] James H. Charlesworth has written a unique volume that explores the Qumran *pesharim* as a historical source for reconstructing Second Temple period history.[11] Unlike other works on the Hasmonean period, Charlesworth focuses on how the Jewish sectarians at Qumran read and applied Scripture to explain events of their time not only in light of the Dead Sea Scrolls, but also in conjunction with the writings of Josephus, paleography, archaeology, and other relevant Jewish texts. Although devoted to reconstructing Qumran history, Charlesworth's

6. Schürer et al. 1973–87. Grabbe's (1992, xxxix) past comments on the problems of this book are still relevant: "It covers many aspects of Judaism in this period, including the history and literature, and should remain the standard detailed reference work for many years to come. However, in the last fifteen years scholarship has rendered parts of the new Schürer out-of-date. Moreover, initial editorial uncertainty as to how far to revise Schürer's text resulted in notes that sometimes contradict the text!"

7. Dąbrowa 2010a. See also Dąbrowa 2010b.

8. Regev 2013.

9. Goodblatt, Pinnick, and Schwartz 2001.

10. H. Eshel 2008, esp. 5–12. A considerable portion of this book consists of lengthy quotations from Josephus's *War* and *Antiquities*.

11. Charlesworth 2002.

investigation represents an innovative model for understanding the Second Temple period that sheds considerable new light on the history of the Hasmonean state.[12]

Josephus the Historian and His Works

Josephus is the only historian whose extant works cover the entire history of the Hasmonean state. He documents this period in his two major books, the *War* and the *Antiquities*. The *War* is his first book.[13] It primarily describes the events of the First Jewish Revolt of 66–73/4 C.E., but also recounts the history of the Jews beginning with the reign of Antiochus IV Epiphanes. Studying the *War* is complicated because Josephus was both its author and one of its major characters. The opening paragraph of his book states that its subject matter is "the war of the Jews against the Romans" (Ἰουδαίων πρὸς Ῥωμαιους πόλεμον; *War* 1.1). This preface shows that Josephus was greatly influenced by the *Histories* of Polybius and the *Gallic War* of Julius Caesar. This should not be surprising since Polybius and Caesar wrote their histories for similar purposes as Josephus, namely to defend Rome, their homelands, as well as their reputations.[14] When reading these three writers, we must remember that their personal ambitions often affected their narratives. This is especially true of Josephus. He simultaneously sought to praise the Romans, himself, his ancestral faith, as well as condemn some of his fellow Jewish rebels. The events of his later life often shaped his accounts of the Hasmonean state; his works often justify his actions during the First Jewish Revolt.

Josephus was a controversial figure during his lifetime. This is largely because of his unusual background. Although his *War* is similar to the histories of Caesar and Polybius, it is truly a unique work because of Josephus's status. The emperor Vespasian gave him Roman citizenship, a pension, and a home in the city of Rome even though he had fought against him and his son, the future emperor Titus.[15] This patronage not

---

12. Many Dead Sea Scrolls have never been used to reconstruct Hasmonean history. These texts will be the focus of a companion volume to the present study that will use them to recount unknown historical episodes that involved the Hasmonean rulers and shaped Second Temple Judaism.

13. See Attridge 1984; Bilde 1988, 192–93; Schürer et al. 1973–87, 1:47–48.

14. See further Bilde 1988, 27–60; Sterling 2000; M. Stern 1974–80, 1:71–80. Cf. Feldman 1984, 772–77. For Polybius's works and relevant Hellenistic literature, see Walbank 1972, 1–31; 1993, 13–29.

15. *Life* 422–23. He lived in Vespasian's former residence. See Mason 2001, 168–69.

only provided him with ample leisure time to write his books, but it also gave him access to the Flavian *Commentarii*.[16] Despite his influential connections, Josephus had powerful enemies. He had to defend his *War* against several Jewish critics, especially the historian Justus of Tiberius. Justus not only had been one of his opponents in the Galilee in 66–67 C.E., but he also wrote an account of the First Jewish Revolt that contradicted Josephus's *War*. Josephus claimed that Justus's book was incorrect since it contradicted the *Commentarii* of Caesar, presumably those of Titus that he, and purportedly not Justus, had read.[17]

Josephus had many advantages that were unavailable to his Jewish contemporaries such as Justin, which contributed to his success as a historian. He had access to libraries and official Roman accounts of the First Jewish Revolt. He also knew many Jews and Romans who had participated in this conflict; he interviewed some of them. He even sent copies of the *War* to Vespasian, Titus, and Agrippa II—all purportedly testified to its truthfulness.[18] Titus even signed a copy, which effectively give the *War* the royal imprimatur.[19] This endorsement for many readers meant that any effort to dispute the *War*'s content could potentially be viewed as a challenge to Titus's credibility.

16. *Life* 342, 358. Cf. *Apion* 1.56. For Josephus's dependence on this source, see Thackeray 1929, 38–40.

17. *Life* 340–42. Justus's patron, Agrippa II, not only acknowledged that Josephus was a trustworthy historian, but he even contributed material to help him write the *War* (*Life* 5.364–67). Justus presumably waited until Agrippa II had died before he disputed the accuracy of Josephus's account of the First Jewish Revolt. See further Rajak 1973.

18. *Apion* 1.50–52. The relationship between Josephus and the emperors Vespasian and Titus should not be understood as indicating that he was closely associated with them or with those in the inner circles of power. Vespasian encouraged the arts and paid the salaries of some teachers of Latin and Greek rhetoric. Although Josephus had more contact with Vespasian and Titus than many of his contemporaries during and after the First Jewish Revolt, it is doubtful that the imperial family had any actual role in the writing of his works. For these issues, see further Suetonius, *Vesp.* 17–18; Hollander 2014. Josephus claims in *Life* 361–62 that he gave copies of the *War* to "many" Romans who had fought alongside Vespasian and Titus. Several prominent legionary legates from this conflict were alive at this time and could have verified its accuracy, including Sextus Vettulenus Cerialis (*Legio V Macedonica*), M. Titius Frugi (*Legio XV Apollinaris*), the tribune Nicanor (*War* 3.344–46), and Masada's conqueror L. Flavius Silva Nonius Bassus. See further, Mason 2009, 57; Cotton and Eck 2005.

19. *Life* 363.

Josephus's use of imperial publicity to support the veracity of his accounts of the First Jewish Revolt suggests that many of his contemporaries doubted the truthfulness of his *War*. This skepticism has not diminished with the passage of time, for questioning Josephus's accuracy has become a major academic enterprise. Recent scholarship, largely beginning in the 1990s, has rejected the positivistic tradition that treated Josephus's works as discrete pieces of historical information that could be used to reconstruct the past. Josephus studies in recent decades has focused on more sophisticated modes of inquiry that seek to explore his literary context, his use of language, his rhetorical artifice, as well as the historical accuracy of his accounts in light of archaeological discoveries.[20]

It is fortunate for scholars interested in the Second Temple period that Josephus later wrote a more detailed work that includes a lengthy account of the Hasmonean state, which also contains additional materials pertaining to the development of Jewish sectarianism. Known as the *Antiquities*, this book recounts history from the creation of the world up to 66 C.E. when the First Jewish Revolt began. It is largely a retelling of biblical history that was written to educate Gentiles about Judaism's past. In this book Josephus offers a more detailed account of the Hasmonean state that sometimes corrects errors, and clarifies confusing sections, in his *War*. He also includes several lengthy descriptions about the favorable relations between the Roman Republic and the Hasmonean monarchs.[21] His purpose in including such material was to show that the First Jewish Revolt was an aberration, and the Jews had long enjoyed favorable relations with the Romans. The rulers of the Hasmonean state figure prominently in these sections.

Josephus intended the *Antiquities* to be his first work. He abandoned the project to compose the *War*. One of his goals in writing the *Antiquities* was to rebut Jewish attacks on his integrity that began around 71 C.E. when he arrived in Rome. He wrote the book primarily for Roman readers. However, he also intended it for subjects of the Roman Empire; this appears to be the same group for whom he later wrote the *Antiquities*.[22]

---

20. See further Bond 2000; Chapman and Rodgers 2016, 1–13; Pastor, Stern, and Mor 2011; Rodgers 2006b; D. Schwartz 2013.

21. See further Mason 1998.

22. *War* 1.1–4, 10–12, 23, 31, 183, 187, 216, 218–19, 359–60, 370, 386–92; 2.204–13, 250–51; 4.491–96; 7.360. Cf. *Life* 361–62; *Apion* 1.50–51. See Bilde 1988, 102–31; Mader 2000, 155–56; Mason 1998, 96. In *War* 1.17 Josephus imitates the classical historians by beginning his *War* where Jewish Scripture ended to produce a continuous historical record of the Jewish people to the present. See further Walbank 1993, 19.

Josephus resumed writing the *Antiquities* following the publication of the Greek edition of the *War*, which appeared before the death of Vespasian in 79 C.E.[23] He encountered some delays. The *Antiquities* was not published until approximately fifteen years later, in 93–94 C.E., during the thirteenth year of the reign of the Emperor Domitian (93/4 C.E.).[24] This was a time of distress. Domitian was beginning his purge of Rome's intellectuals for their unflattering representations of him. He executed Hermogenes of Tarsus for including allusions to him in his history.[25] Domitian also ordered the death of Helvidius Priscus for a farce that supposedly criticized his divorce.[26] He did not restrict his persecution to those who wrote about him, but he also punished those who criticized the monarchy. He had Rusticus Arulenus and Herennius Senecio executed because they praised some deceased critics of Nero and Vespasian.[27] These imperial sentences show that Josephus lived during a dangerous age even for those who had received imperial patronage.

Jews like Josephus were in potential danger during the reign of Domitian because of their supposed loyalty to Judea and its priests. Many pagans were also suspicious of Jews because the First Jewish Revolt had been a long and costly war. Although a Roman citizen, Josephus expressed fear for his safety even though Vespasian had favored him.[28] He and other Jews

23. Josephus mentions (*Life* 361) that he presented a completed copy of the *War* to Vespasian. The book is generally dated between 75 C.E., when Vespasian dedicated the Temple of Peace (*War* 7.158, 79), and 79 C.E., the year of his death. See further Attridge 1984, 192–93; Bilde 1988, 79; Laqueur 1920, 6; Weber 1973, 56–58; Rajak 1983, 195; Smallwood and Rajak 2012. Some scholars have noted a marked difference in Josephus's attitude towards Titus and Vespasian within the narrative, suggesting a publication date under Titus, 79–81 C.E. See S. Cohen 1979, 87; Price 2001, 223; Barnes 2005, 139–40; S. Schwartz 1990b, 13–15. It has further been suggested that *War* 7 was a later addition under Domitian. This thesis is primarily based on the more pronounced role of the third Flavian emperor in this book and its inferior style compared to *War* 1–6. See further S. Cohen 1979, 87; Thackeray 1929, 31–35; Barnes 2005, 139–40. See, summatively, Mason 2001, 148 n. 1493; C. Jones 2002, 113–14; D. Schwartz 2011a.

24. Josephus provides this date in *Ant.* 20.267. For discussion, see Attridge 1984, 185–92; Bilde 1988, 103–4. If he completed the book in 93/4 C.E., then his claim (*Ant.* 3.218) that the Urim and the Thummim ceased to function 200 years earlier would date its cessation just before the death of John Hyrcanus.

25. Suetonius, *Dom.* 10.1.

26. Suetonius, *Dom.* 10.4.

27. Suetonius, *Dom.* 10.3–4; Tacitus *Agr.* 2.1; Pliny, *Ep.* 7.19.4; Cass. Dio, *Hist.* 67.13.2. See further Mason 2009, 76.

28. *Life* 425; Goodman 2007, 440–42.

living in Rome were constantly reminded of the First Jewish Revolt since the Flavians had transformed its Forum to commemorate their victory over the Jews. Some Romans even publically expressed their disgust at Jews like Josephus who resided there. The poet Martial was among the most prominent of the opponents of the Jews at this time. His *Liber spectaculorum* not only celebrates the construction of the Flavian amphitheater, where Romans came to watch gladiators and *bestiarii* engage in a bloody orgy of death, but he portrays Jews as anthropomorphized animals like those killed in it.[29] This unflattering portrait of Jews reflects the type of hostility Josephus encountered as a citizen in Rome.

Josephus's economic situation became worse when Domitian ended the pension that Vespasian had granted him. This forced Josephus to earn his living from sales of his *War* and money supplied by his new patron Epaphroditus.[30] It was this loss of imperial support, and the accusations of his critics, that eroded confidence in the *War*. The increasing public disapproval of this book hampered Josephus's ability to secure support for his future writing projects.[31] It is possible that he even postponed publication

29. Mart. *Spect.* 2.2; 4.4; 7.30, 35, 55, 82; 10.50; 11.94; 12.57. For references to the Flavians and Jews in this work, see further H. Chapman 2012.

30. *Life* 430. This man is the only literary patron Josephus mentions in his works (*Ant.* 1.8–9; *Apion* 1.1; 2.278). The extant references to him supports the thesis of Laqueur (1920, 23–36) that he should be identified with the freedman M. Mettius Epaphroditus, whom the *Sudas* states was a *grammaticus* and former tutor to the son of the Egyptian prefect Marcus Mettius Modestus. Epaphroditus was manumitted in Rome and possessed a library of over 30,000 scrolls. He purportedly died at the age of seventy-three. He was recognized with a statue that bears his name (*CIL* 6.9454). His position suggests that he had some contacts with Rome's aristocratic families, but was not among the elites. Others identify Epaphroditus with the imperial freedman, Ti. Claudius Aug(usti) lib(ertus) Epaphroditus who served under Nero as a *libellis* and was involved in uncovering the Pisonian conspiracy against the emperor in 65 C.E. See Hollander 2014, 279–93; Mason 2001, 172; Rajak 1983, 223–24; S. Schwartz 1990b, 16–17; Sterling 1992, 239–40. Recently, C. Jones (2002, 114–15) has suggested that Josephus's patron was actually a freedman named Epaphroditus, who served in the office of the *ab epistulis* under one or more Flavian emperors and was commemorated at Rome with a large funerary altar.

31. In *Ant.* 20.267–68 Josephus appears to acknowledge that there are inaccuracies in his *War* and states he wanted to publish a new version of it. This not only suggests that he faced public criticism over his *War*, but that he intended the *Antiquities* to be a more accurate work that also corrected errors in his first book. Josephus (*Ant.* 20.266) also mentions that he wrote *Life* to affirm his qualifications as a historian of the First Jewish Revolt and to defend his character. See further, S. Cohen 1979, 128–29; P. Stern 2010, 91.

of his *Antiquities* until after the death of Agrippa II to avoid angering this leading Jewish supporter of his writing who also resided in the city of Rome.[32] Even while he was alive, Josephus appears to have gone to great lengths to avoid any overt criticism of Agrippa II. In his books he portrays Agrippa II positively as a mediator between the Jews and the Romans. Josephus never describes him as taking part in direct military action against Jews. Because Agrippa II was awarded the *ornamenta praetoria* around 75 C.E. for his service in the First Jewish Revolt, he certainly fought in this war alongside Vespasian and Titus despite Josephus's implication otherwise.[33] It is probable that Josephus did not want to put Agrippa II in a difficult position by highlighting his past military service to the Roman Empire during the First Jewish Revolt, which could have eroded Jewish support for him in his homeland. Because it was not his intent to document everything that occurred during the First Jewish Revolt, it is important to go beyond Josephus's books to gain a full understanding of the Second Temple period. This is especially true of his historical accounts of the Hasmonean state. He sometimes changed them to make them more accurate, and to comment upon recent incidents in the city of Rome that affected him and other Jews.

A look at Josephus's books reveals that he updated his works to reflect later historical events and concerns of the Jewish community of the first century C.E. This is especially true of the *War*. Josephus's treatment of Aulus Alienus Caecina in *War* 4.634–44, and the lack of references to much of book 7 in the ancient summary of the *War*'s content, suggests

---

32. It is doubtful that Agrippa II was alive when the *Antiquities* was published since Book 20 is critical of him. The death of Agrippa II has been the subject of much academic debate since it bears on the dating of *Life*. This book appears to presuppose that he is no longer alive (*Life* 359). Phot. (*Bibl.* 33 s.v. "Ioustos" *PG* 103:66) writes that he died after 100 C.E. in the third year of Trajan. This would extend the gap between the *Antiquities* and the *Life* even though Josephus (*Life* 430; *Ant.* 20.266–67) closely connects the writing of the two works. The extant evidence from coins and other sources suggest that Photius is mistaken. It is probable that he conflated two passages from chs. 13 and 15 of Jerome's *De Vir. ill.* (*PL* 629–54) in which a reference to Josephus appears in connection with a description of Clement of Rome, whom he states died in the third year of Trajan. Josephus wrote *Life* and *Ant.* 17–20 during the reign of Domitian (before September 96 C.E.) and after the death of Agrippa II (perhaps in or before 93/4 C.E.). See further Attridge 1984, 210–11; Bilde 1988, 103–6; S. Cohen 1979, 170–80; Mason 2009, 147; S. Schwartz 1990b, 19–20.

33. Cass. Dio, 65.15.3–4. This honor gave Agrippa II the senatorial rank of praetor. See further Wilker 2011; Hollander 2014, 252–304, esp. 268.

that he inserted additional material in later editions of this book.[34] His account of the siege of Masada, contained in Book 7 of the *War*, provides one example of a later updating that is relevant to the examination of Jewish sectarianism.[35] There is ample evidence that Josephus revised this section of the *War* to deal with Jewish disturbances of the post-Flavian era. It appears that Book 7 was written in the time of Domitian, and revised during the reign of Nerva or Trajan.[36] The end of his account of Masada was apparently the original conclusion of the *War* since he wrote that the entire country was now subdued and no enemies remained (*War* 7.407–9).[37]

The issue of Josephus's later redactions of his works is also important to consider before using his writings to examine Jewish sectarianism during the period of the Hasmonean state. He actually wrote that there were four major Jewish sects: the Sadducees, the Pharisees, the Essenes, and the "Fourth Philosophy."[38] This latter sect gave rise to the *Sicarii*, which became especially active during the two decades following the death of Agrippa I in 44 C.E.[39] Because the *Sicarii* did not emerge until the first century C.E., it is clear that Josephus used his sources regarding the practices of the three major Jewish sects of the Hasmonean period to understand and explain the later development of the *Sicarii*, as well as the Zealots, of his own time.[40] His account of their failed effort to foment a revolution in Alexandria and Cyrene (*War* 7.409–41) appears to form a distinct unit.[41] It highlights the deeds of those who had escaped from the Romans. In this section Josephus displays a different attitude to the *Sicarii* than elsewhere in the *War*. Instead of portraying these rebels as a group

34. Barnes 2005, 139–40; S. Cohen 1979, 87; Thackeray 1929, 31–35. For the ancient table of contents appended to the *War* that helps us to reconstruct some of the later changes to the book, see McLaren 1998, 79.

35. The archaeological evidence suggests that Josephus modeled his account of Masada after the siege of Gamla. For this reason, it is important to consider the literary quality of Josephus's narratives when using his works to reconstruct history. See further Atkinson 2006.

36. See further M. Stern 1974–80, 1:72 nn. 8–9.

37. In the beginning of the *War* Josephus mentions the destruction of the local fortresses (*War* 1.29), which suggests that the Masada story was included in the original work. For Masada, see further Atkinson 2006; 2010.

38. *Ant.* 18.10, 23.

39. *Ant.* 20.186–87; *War* 2.254–57.

40. For example, Josephus writes that many beliefs of the Sicarii are similar to those held by the Pharisees (*Ant.* 18.23).

41. Brighton 2009, esp. 93–140.

that does not represent traditional Jewish values, as he does in Books 2–6, he expresses pity for them as they underwent torture and shows some hostility to Rome's policy in Judea.[42]

The additions concerning the *Sicarii* in Josephus's works reflect his changed attitude toward Roman rule of his former homeland during the post-Titus period. For this reason, it is important to take into consideration Josephus's social situation in Flavian Rome when reading his *War* and *Antiquities*, and how events there shaped his accounts of the Hasmonean period.[43] Although Josephus's accounts contain much ancient information about Jewish sectarianism of the first century B.C.E., he often inserts this material in his books to help his non-Jewish readers understand those groups he considered disruptive, as well as to distinguish them from pious and sensible Jews like himself. His descriptions of Jewish sectarianism were primarily intended to help his Gentile readers understand recent Jewish conflicts of the first century C.E. They should not be read as accurate reflections of Jewish sects of the Hasmonean period since they are shaped by later events. For this reason, his accounts of the Hasmonean monarchs and their sectarian affiliations in the *War* and the *Antiquities* are often biased.

The *Antiquities* is a work that must be read in light of Flavian Rome. Josephus also appears to have sometimes redacted his sources to explain or defend his own status as a Roman citizen in Flavian Rome of the late first century C.E. Flavian Rome is a hidden character whose influence can be detected in much of his accounts of the Hasmonean state. He appears to have added material to the *Antiquities*, as well as his *War*, during Domitian's reign. At this time Josephus's prominent Jewish supporters, Agrippa II and Berenice, had left the city of Rome. He apparently underwent a period of self-reflection regarding his status as a Jew. Hanan Eshel suggests that he ended his *War* with the tragic account of the mass suicide at Masada because he was convinced that Judaism could not survive without the Jerusalem temple. During the fourteen years he spent writing his *Antiquities* he apparently changed his attitude towards Judaism. He realized that it had survived in Judea and the Diaspora without a temple and could exist without a sanctuary. This caused him to become more optimistic about its future in some sections of the *Antiquities*. In this book he also tried to persuade his readers to change

42. *War* 7.417–19.

43. Popović (2011, 3) comments on this problem: "One of the fundamental issues is whether Josephus' accounts are proper historical sources for understanding pre-70 C.E. Judaea or whether they are instead historical sources for understanding the historical context of Josephus in Flavian Rome." Cf. Regev 2013, 28–31.

their views about Judaism and support the Pharisees and Jewish leaders such as himself.[44]

One of the most important differences between Josephus's two major books is the anti-monarchical stance in the *Antiquities*. As Mason notes, Josephus's account of the Judean constitution is that of a "decidedly anti-monarchical, senatorial aristocracy" that lead him to introduce a senate into his biblical paraphrase.[45] In his account of the Mosaic legislation pertaining to kings, Josephus reaffirms aristocracy as the ideal constitution. He emphasizes there is no other necessary form of government since God alone is the lawful ruler. Although he highlights Saul, David, and Solomon as heroic figures, he diminishes their accomplishments by weakening their positions as monarchs.[46] Josephus does not focus on the eternal promise to David, but emphasizes the authority of Moses and his aristocratic constitution. He does this because any hint of messianic zeal in his writings would have been a particularly sensitive issue for the Romans. Although he downplays messianism in his *War*, he suggests that it was a potent force that contributed to the rebellion against the Romans when he writes that the Jews were incited to war by an ambiguous oracle found in their sacred writings that someone from their land would rule the world.[47]

Josephus cautiously avoided messianism in his history of the Hasmonean period.[48] He appears to have been reluctant to document any Hasmonean history that involved the violent messianism of the type that had contributed to the outbreak of the First Jewish War. Instead, he stresses that the Hasmonean family's rule had gone well until they had established a monarchy and allowed sectarian factions to influence politics. Josephus wrote his books partly to support the aristocracy, namely the rule of the Pharisees and their leaders. For Josephus, these groups represented caution and Roman aristocratic values. They were opposed to the religious zeal of the Zealots and related Jewish groups that had caused the rebellion

---

44. For this this interpretation, see H. Eshel 1999. Note also the statement in support of the Jews in *Ant.* 14.185–89.

45. Mason 2009, 90–91. For anti-monarchical passages, see *Ant.* 4.223; 6:36; 11:111; 14.91. For the senate, see *Ant.* 5.15, 43, 55, 135.

46. Rodgers 2009, 181.

47. *War* 6.312–13. Cf. *War* 4.388. Josephus notes that there was a debate as to whether this man would be a Jew or if the prophecy referred to Vespasian. He emphasizes that the Jews were wrong to have focused on this oracle, and that messianism brought disaster to them and the destruction of Jerusalem. For this oracle in Roman literature, see Tac. *Hist.* 5.13; Suet. *Vesp.* 4.5.

48. Mendels 1998, 294–313.

against Rome.[49] For Josephus, the priests and the aristocrats were the only legitimate Jewish leaders. Although they may have participated in the First Jewish Revolt, he emphasizes that they could henceforth be counted upon to support Rome.[50] Josephus was convinced that the Romans were the masters of the world, and that it was God's plan for them to govern much of it. God, he believed, had vowed to destroy the Jerusalem temple because the Jews had rejected everything that was Roman.[51]

The failure to recognize that Josephus revised the *Antiquities* has led to some misunderstandings concerning the development of Jewish sectarianism during the Hasmonean period. Joseph Sievers, for example, shows that that no chronological conclusions can be drawn from his placement of Jewish sectarian divisions to the time of Jonathan. Through a close reading of the sectarian references in the writings of Josephus, and the ancient table of contents appended to his works, Sievers demonstrates that *Ant.* 13.171–73 was inserted into a later edition of this book.[52] Consequently, the placement of Josephus's description of Jewish sects in his account of Jonathan should no longer be understood to imply that sectarian divisions actually began during his high priesthood.

The *Antiquities* contains a very different depiction of Jewish sectarianism during the period of the Hasmonean state than the *War*.[53] In his *War*, Josephus depicts the Pharisees as a religious party that plays a minimal role in politics and emphasizes that they were not closely associated with the

49. H. Eshel 1999, 233; Mason 2001, 7.

50. S. Schwartz (1990b, 15, 69–88) observes that Josephus greatly idealizes the priests in his *War* and *Antiquities*. He accomplished this by emphasizing that the priesthood not only survived as a distinctive class in the post-70 C.E. period, but that its members were now seeking Roman favor. The priests had financial reasons to court the Romans: they wanted to regain their confiscated property (*War* 7.216–17). S. Schwartz (1990b, 91) also comments that *Ant.* 14.20–28 suggests the temple cult must have continued following 70 C.E. and that the prayers of the priests were still regarded as beneficial. Although Josephus at times mentions examples of his own prophetic abilities (*War* 3.351–53, 399–408), he does not refer to himself as a prophet in his works. It is probable that he does so because he believed that his prophetic abilities derived through his function as a priest, and because his audience may have been suspicious of prophets. For this reason, he emphasizes that only great leaders of the past, such as John Hyrcanus, were prophets. For this interpretation, see Grabbe 2003, 203–4.

51. Josephus stresses αἰτία to argue that the Jewish rejection of Rome was the underlying cause of the disastrous revolt. See further Varneda 1986, 7, 12–13, 17–18.

52. Sievers 2001a.

53. See D. Schwartz 1983. D. Schwartz's article was written in part to counter Morton Smith's (1956, 74–78) thesis that Josephus's *War* contains a more historically

anti-Roman rebels. However, in his *Antiquities* he portrays the Pharisees as actively involved in politics, especially during the reign of Alexander Jannaeus. The *Antiquities* is likely more accurate since he wrote this book at a time when the Jewish rebels were no longer a concern to Rome. Therefore, he could truthfully describe the past political activities of the Pharisees without any fear of offending his Roman patrons.

Because they present different depictions of the Hasmonean rulers, the *Antiquities* and the *War* should not be harmonized. Rather, their divergent portrayals of the same persons and events must be examined individually, in light of other textual, archaeological, and numismatic evidence when available, to determine which, if any, reflects historical reality. Josephus, moreover, did not merely insert additional materials in his *Antiquities*. This book is unique among his writings since he effectively changed its meaning through the addition of an appendix known as *Life* that reflects debates of the Flavian era.

The book known as *Life* recounts the brief time during which Josephus was commander of the Galilee (ca. December 66 C.E. until May–July 67 C.E.). It also contains some historical information of relevance to the present study. Because this book is actually an appendix to the *Antiquities*, it shares its literary origin. Since Josephus intended *Life* to be part of the *Antiquities*, the two works should be read together as a single composition.[54] The content of *Life* is important to the present study because it occasionally helps in detecting and understanding later changes to the text of the *Antiquities*.[55]

accurate portrayal of the Pharisees than his *Antiquities*. See also S. Cohen 1979, 144–51; Fuks 1990; S. Schwartz 1990b, 172–200. D. Schwartz (2013, 79–82) notes that Josephus downplays strife in the *Antiquities*.

54. Rodgers (2006a) points out that Nicolaus of Damascus appended a now lost autobiography to his universal history. Josephus may have been influenced by Nicolaus, and decided to add an autobiography to his *Antiquities* to update it in light of later historical events and debates concerning his role in the First Jewish Revolt.

55. The *Life* is generally dated to 94–95 C.E., but no later than 96 C.E. See *Ant.* 20.266; *Life* 430. In *Life* 359–60 Josephus appears to presuppose that King Agrippa II is dead. A brief comment by Phot. (*Bibl.*, Codex 3) states that Agrippa II died in the third year of the Emperor Trajan in 100–101 C.E. Although some, such as Laqueur (1920, 247–78), have used this reference to propose a later date for *Life* and *Antiquities*, the earlier dating is preferred. See further Bilde 1988, 103–6; Mason 2009, xxi, and n. 6. There is no evidence that Josephus ever referred to the work as *Life*. It was issued as an appendix to the *Antiquities* and became regarded as part of this book in the manuscript tradition. Because it opens with a connecting particle, it did not need any title. Although it was clearly intended to form part of the *Antiquities*, I will follow scholarly convention and refer to the appendix to this book as *Life*.

Josephus intended *Life* to be a defense of his character and to demonstrate the truthfulness of his previous writings, especially the *War*.[56] In *Life* he introduces his readers to Jewish sectarianism partly to enhance his own credentials. He claims to have studied the ways of the Pharisees, the Sadducees, and the Essenes during his youth. He even comments that he also spent three years as a devotee of a desert hermit named Bannus.[57] Josephus describes them as philosophical schools both to imply that he was a lifelong seeker of Jewish wisdom, and to show that Judaism emphasized the pursuit of virtue like the classic Greco-Roman philosophical traditions.[58]

Life contains several contradictions with Josephus's previous works. It sometimes conflicts with the *War* concerning his activities in the Galilee. This is particularly true in *Life* 28–413 and *War* 2.568–646. Perhaps the most significant difference is his inclusion of Justus of Tiberius as a character in *Life*; he is absent in the *War*. Josephus in *Life* portrays his conduct during the First Jewish Revolt and the Jewish sects favorably. He does so in part to argue that priestly Jews like himself were best qualified to represent the Jewish community to the Roman people.[59] Because Josephus wrote *Life* as an apologetic text, it should not be surprising that its details sometimes differ from the *War*. It is far from a complete description of the career of Josephus; it is instead first and foremost a personal apology regarding specific issues.[60] Because Josephus appended it to his *Antiquities*, *Life* to some extent should be regarded as a revision of the former work

56. See further, S. Cohen 1979, 114, 126–28; Mason 1997. Rajak (1983, 154, 345–68) emphasizes that even though *Life* was largely intended as a reply to Justus, it still addresses later concerns of the surviving Jewish aristocracy in the Diaspora.

57. *Life* 10. Klawans (2012, esp. 44–91, 137–38) proposes that Josephus's descriptions of the Pharisees, especially his explanations of their doctrines of fate and free will, support his claim to have adopted the ways of this sect. However, it is important to note the placement of this material in *Life*. Its purpose is to show that Josephus gave up the most rigorous philosophies of his day to pursue a responsible political life. Mason (1991; 2001, 20 n. 87) also suggests that Josephus merely deferred to the Pharisaic majority rule in Jerusalem and never actually became an ardent Pharisee in practice. His view is followed by Siegert, Schreckenberg, and Vogel (2001, 163). Baumbach (2005, 21–50) argues that the Pharisees were the most beneficial party for Josephus's career.

58. *Life* 2. See Mason 2009, 208–13.

59. For the importance of these features in *Life*, see P. Stern 2010; Rodgers 2006a.

60. McLaren 1988, 69. See also S. Cohen 1979, 109. For further discussion on the apparent (not necessarily real) conflict between *Life* and *War*, see Attridge 1984, 187–92; Rajak 1983, 154–66; Rappaport 1994.

since it reflects his later views on his participation in the First Jewish Revolt and the changed relationship between the Roman Empire and the Jews following this conflict.

It is also important to consider Josephus's use of literary assistants when reading his works since it is plausible that some of his changed attitudes in his books reflect their activities. He states that he used them to improve his Greek style when he wrote his *War*. The result is a fairly polished narrative that is reminiscent of the best writings of the Greco-Roman historians. But he did not use them when he wrote his *Antiquities*.[61] Consequently, in this book he often copied extensive passages from his Greek sources largely verbatim. This work is especially useful for historical study because it often preserves lengthy quotations from his sources. Unfortunately, these often offer conflicting chronologies. In some sections the origin of the historical material he derived his information from is unknown. Chapter 13 of the *Antiquities*, beginning with paragraph 218 that covers the period from the rise of Jonathan to the death of Queen Shelamzion Alexandra, for example, is unique and of unknown derivation.

Josephus occasionally cites his Greek sources. These references are useful for understanding his methods of research and writing.[62] For the

61. Thackeray (1929, 18–19) is the greatest proponent of the assistant theory. He adheres to the thesis that Josephus had received considerable help in writing the *Antiquities*, and that only *Ant.* 20 and *Life* were written by Josephus himself, cf. Josephus's reference to assistants in *Apion* 1.50. Richards (1939) opposes this view, citing consistent literary evidence which assumes that Josephus wrote the entire draft of the *Antiquities* himself, some of which was revised by Greek helpers for a second edition. Rajak (1983, 233–36) offers a comprehensive overview of arguments and counterarguments; she points out a series of methodological flaws in Thackeray's thesis, not least the fact that Josephus does not mention any help in writing the *Antiquities*, and that the various styles that Thackeray believes to have found must be attributed to Josephus's personal reading material at the time of writing. See also Shutt (1961, 29–35), whose own linguistic analysis of the common terms and constructions in *War* and *Antiquities* implies a single authorship. He sees the assistants' presence only in polishing and improving on Josephus's Greek in the *War*. Because Josephus mentions the literary assistance he received when he wrote his *War*, I accept the thesis that assistants helped him improve his style when he wrote this particular book. However, the final product should be viewed as the work of Josephus because he selected and reshaped his sources to emphasize particular historical themes and to portray each Hasmonean ruler favorably or unfavorably.

62. Josephus used 1 Maccabees as a major source for the *Antiquities*, but he also used unknown works to recount additional historical events. See, e.g., *Ant.* 13.35–36, 58–80, 106–21. He also quotes from, or refers readers to, several historians in his *Antiquities* such as Nicolaus of Damascus (13.250–51, 347), Strabo (13.286–87, 319,

period between Antiochus IV Epiphanes to the accession of Archelaus (6 C.E.), Josephus primarily used Nicolaus of Damascus. As Herod the Great's Gentile advisor and envoy, Nicolaus is not the most reliable source for Hasmonean history. In his *Universal History* he glorified Herod, and minimized the achievements of the Hasmonean rulers to legitimize the reign of his patron. This is particularly true of his account of Alexander Jannaeus. It is often polemical and does not preserve an accurate report of his military accomplishments or his expansion of the Hasmonean state. Josephus often portrays Hyrcanus II unfavorably in the *Antiquities*. However, the Roman documents he cites in *Ant.* 14 praise him and show that Julius Caesar favored him more than Herod's father, Antipater. Nicolaus appears to have given Antipater some of the credit for the achievements of Hyrcanus II: he likely did this to justify his benefactor Herod the Great's establishment of a new Jewish monarchy that replaced the Hasmonean dynasty. Josephus occasionally incorporates Nicolaus's prejudices against the Hasmoneans in the *Antiquities*.[63] But not all of the unevenness and contradictions in this book should be attributable to Josephus or his sources, but rather to his method of writing history.

Josephus and His Methods of Writing History

It is important to consider the way Josephus produced his books to make sense of his conflicting accounts of the Hasmonean rulers. There were no firm lines in antiquity between writing and publication. Books were first presented orally in public recitations before they appeared in written form. They were then often distributed in drafts or copies as gifts to a small circle of associates, and periodically revised afterwards. In his

347), and Timagenes (13.344). In one instance he merely refers to "some writers" (13.337) as a source of history for the reign of Alexander Jannaeus. The Christian writer M. Minucius Felix mentions a now-lost work on this period by Antonius Julianus titled *de Judeis*. This is presumably the procurator of Judea during the First Jewish Revolt. Josephus likely consulted this work, and another lost history of the First Jewish Revolt. See further Schürer et al. 1973–87, 1:33–34. It is doubtful that Josephus knew the works of the Hellenistic Jewish historians, with the exception of Artapanus. Rather, he likely obtained this material from Alexander Polyhistor's Περὶ Ἰουδαίων. It is probable that Josephus had access to a Seleucid chronicle. See further *Ant.* 1.240; *Apion* 1.218; Sterling 1992, 263–84. For possible sources used by Josephus, see Attridge 1984, 210–27; Bilde 1988, 80–89; Babota 2014, 9–34; Dąbrowa 2010a, 13–16; D. Schwartz 2013, 6–10, 100–104.

63. See further Regev 2013, 28–29; Wacholder 1962, 4–36; Schürer et al. 1973–87, 1:28–32; T. Landau 2006, 1–68.

apologetic work *Against Apion* (1.47–57), Josephus implies that his *War* was criticized in literary circles during his oral presentations of it before its printed publication. In defending himself he had to be careful of criticizing his enemies, such as Justus of Tiberius, who had powerful patrons. He also had to flatter the rich, some of whom were his actual or potential benefactors.[64] Because Josephus's books, like those of his contemporaries, were written for his peers they often reflect the concerns and interests of his readers.

Josephus wrote his works, especially his *War*, for an educated audience in Rome. He was not the only historian of his time to have done so. In *War* 1.1–3 he states that other writers are currently producing histories of the First Jewish Revolt.[65] He appears to have heard several of them presented orally. Josephus even implies that he has been engaged in an ongoing oral debate with some of these authors. He writes that many of his contemporaries criticized his deficient Greek style, which caused some to question his credibility as a writer.[66] To make his books more popular, he had to pay attention to their literary style and oral quality.

Josephus suggests that his public presentations forced him to produce books that were entertaining. This accounts for some of his more unusual and interesting digressions that sometimes interrupt his narratives.[67] Josephus's concern for the entertainment value of his books also compelled him to include a few sensational stories about some of the Hasmonean monarchs and Jewish sects to interest his audience and attract new patrons. For this reason, it is important to consider the literary qualities of his accounts of the various Hasmonean rulers, which at times contain many novelistic features that Josephus undoubtedly included for the enjoyment of his listeners and readers.

64. See further Attridge 1984, 200–203. For the oral recitation of historical works in Rome, see further Mason 2009, 7–15, 45–67; Goldsworthy 2006, 186–90.

65. The Greek in this passage suggests that the *War* has been subjected to an extensive scholarly debate and multiple revisions prior to its publication. See further Mason 2009, 58.

66. For his Greek style, see *Ant.* 20.263; *Life* 40; cf. *War* 1.16; *Apion* 23–24.

67. Polyb. (2.56) criticizes the tendency of historians to include such sensationalistic materials. All ancient historians paid careful attention to rhetoric when they wrote their historical accounts. Nevertheless, the criticism of Polybius and other writers suggests that ancient historians considered the pursuit of truth their main goal, and that they often despised those who viewed history as subordinate to rhetoric. See, e.g., Cic. *De or.* 2.15.62.

In his letter to the historian Lucceius, Cicero urged him to produce history that was full of what we would term today romantic sensationalism.[68] Cicero's approach to history contrasts with that of the standards of Thucydides and Polybius, both of whom stress rational explanation. Josephus tends to follow the chronological approach of Polybius while integrating the dramatic style of Thucydides to convey the story of the Hasmonean period through character studies of prominent individuals. Josephus often measures them by their relationship with the Roman Republic.

Like Polybius, Josephus wanted to explain why the Roman Empire dominated much of the known world. His accounts of the Hasmonean state often emphasize the history of the Roman Republic's involvement in the Egypt and Syria to explain its domination of much of Europe, North Africa, and the Middle East in his day. Like the historian Appian, Josephus often pays little attention to chronological accuracy. He juxtaposes and transposes events from different times to produce what appears to be a sequential account of the Hasmonean state. The result is a narrative that is often chronologically inaccurate: yet, it met standards of contemporary historiography.[69] However, it is difficult to determine the extent to which this is the product of Josephus or his sources since, like other Roman historians, he seldom acknowledges the works he consulted. He often merged earlier materials into his narratives without citing them.[70] His method of writing and documentation was not only common, but it was also the result of ancient research methods.

Josephus made extensive use of Rome's public libraries as well as the private libraries of his patrons and other influential Romans.[71] These libraries certainly included many ancient texts. A recent study of surviving scrolls from fifty literary collections and libraries from the second century B.C.E. to the third century C.E. found that many of these manuscripts were used for 150 to 500 years. The average lifespan of these texts was

---

68. Cic. *Fam. 5.12.*

69. Atkinson 2011, 7–17.

70. For Josephus's splicing of his sources, particularly 1 Maccabees and Nicolaus of Damascus, and the resulting chronological contradictions in his books, see further D. Schwartz 2013, 96–100.

71. Atticus in the first century B.C.E. was famous for his extensive library. He not only purchased many books, but he copied and loaned them. Josephus borrowed books from his friends and his literary associates. Josephus's patron, Epaphroditus, owned some 30,000 works (*Ant.* 1.8–9; *Life* 430; *Apion* 1.1; 2.1, 296). For the loaning of books, see further, Cic. *Att.* 1.4.3; 1.7.1; 1.10.4; 1.11.3; 2.4.1.

between 200 and 300 years.[72] The famed physician and philosopher Galen mentions that the libraries on the Palatine hill were between 200 and 450 years old at the time of the fire of 192 C.E.[73] Given the great age of some of the scrolls found in ancient libraries, it is probable that Josephus had access to collections that may have included originals or copies of now-lost historical works from the Hasmonean era.

Because the ages of the manuscripts discovered in ancient libraries and literary collections demonstrate that scrolls survived for centuries, this study goes beyond Josephus to use books written by much later writers since it is probable that they consulted works or copies of texts from the Hasmonean period that are no longer extant. Such information is especially important to consider since sometimes, as in the case of George Syncellus, Byzantine authors clearly had access to Jewish historical works that predate the writings of Josephus.[74] However, these Christian works are only used when their information about the Hasmonean period is supported through textual, epigraphical, numismatic, or archaeological evidence.

Even if Josephus and later historians had access to ancient texts from the Hasmonean era, it is important to consider how their methods of research may have affected their writings. Because books in public libraries did not usually circulate in antiquity, scholars had to make notes or memorize their contents.[75] Many inconsistencies in the writings of Josephus are undoubtedly due to his having memorized passages from books in libraries. He did not always check his completed work with his original sources. In some instances he appears not to have actually read the works he cites. Rather, he sometimes appears to have relied on oral knowledge about ancient texts and their contents he acquired from others.[76]

---

72. See Houston 2009.

73. Gal. *On the Avoidance of Grief* 13. This conflagration destroyed much of his extensive personal library that he had stored in nearby warehouses. The recently discovered text of Περὶ Ἀλυπίας documents some of the contents of Galen's literary collection and provides important information about Roman libraries that reflect conditions of the preceding century when Josephus wrote his books. See further Rothschild and Thompson 2011; Nicholls 2011.

74. S. Schwartz 1990a.

75. Ancient writers often relied on their memories and used mnemonic techniques such as those preserved in *Rhet. Her.* 3.22 in lieu of taking notes. For the common practice of memorizing extensive passages from books, see Cic. *Tusc.* 1.24.59–64; (Pseudo) Plut. *Mor.* 513B; Paus. 6.19.5; Plin. *HN* 7.24; Quint., *Inst.* 11.2.7; Strabo, *Geogr.* 13.1.55. The compiler of the epitome of Jason of Cyrene's five-volume work into the book known as 2 Macc 2:25 states that he undertook this project to help those who wanted to memorize the entire work.

76. Pucci 2006.

But there is another reason to be doubt the accuracy of those passages in which Josephus cites from a named historian.

In those instances where Josephus mentions his sources, we cannot necessarily conclude that he reproduces them verbatim. Rather, he frequently inserts his own viewpoints into them, which makes it difficult to distinguish materials he copied from his own opinions. For this reason, the accounts of the Hasmoneans in his books, including quotations from other historical works, should be considered to convey thoughts of Josephus. He not only carefully selected his sources, but he is responsible for their redactions and their chronological placement in his narratives. This is especially true of his account of Judah Aristobulus in his *Antiquities*.[77] This section of the book is largely devoid of historical value, but would have been quite entertaining to recite before a live audience. When reading Josephus's accounts of the Hasmonean period it is important to consider their oral quality as works that were written to be both didactic and entertaining. This was expected of any good historian in antiquity. Josephus was clearly at the top of his craft; while reading his accounts of the Hasmonean state we can easily understand why he was so popular in his day.[78]

Like his contemporary historians, Josephus paid much attention to style. He often imitates the literary structures and forms of his predecessors. For the *War*, he was especially influenced by Dionysius of Halicarnassus. In his *Antiquities*, Josephus frequently imitates Thucydides. His presentation of conflict is often reminiscent of the writings of Caesar and Polybius. Josephus was particularly influenced by the understanding of fate as depicted in Polybius. Because Josephus wrote for pagans, he must have adopted these familiar literary models to influence his Gentile audience and his patrons. His books also suggest some dissatisfaction with works on Judaism that were available in his day, such as those of Alexander Polyhistor. He at times attempts to explain Jewish customs and to clarify misperceptions concerning Judaism that were widely held among pagans in the first century C.E. Because Josephus was not satisfied with the writings about Judaism available in his time, neither should we be. And we must also not be content with Josephus's works either. Rather, the contemporary researcher must go beyond his books to seek other sources both to verify the contents of his histories of the Hasmonean state and to uncover events he did not include in his *War* and *Antiquities*.

77. *Ant.* 13.301–19.

78. According to Eusebius (*Hist. eccl.* 3.9), after Josephus's death a statue of him was erected in Rome. His books were considered so important they were preserved in the city's public library.

The remainder of this book offers a comprehensive reconstruction of the Hasmonean state that goes beyond the writings of Josephus to incorporate all the extent historical, literary, epigraphical, and archaeological evidence. It begins, in Chapter 2, with a brief history of the Hasmonean family from their revolt against the edict of Antiochus IV Epiphanes to their creation of a state by Simon. It ends here because Simon was the last surviving son of Mattathias who had fought in the rebellion against the Seleucid rulers. Although he technically established a state, it was not until the reign of his son, John Hyrcanus, that the Hasmoneans kingdom actually became independent of the Seleucid Empire. The remaining chapters examine in depth each Hasmonean ruler from John Hyrcanus to the 30 B.C.E. murder of Hyrcanus II. The conclusion explores how Josephus's political and social situation in Flavian Rome affected his accounts of the Hasmonean rulers documented in this study, as well as the extent to which the Parthians of the first century C.E. influenced his perceptions of the Hasmonean rulers and his telling of their stories.

Chapter 2

THE CREATION OF THE HASMONEAN STATE

The Hasmonean Family: Their Background

The Hasmoneans were a Jewish family that fought the Seleucid rulers during the mid-second century B.C.E. to create an independent Jewish state, which they at first governed as its political leaders and high priests and then as its kings.[1] It was the Hasmonean family's religious zeal that brought them to power, and which helped them to maintain an independent state for nearly eighty years. Even after its termination, several members of the Hasmonean family fought the Romans for three decades to revive it. Unfortunately, relatively little is known about the Hasmoneans before the beginning of their rebellion against Seleucid rule. We are even uncertain as to origin of the family's name.

The name Hasmonean is apparently derived from an unknown ancestor named *Hašmônay*.[2] Josephus and 1 Maccabees record that the Hasmoneans belonged to the priestly course of Joiarib. According to Josephus, it is the

---

1. In addition to the works of Josephus, the major extant sources for the early Hasmonean period are 1 and 2 Maccabees. See further Atkinson 2013c, 8–16; 2015b.

2. *War* 1.36; *Ant.* 11.111; 20.190, 238; *Life* 1.4. The meaning of the name "Hasmonean" is unknown. Josephus claims it derives from a family patriarch named Asamonaeus. Although the name is conspicuously absent in both 1 and 2 Maccabees, Josephus and the rabbis use it frequently. See further Atkinson 2015b; Goldstein 1976, 17–20. See also *War* 2.344; 5.139; *Ant.* 20.190, 347. It is possible that the Hebrew name "Hasmonean" (חשמון) is a corruption of the name of Mattathias's grandfather, Simeon (= Shim'on; שמעון), mentioned in 1 Macc 2:1. The Hasmonean family is also known as the Maccabees, and their revolt against the Seleucid monarch Antiochus IV Epiphanes is frequently called the Maccabean Revolt. However, the name "Maccabee" is actually the nickname given to the family's most famous member, Judas (Judah) for his prowess in battle. It is related to the Hebrew and Aramaic root *mqb* and likely means "hammer-like." See further Bar-Kochva 1989, 147–48. The present study will use the name Hasmonean to refer to all members of this family who trace their descent to Mattathias.

elite of the priestly courses.[3] He may have highlighted Joiarib's prominence to justify their usurpation of the high priesthood from the family of
priests that previously held the title.[4]

The Hasmonean dynasty figures prominently in the works of Josephus.
This should not be surprising since he proudly claimed descent from them:
his "royal ancestry."[5] Although he tells us a great deal about his ancestors,
his *War* and *Antiquities*, which contain the most extensive accounts of the
Hasmonean family, lack many details. This is particularly true regarding
the beginning and the nature of their revolt against the Seleucid Empire.

The events in Jerusalem from 169 to 167 B.C.E. that led Antiochus
IV Epiphanes to issue a decree that purportedly outlawed the practice of
Judaism, and which led some members of the Hasmonean family to rebel
against Seleucid rule, are controversial. Five major sources document

---

3. *Life* 2; 1 Macc 2:1; 14:29. Josephus explains the origin of the priestly
day-courses in *Ant.* 7.365–67, which is a paraphrase of 1 Chr 24:1–19. According to
biblical tradition, Joiarib is the first clan recognized by lot. Because Joiarib occupies
a subordinate place in the listing found in Neh 12:1–7, 12–21, this may indicate that
1 Chronicles was redacted during the Hasmonean period to enhance the Hasmonean
family's ancestry. See Schürer et al. 1973–87, 2:250 n. 50; Goldstein 1976, 17; Mason
2001, 4 n. 10. Because the Greek translation of the biblical book of Joshua appears
to have been revised to support the Hasmoneans, it is probable that other biblical
texts were likewise redacted during the Hasmonean period. See further de Troyer
2003, 9–58. It has been suggested that the Hasmoneans were actually Zadokites. See
Schofield and VanderKam 2005; VanderKam 2004, 270 n. 90; Rooke 2000, 281–82.
H. Eshel (2008, 55), however, comments that since there is no explicit statement
saying that the Hasmoneans were Zadokites we should not assume that they were
from this family. Klawans (2012, esp. 18–23) has criticized scholars for overempha-
sizing the importance of the Zadokite priesthood in the Second Temple period since
Josephus provides no indication that Zadokite descent was a particularly important
issue or that the Hasmoneans were Zadokites. Babota (2014, 269–84) argues that
Jehoiarib was never important in the early restoration or pre-exilic period and that
priests from this watch were never high priests before the Hasmoneans. He concludes
that the Hasmoneans were priests of the "sons of Aaron" as all other priests were.
Because no ancient source claims the Hasmoneans were descended from Zadok, it is
doubtful they were related to him. See further Charlesworth 2002, 31.

4. Menelaus (172–162 B.C.E.) is the first recorded high priest in the Second
Temple period to belong to a family other than one directly descended from Joshua
(1 Macc 7:14), the first high priest of this era. See further VanderKam 2004, 18–42,
203–26.

5. *Life* 2–3. Josephus also mentions that his ancestor Simon Pellus was a
contemporary of the father of John Hyrcanus, the high priest Simon. His mother was
descended from the Hasmoneans.

the revolt led by the Hasmonean patriarch Mattathias against this edict.[6] How much of these stories are legend remains uncertain. According to the traditional accounts preserved in the extant sources, the Hasmonean revolt began when Mattathias defied the decree of the Seleucid monarch Antiochus IV Epiphanes that banned the observance of Jewish Law.[7] His family's war against the Seleucid rulers lasted for nearly twenty-five years.[8] During the reign of his son Simon, in the Seleucid year 170 (= 143/2 B.C.E.), the Hasmoneans gained independence for Judea.[9] His legitimacy to rule this new state largely rested in his having fought in the original revolt against the Seleucid Empire led by his father, Mattathias. All Hasmoneans in some manner sought to invoke the memory of Mattathias to show they were committed to their ancestral faith and the creation of an independent Jewish state.

According to the extant accounts, Mattathias was a priest from the northwestern Judean town of Modein. The author of 1 Maccabees implies that he and his family had lived there for generations.[10] The apparent association of the town's residents with the territory of Judea may have contributed to the Hasmonean family's hostility towards the Seleucid's Samaritan allies. The religious and cultural affiliation of the residents of Modein with Judea also appears to have created tensions that eventually incited Mattathias to lead a revolt against the Seleucid authorities.[11] After

6. 1 Macc 1; 2 Macc 3–7; Dan 7–12; *War* 1.31–35; *Ant.* 12.237–64.

7. 1 Macc 1:16–64; 2 Macc 5–7; *War* 1.34–35; *Ant.* 12.242–64.

8. 1 Macc 2:1–28; *War* 1.36–37.

9. 1 Macc 13:33–42; *Ant.* 13.213. This event may be documented in the *Megillat Ta'anit* under the year 27 Iyyar or 3 Tishri. See further, Goldstein 1976, 78–79; Sievers 1990, 109–12; Schürer et al. 1973–87, 1:190; VanderKam 2004, 272.

10. 1 Macc 2:70; 13:25. Cf. *Ant.* 12.265. According to 1 Macc 2:1, Mattathias moved from Jerusalem to Modein with his five sons. Elsewhere, the author of 1 Maccabees (2:70; 9:19) writes that Modein was the family's ancient home. Bar-Kochva (1989, 199 n. 8) suggests that the family's ritual functions as priests of the Joiarib clan was its only connection with Jerusalem.

11. Modein is placed in the mountains northwest of Jerusalem. See 1 Macc 3:10–38; 11:34; *Ant.* 12.287; Goldstein 1976, 410; Sievers 1990, 27 n. 1. The site is often identified with el-Medieh, which is approximately seven miles (twelve kilometers) east of Lod. See further, Boettger 1879, 187–88. Based on this location, it has been proposed that the city was part of the province of Samaria. See Babota 2014, 38. Some place Modein at Khirbet Umm el-'Umdan where a structure that has been identified as a Hasmonean period synagogue has been discovered. See Runesson, Binder, and Olsson 2008, 57–58. It has been suggested that the decision of the Hasmonean family to ally with Judea to the south explains why Apollonius, the governor of Samaria, initially opposed their resistance movement. This assumes

the death of Mattathias (ca. 166 B.C.E.), his five sons continued his revolt against the Seleucid monarchs. According to 2 Macc 2:2–5, their names were John, Simon, Judas, Eleazar, and Jonathan.[12] They were presumably born in Modein and considered themselves Judeans. Given the importance of the town in the historical accounts of the Hasmoneans, it is probable that Simon's son, John Hyrcanus, was also born there.[13] It was in this small and relatively insignificant place that the Hasmonean family came to prominence when their patriarch, Mattathias, first displayed his family's Phinehas-like religious zeal and used violence to oppose the Seleucid Empire's religious and political domination of this homeland.

The Hasmonean Revolt against the Seleucids

According to 1 Macc 1:26, Mattathias "burned with zeal for the law, just as Phinehas did against Zimri the son of Salu."[14] His fiery temper erupted when officials sent by Antiochus IV Epiphanes arrived in his village with an order that everyone offer a public sacrifice according to the Greek fashion.[15] When a Judean approached the altar to comply with the imperial edict, Mattathias killed him and the royal official before destroying it. He then called upon "all who are zealous for the sake of the Torah, who uphold the covenant, to follow me."[16]

The author of 1 Macc 2:26 and 54 compares Mattathias's act with the zeal of Phinehas, who used violence during the Exodus to compel Jews to observe the Torah, for two major reasons. First, like Phinehas,

---

that Modein was in the border zone between Samaria and Judaea, and that Mattathias and his family considered themselves to be Judeans. For this interpretation, see S. Schwartz 2001, 33. Because the Samaritans were not included in the persecution of the Jews by Antiochus IV Epiphanes, it is probable that Modein was located in Judea and its residents were ideologically connected with Jerusalem as suggested by the ancient Jewish and Christian descriptions of the site, which imply that it was always considered part of Judea. See further Scolnic 2010.

12. The list in 2 Macc 2:22–23 replaces John with Joseph. The author of 1 Macc 16:2 states that "Judas and John" are Simon's "two eldest sons" while v. 14 mentions an additional brother named Mattathias.

13. Hyrcanus's grandfather, Mattathias, and his uncle, Jonathan, were buried in Modein, which suggests this was the ancestral village of the family and his probable place of birth. See also 1 Macc 2:70; 13:25; *War* 1.36.

14. For this biblical story, see Num 25:6–8; Sir 45:23–26.

15. 1 Macc 1:51; 2:15–30. Because this story only appears in 1 Maccabees its historicity is uncertain. Cf. *War* 1.36.

16. 1 Macc 2:27.

Mattathias and his sons enforced their interpretation of the Law upon their fellow Jews. Second, since Phineas and his descendants received the high priesthood because of their zealous acts, the writer of 1 Maccabees appealed to this tradition to validate the actions of the descendants of Mattathias who served as high priests. Mattathias's appeal to strict Torah observance, which included the forced circumcision of the sons of those Jews who had obeyed the Seleucid prohibition against circumcision, formed the basis for his opposition to the Seleucid rule.[17] According to 1 Macc 2:48, through such violent acts, he and his followers saved the Torah from the hand of the Gentiles. His example of religious zealotry and military resistance became the foundational ethos of the entire Hasmonean dynasty, and would later serve as a model for the zealots who opposed Rome during the First Jewish Revolt of Josephus's day.[18] But of all the sons of Mattathias, none was more zealous and violent than Judas.

Judas was the oldest and most famous son of Mattathais.[19] He assumed leadership of the revolt immediately after his father's death, and quickly achieved renown as a warrior and a military commander. The author of 1 Macc 3:1–9 recounts his valor and portrays him as the savior of his people. In 164 B.C.E. he captured Jerusalem, cleansed the temple, and reinstituted the sacrificial rites. His achievement has subsequently been celebrated with the Festival of Hanukkah.[20]

17. 1 Macc 2:46. For the use of the Phinehas tradition by the Hasmoneans, see Collins 2003, 12–14.

18. See further Regev 2013, 107–8. Dąbrowa (2010b, 8–12) also stresses the religious character of Hasmonean resistance and its aim to defend the Jewish religion. The legend (1 Macc 2:49–68; *Ant.* 12.283–84) that Mattathias before his death chose Simon to lead the rebellion reflects traditions that highlighted the movement's religious focus to show that Simon's piety led to the creation of an independent state. See Sievers 1990, 36–37.

19. 1 Macc 2:1–9:22; 2 Macc 8–15; *War* 1.36–47; *Ant.* 12.265–434.

20. 1 Macc 4:36–59; 2 Macc 10:1–8; *Ant.* 12.316–25. The book of 2 Maccabees contains a theological interpretation of the cleansing of the temple by Judas. See Wheaton 2012. The disagreements between 1 Maccabees and 2 Maccabees makes it difficult to determine the exact sequence of events associated with this holiday, particularly whether Antiochus IV Epiphanes died before or after Judas rededicated the temple. They also give different explanations why the festival continued for eight days, why it began on the 25th of Kislev, and why it was originally associated with the Festival of Tabernacles. See VanderKam 2004, 23–40. The nature of the Seleucid imposed cult in the Jerusalem temple is the subject of a longstanding academic debate. For this issue, see further Atkinson 2015a; H. Eshel 2008, 13–27; Grabbe 1992, 258–59.

After Judas died in battle, his brother Jonathan took over command of the rebellion.[21] It was during his reign that the Hasmoneans began to negotiate with their former Seleucid foes to bring stability to their fledgling kingdom, and to win both political recognition and higher offices from them. The family's unique combination of religious zeal and political acumen proved to be its greatest strength, and allowed them to create a small state amidst larger hostile powers and maintain its independence for nearly a century. But at this time the movement's future was uncertain under Jonathan.

Although Jonathan was an exceptional warrior like his father and brother, Judas, he proved to be the family's most astute politician thus far. He quickly realized the advantages to be gained by supporting one of the contenders seeking to rule the Seleucid Empire. At this time, Demetrius II and Alexander Balas were fighting one another to control Syria.[22] Because neither was able to defeat the other, it was inevitable that they would look south to the Hasmoneans for help. But they soon found that Jonathan's support came with a hefty price tag.

During his reign, Jonathan attempted to retain power through diplomacy with several Seleucid rulers. But he did not entirely trust them. He also realized that he needed to appease the pharaohs of the Ptolemaic Empire adjacent to his border. It was an opportune time to make overtures to them. Ptolemy VI Philometor and his co-ruler, his sister-wife Cleopatra II, were friendly towards the Jews.[23] They had welcomed Onias IV after he left Judea following the deposition and murder of his father, the high priest Onias III. The royal couple allowed Onias IV and his supporters to settle in Egypt and construct a Jewish temple in the town of Leontopolis.[24] Philometor later betrothed his daughter, Cleopatra Thea, to Alexander Balas, the new ruler of Syria.[25] Jonathan sat on the royal dais between the groom and the bride's father at the wedding as an honored guest; he

21. 1 Macc 9:23–12:53; *War* 1.48–49; *Ant.* 13.1–212.

22. For Demetrius II (145–38, 129–25 B.C.E.), see Atkinson 2012c, 106–11; Ehling 2008, 164–78; Grainger 1997, 42–44. For Balas (150–46 B.C.E.), see Grainger 1997, 6–7.

23. For these Egyptian rulers, see Atkinson 2012c, 117–24; Hölbl 2000, 127–52. Philometor ruled from 181 to 145 B.C.E. and Cleopatra II reigned from 130 to 127 B.C.E.

24. *Ant.* 13.62–73; *War* 7.426–31. For this temple and its Jewish community, see further Collins 1999, 69–72; Bohak 2010; Huß 2001, 590.

25. Alexander I Balas of Smyrna was the first successful usurper in Seleucid history. For his reign, see Grainger 1997, 6–7. For Cleopatra Thea, see Grainger 1997, 45–47. The couple had one child, Antiochus VI Dionysus.

also gave the couple lavish gifts of gold. Jonathan's appearance at this event was a public declaration that the Hasmoneans were now allies of the Seleucid Empire and their Ptolemaic backers.[26] This not only gave Jonathan's fledgling kingdom a measure of political stability, but also the necessary religious recognition his family needed to rule it.

In exchange for Hasmonean support, Balas recognized Jonathan as the Hasmonean high priest. The ceremony took place in 153/2 B.C.E. during the Festival of Tabernacles. Jonathan not only became the first Hasmonean to hold this sacred office, but this holiday effectively became a yearly celebration of his family.[27] Balas sent Jonathan a purple cloak—the color of royalty in antiquity—and a crown as tokens of his new office and numbered him among the prestigious order of the king's "Friends."[28] All subsequent Hasmonean rulers would follow Jonathan's example and seek treaties with foreign countries to retain power. Unfortunately, the Hasmoneans often found themselves entangled in Seleucid and Ptolemaic dynastic feuds that frequently led to wars on Judean soil. This fighting forced the various members of the family to support one claimant for the Seleucid throne over another.

Balas fell out of favor with his father-in-law. Philometor returned to Ptolemais to annul the marriage of his daughter, Cleopatra Thea, to Balas and forced her to wed Demetrius II.[29] When Philometor arrived in Hasmonean territory, Jonathan had no choice but to abandon Balas and accompany Philometor to Syria. During the journey, it appeared that Philometor was preparing to annex Judea: he placed garrisons in many of is towns.[30]

Philometor and Demetrius II fought Balas. During the engagement a Syrian war elephant startled Philometor's horse. Balas's men threw him to the ground and fatally wounded him. However, Philometor clung to life for five days. Before he died, his men brought him Balas's severed head. These events affected the Hasmonean dynasty since Jonathan had attended Balas's wedding as an honored guest. It also gave Jonathan an

26. For these events, see further 1 Macc 10:51–58; *Ant.* 13.80–83; Bevan 1927, 94–95; Gruen 1984, 666–67.

27. 1 Macc 10:15–21; *Ant.* 13.43–46. For the Hasmonean appropriation of Tabernacles, see further Rajak 2001, 39–60.

28. 1 Macc 10:15–20. For this institution, see Savalli-Lestrade 1998, 77–78.

29. Demetrius II Nikator (145–38 and 129–25 B.C.E.) was the son of Demetrius I and perhaps Laodice V. For his reign, see Grainger 1997, 42–44. Cleopatra Thea ruled from 125–121 B.C.E., see further Whitehorne 1994, 149–73.

30. 1 Macc 10–11; *Ant.* 13.86–115; Diod. Sic. 32.9; App. *Syr.* 67; Just. *Epit.* 35.2.1–4.

opportunity to increase his power at the expense of the Seleucid Empire, providing that he chose the winning side in the forthcoming Seleucid civil war.

Jonathan took advantage of the turmoil caused by the new civil war between Demetrius II and the pretender Tryphon, which greatly weakened the Seleucid Empire, to increase his power in Judea.[31] Tryphon had no authority to govern in his own name. Rather, he exercised power through the boy prince Antiochus VI Dionysus, whom he had kidnapped.[32] At this time the Hasmonean family realized that no single monarch was powerful enough to rule securely over the entire Seleucid Empire. The two contenders for the throne of Syria likewise recognized they needed outside help to retain power over a portion of Syria. Demetrius II took action first: he gave Jonathan significant land concessions and ordered the removal of Seleucid garrisons from Jerusalem in exchange for Hasmonean troops to fight Tryphon.[33]

Jonathan supplied troops to help Demetrius II subdue a revolt in Antioch. Now confident that he could defeat Tryphon alone, Demetrius II reneged on the promises he had made to the Hasmoneans. Jonathan subsequently switched sides and backed the young Antiochus VI and Tryphon.[34] In early 144 B.C.E., Tryphon proclaimed Antiochus VI king of the Seleucid Empire.[35] Tryphon let Jonathan keep all the privileges Demetrius II had given him, including the office of high priest. He also appointed Jonathan's brother, Simon, governor of the coastal area "from the Ladder

31. The actual name of Tryphon was Diodotus. He is commonly known by the nickname Tryphon. See Diod. Sic. 33.4a; Strab. 16.2.10; *Ant.* 13.131. For the events of Tryphon's reign, see Atkinson 2012c, 107–10; Ehling 2008, 164–89; Grainger 1997, 69–70.

32. Diod. Sic. 32d. Antiochus VI Dionysus (from 144–142/41 B.C.E.) was the son of Cleopatra Thea and Alexander Balas. Tryphon governed on behalf of Antiochus VI during this time and then alone from 144/43 to 138/37 B.C.E. See Just. *Epit.* 36.1 *Ant.* 13.6.1. App. (*Syr.* 11.68) mistakenly identifies Antiochus VI as Alexander II Zabinas. See further Grainger 1997, 69–70. Zabinas and Balas minted coins with portraits that depict them wearing the scalp of a lion that imitated the currency minted by Antiochus IV Epiphanes and his successors. This image was intended to portray them as the rightful successors to the Seleucid Empire. See N. Wright 2011a.

33. See 1 Macc 11:42–53; Downey 1961, 122–24; cf. Diod. Sic. 33.4.2.

34. 1 Macc 11:38, 41–52; *Ant.* 13.133–44. Dąbrowa (2010a, 54) suggests that Demetrius II realized that keeping his promise to the Hasmoneans no longer served his own interests, but actually strengthened the power of Jonathan.

35. The numismatic evidence shows that Tryphon proclaimed Antiochus VI king in S.E. 169 (= 144/3 B.C.E.). See Houghton 1983, 79.

of Tyre to the borders of Egypt."[36] Jonathan also sent an embassy to Rome to renew the treaty with the Roman Republic his brother Judas had made.[37] It was at this time that Jonathan made a momentous decision that would affect all his successors, and help lead to the creation of an independent Jewish state.

Because the Seleucids were no longer reliable allies, the Hasmoneans were forced to seek some relationship with the Roman Republic to ward off further Syrian incursions into their territory. Jonathan decided to follow the example of his late brother, Judas, and send a delegation to Rome to renew his family's treaty. His mission to Rome in 144 B.C.E. took place a year or two after the Republic's victory in the Achaean war and the ascension of Demetrius II. The Romans at this time wanted to prevent Syria's monarchs from expanding their territory, especially along the coast and in the lands occupied by the Hasmoneans. Jonathan likely realized this and took advantage of the Seleucid Empire's continuing civil wars to court the Roman Republic. Because the Romans had intervened to stop Antiochus IV Epiphanes's second invasion of Egypt in 168 B.C.E., it was probable that they could return to the Middle East to interfere in affairs of the Seleucid Empire.[38] All subsequent rulers of the Seleucid Empire had to consider the possibility of a Roman invasion before they decided to attack the kingdoms along the shore of the Mediterranean. This gave Jonathan some security.

Jonathan's military campaigns appear to have been carefully planned to prepare for the creation of an independent state. Sievers believes the wars of Jonathan were part of a coordinated effort by the Hasmoneans to secure and enlarge Judean territory since the towns he captured were all at strategic locations.[39] However, Bar-Kochva suggests that Jonathan's earlier treaty with Demetrius II was intended to solve Judea's deteriorating economic situation that had been brought about by the continual Seleucid wars and the shortage of agricultural land.[40] Although the Hasmoneans were undoubtedly in need of additional arable lands, Jonathan's campaigns were limited to

36. 1 Macc 11:59.

37. 1 Macc 12:1–4.

38. When Antiochus IV invaded Egypt in 168 B.C.E., the Roman legate C. Popilius Laenas met him and demanded that he return to Syria or face the might of Rome. Antiochus returned home in disgrace. See Polyb. 29.27.1–8; Diod. Sic. 31.2; Livy, *History* 45.12.1–8; App. *Syr.* 66.350–52; Just. *Epit.* 34.3.1–3. Cf. Dan. 11:29.

39. Sievers 1990, 97–99. Jonathan captured the following cities: Ascalon and Gaza (1 Macc 11:60–62; *Ant.* 13.148–53), Hazor (1 Macc 11:63–74; *Ant.* 13.154, 158–62), Beth-Zur (1 Macc 11:65–66; *Ant.* 13.155–57), and Adida (1 Macc 12:38).

40. Bar-Kochva 1989, 53–54.

sites of strategic economic and military, not necessarily agricultural, importance. This suggests that he had a coordinated plan to win independence through both conquest and treaty. Demetrius II was unable to curtail this Hasmonean expansion because of his war with Tryphon.

Tryphon became worried of the growing power of the Hasmoneans. He tricked Jonathan to accompany him to Ptolemais with only a small bodyguard. Tryphon arrested him. Simon's efforts to pay the requested ransom to release his sibling proved futile. Tryphon murdered Jonathan in 143/2 B.C.E. Simon gained possession of his brother's bones and buried them beside his parents and his three siblings in Modein.[41] If Tryphon thought that getting rid of Jonathan would weaken the Hasmoneans, he and the other Seleucid rulers would soon learn that his brother, Simon, was a far more formidable foe.

The Creation of the Hasmonean State

Simon was the sole surviving son of Mattathias. His father's apparent popularity may explain why he was able to succeed Jonathan as his nation's high priest and political leader.[42] Despite his pedigree, there was apparently considerable controversy over Simon's appointment; some apparently wondered whether his sons would automatically inherit secular rule and the high priesthood. Many Judeans undoubtedly worried that the Hasmonean family would become a Hellenistic-style dynasty in which these offices were restricted to the descendants of Mattathais. Although the Hasmoneans had not yet adopted the title of king, Simon's authority was essentially that of a Hellenistic monarch. He was supreme civil governor; the commander of the army; and it would soon become clear that his descendants were to succeed him. But what was perhaps most problematic was that Simon was first and foremost the nation's religious leader. To oppose him could even carry the death penalty![43] Simon's reign is important since it marks the institutionalization of both Hasmonean

41. *Ant.* 13.211–12.

42. 1 Macc 13:1–16:17; *War* 1.50–54; *Ant.* 13.213–28. Jonathan had both male and female children (1 Macc 13:16; *Ant.* 13.204; *Life* 1.1.4). According to 1 Macc 13:16, Simon sent two of them to Tryphon as part of a ransom to free Jonathan; they were presumably killed. The Vulgate of 1 Macc 13:23 reads: "Occidit Ionathan et filios eius." Although this is a scribal addition, it appears to reflect historical reality. Josephus emphasizes that Tryphon tricked Jonathan to make it clear that Simon played no part in his brother's assassination (*Ant.* 13.205), or the murder of Jonathan's children.

43. 1 Macc 14:43–46.

rule and the family's charisma: there would no longer be any spontaneous calls for a leader like Mattathias to save the Jews from the Seleucid rulers. The Hasmoneans now sought political stability by restricting virtually all authority to a single person.[44]

There is a discrepancy in the extant sources concerning the year when Simon began to acquire his unpreceded powers. This may suggest some effort on the part of the ancient chroniclers to conceal some of the obstacles he encountered when he implemented the principle of dynastic rule. The trouble in determining what happened at this time is partly due to the apparent confusion in the sources concerning both the length of Jonathan's tenure as high priest, and whether he was preceded by an unknown high priest.[45] Let us try to sort out these uncertainties beginning with his official declaration of independence from the Seleucid Empire.

44. See further Regev 2013, 113–17.

45. Josephus in *Ant.* 20.238 mistakenly writes that he was high priest for seven years. Alexander Balas recognized Jonathan as high priest in 152 B.C.E., which gives him a term of ten years. 1 Macc 13:41–42 does not provide a date for the death of Jonathan. It synchronizes the first year of the political rule of Simon, his brother and successor, with 170 of the Seleucid Era. This Seleucid date indicates that Tryphon murdered Jonathan in 143/2 B.C.E. The following scholars accept this date: Ehling 2008, 175–76; Goldstein 1989, 316–19; Habicht 1989, 362–69; Klausner 1972a, 196–99; Schürer et al. 1973–87, 1:190; VanderKam 2004, 264. The chronology of Josephus complicates matters; he writes in *Ant.* 12.414 that after the death of Alcimus, Judas became high priest for three years. See also *Ant.* 12.434; cf. *Ant.* 12.419. However, Josephus in *Ant.* 20.237 states that after the death of Alcimus there was no high priest for seven years. His statement that the high priesthood was vacant for four years in *Ant.* 13.46 is clearly an error. The claim of Michael Wise (2005) that Judas may have been recognized as high priest during the interregnum, traditionally dated between 159 and 152 B.C.E., is largely based on the restoration of the names "Judah, Jonathan, Simon" (יהודה יונ[תן שמעון) in line 10 of 4Q245. Although Jonathan and Simon are plausible restorations of these lines, the name Judah is a mere conjecture and goes against the extant historical evidence that identifies Jonathan as the first Hasmonean high priest. It is plausible that 1 Maccabees and Josephus tried to suppress the memory of an unknown high priest who had officiated from 159 to 152 B.C.E. The existence of such a priest would explain why Jonathan had to be appointed high priest: if the office had been vacant, it should have been easier for the Hasmoneans to supplant the line of Zadok with Joiarib. It is possible that Jonathan replaced a sitting high priest, which may account for some of the opposition to his holding this office in the extant narratives, as well as the difficulties Simon later faced in gaining public recognition from his citizens when he assumed the high priesthood. See further, Babota 2014, 131–34; H. Eshel 2008, 54–55; Gruen 2016, 228–29; VanderKam 2004, 264–51.

According to 1 Macc 13:41–42, the letter of Demetrius II to Simon marks the beginning of the Hasmonean State: "In the year 170 (= 143/2 B.C.E.), the yoke of the Gentiles was lifted from Israel and the people began to write as the dating formula in bills and contracts, 'In the first year, under Simon, high priest, commander, and chief of the Jews'." Although it is possible this new system of dating began with the liberation from Seleucid rule and taxes, the *Megillat Ta'anit*, 1 Maccabees, and Josephus suggest it marks the beginning of Simon's tenure as high priest and political leader of an independent state.[46] However, the author of 2 Macc 1:7 dates this event to the Seleucid year 169 B.C.E.[47]

Although Demetrius II recognized Simon as high priest in 143/2 B.C.E, the situation in Judea was different. The people appear to have been reluctant to allow him to accept a religious position a foreign king had bestowed upon him. The writer of 1 Maccabees includes a document (14:27–49) that is introduced as a spontaneous proclamation of praise for Simon because of his military successes, but which states that the "people" (ὁ λαός; 1 Macc 14:35) appointed him high priest in 140 B.C.E.[48] VanderKam proposes that the declaration of the people in 1 Macc 14:27 actually took place earlier, at the gathering in Jerusalem recorded in 1 Macc 13:1–9. He suggests this meeting was with the soldiers who had escaped from Tryphon at the time of Jonathan's death. With no leader to protect them, the Jewish authorities subsequently recognized Simon as high priest. Simon then called together the people of Jerusalem, who were dismayed at these events because they had not been involved in the earlier gathering. They formally affirmed his appointment in public.[49] But the ordination process was likely more complicated.

Sievers suggests that Simon was first accepted as high priest by the people, then by Demetrius II, by the priests and other officials in his third year, and finally by the larger assembly of people, priests, and leaders as recorded in the decree of 1 Macc 14.[50] Although Demetrius II was among

---

46. See further, Ehling 2008, 175–76. The *Megillat Ta'anit* likely refers to this liberation under 27 Iyyar (or perhaps 3 Tishri), when Demetrius II returned the crown-tax (בלילאי) to the Jews. See further, Sievers 1990, 110–12; Schürer et al. 1973–87, 1:190–91; Zeitlin 1922, 83–84.

47. This book begins the Seleucid Era in 311 B.C.E., while 1 Maccabees counts the commencement of the Seleucid year from spring 312 B.C.E. See further, Goldstein 1983, 145–48; Babota 2014, 237–38.

48. 1 Macc 14:26.

49. VanderKam (2004, 276–83) cites *Ant.* 13.197 to support this reconstruction.

50. Sievers 1990, 122–24. Regev (2013, 114–17) comments that the need to reconfirm the nomination by the assembly three years after Simon had served as high

those who acknowledged Simon as high priest, this should not be taken as a sign of his complete independence from Seleucid rule. The Heliodorus stele shows that since the time of Seleucus IV (187–175 B.C.E.) the Seleucid monarchs sought to exercise a tight control over the finances of the Jerusalem temple and the provinces of Coele-Syria and Phoenicia. This inscription indicates that the Seleucid rulers believed they had the right to appoint the priests in regions under their control, including Judea.[51] However, the various contenders for the Seleucid throne were weak at this time and needed Judean support to fight off their political rivals. This explains why Antiochus VII Sidetes later sought an alliance with Simon, and was willing to recognize him as high priest.[52] Nevertheless, the Seleucid rulers only maintained their treaties with the Hasmoneans when it was convenient for them to do so.

It appears that our sources describe different moments in the career of Simon when the Seleucid rulers and the Jews separately confirmed him as high priest. The surviving documentation also suggests that considerable controversy surrounded this appointment. Based on the extant evidence, there is no reason to connect Simon's public recognition as high priest in 140 B.C.E. with his earlier appointment to this office by Demetrius II in 143/2 B.C.E. Such efforts represent attempts to reconcile the contradictory chronologies in 1 Maccabees and the *Antiquities*; neither book presents a complete account of this period. The extant evidence suggests that Simon did not receive immediate and unanimous acceptance as high priest. It is plausible that some Jews opposed him because they believed his brother, Jonathan, had unjustly taken supreme religious power from a rightful high priest.

If some Jews believed that Jonathan had usurped the high priesthood from a legitimate high priest, this may account for the opposition Simon faced when he succeeded his sibling to this office. The observation of John Collins and Peter Flint that the author of *4QPseudo-Daniel ar* (4Q245) was not specifically anti-Hasmonean, but accepted a "mixed" line of priestly succession as long as the offices of priest and king remained separate, would account for this text's apparent mention of Jonathan and Simon but not John Hyrcanus.[53] Unlike his predecessors, Hyrcanus

priest and political leader shows the necessity for public legitimization of his positions. For the chronological problems in 1 Maccabees pertaining to the appointment of Simon, see further Goldstein 1976, 467–48, 475, 492–94, 500–501.

51. See Atkinson 2013c, 8–16; Cotton and Gera 2009; Cotton and Wörrle 2007; Grüll 2010.

52. Dąbrowa 2010a, 59.

53. See further, Collins and Flint 1996, 158.

represented a major change in Hasmonean policy since he effectively merged the offices of high priest and monarch even though he did not call himself a king. His reign represented a major departure from Hasmonean succession since he was the first of the second generation of his family to govern: he had not fought alongside Mattathais and his sons against the Seleucid rulers.

Simon had a long record of military leadership by the time he became his nation's high priest and political leader. In an apocryphal tradition that was apparently written to justify his right to succeed his brother as commander of his family's movement, the author of 1 Macc 2:65 reports that Mattathias once said to his sons, "Behold your brother Simon: I know he is wise in counsel; always listen to him; he shall be your father."[54] This story may have been created to counter later opposition to his family's consolidation of political and sacred powers by tracing Simon's authority to his father, the famed Mattathias. It was because Simon had fought the Seleucid rulers since the beginning of his family's revolt that he came to be accepted as Jonathan's replacement. He was, moreover, a competent military commander. He and Jonathan had led forces together. Antiochus VI had even appointed Simon "governor from the Ladder of Tyre to the borders of Egypt." Bar-Kochva observes that Simon appears to have been in charge of an early campaign when he led cavalry against Seleucid forces.[55] Simon was clearly qualified to lead his nation's military, which was deemed an essential precondition at this time for Hasmonean rule.

While his brother, Jonathan, was a prisoner, Simon travelled to Jerusalem where, according to 1 Maccabees, the people there appointed him their leader (ἡγούμενος) in place of his siblings, Judas and Jonathan, to fight the Seleucids.[56] Although Simon was the most qualified to assume secular rule, the question of what role religion would play in the new state was controversial. The extant sources suggest that internal opposition to Simon's appointment as high priest limited his religious authority.

The author of 1 Maccabees mentions that it was agreed by "the *Ioudaioi* and the priests that Simon should be their chief and high priest in perpetuity until a true prophet shall arise."[57] The Greek phrase "in perpetuity" (εἰς αἰῶνα) does not say anything about the hereditary character of this office. Rather, it implies that Simon could be removed from the high priesthood before his death since the expected prophet presumably could arrive and either assume power or designate another person to replace

54. This story is repeated in *Ant.* 12.283–84.
55. 1 Macc 10:67–89; Bar-Kochva 1989, 78–79.
56. 1 Macc 12:53–13:9.
57. 1 Macc 14:41.

him.[58] This limitation may provide additional evidence that the *Ioudaioi* and the priests were unwilling to grant Simon the high priesthood forever, or give him the right to pass the office to one of his sons. Because he was not declared king, there also may have been some opposition to him serving as both secular leader and high priest. Many Jews also may have opposed his family's creation of a political and religious dynasty.[59]

It was essential for Simon to maintain peace in his kingdom, and prevent the Seleucid rulers from attempting to take its lands, if he was to establish a dynasty and an independent state. For this reason, Simon sought to secure his position through international treaties that would help keep the Seleucid rulers out of Judean affairs. According to 1 Macc 12, about the time Simon received popular accumulation as high priest and political leader he sent a delegation to Rome under the leadership of a man named Numenius. The author of 1 Maccabees states that Jonathan earlier had sent "Numenius son of Antiochus and Antipater son of Jason" to Rome.[60] Their task was to renew Judas's treaty with Rome.[61] Because the Senate gave his delegation letters of safe conduct for their return, this was a tacit acknowledgment that the Republic backed the Hasmoneans. The writer of 1 Maccabees implies that Simon's mission was successful since it prompted Demetrius II to recognize him as high priest to avoid any potential confrontation with the Roman Republic.[62]

58. The expectation of a future prophet is not new, but is mentioned in connection with the cleansing of the temple by Judas in 1 Macc 4:46 and his disposition of the polluted stones of the altar. Wacholder identifies this unnamed prophet with Elijah and suggests that the author of 1 Maccabees may have been influenced by Eupolemus's *On the Prophecy of Elijah*. However, this may not have been an actual book, but merely a chapter in Eupolemus's *On the Kings of Judaea*. See further Euseb. *Praep. evang.* 9.30.1; Atkinson 2013b; Wacholder 1974, 21–24.

59. Simon may have agreed to other unrecorded concessions to become Judea's religious and political leader. For this possibility, see further Sievers 1990, 127; Goldstein 1976, 504–5.

60. 1 Macc 14:22, 24. The two also served as Simon's ambassadors.

61. 1 Macc 12:1–16; *Ant.* 13:163–70. *War* 1.48. Both 1 Maccabees and Josephus also include a description of the Hasmonean family's letters to the Spartans. The majority of experts doubt their authenticity. For this issue, see Hengel 1974, 1:72; 2:50–51 n. 124; Grabbe 1992, 264; Sievers 1990, 98–99; Schürer et al. 1973–87, 1:184.

62. 1 Macc 14:40. It is possible that Demetrius II knew that Simon had sent this embassy, and therefore recognized him as Judea's political and religious leader before the Romans had given their response.

Several scholars suggest that Demetrius II actually granted the Hasmoneans political independence to help him defeat Tryphon, and that his proclamation to Simon followed the death of Antiochus VI.[63] Despite the uncertainty over the exact sequence of events, Simon's treaties with Rome played a major role in creating the necessary conditions for the transformation of his small kingdom into a full-fledged state that was recognized by the Seleucid emperors. Syria's monarchs had no choice but to do so, and accept the loss of lands they had long claimed as part of the Seleucid Empire, because of the potential threat of Roman interference in the Middle East and the growing military power of the Hasmoneans. Simon's alliance with the Roman Republic gave him the freedom to increase the size of his forces, which increasingly became a threat to the Seleucid Empire.

According to 1 Macc 14:38–40, the Roman Republic officially recognized the Jews as their allies. This was apparently the direct result of the embassy Simon had dispatched under Numenius to Rome to confirm the former treaties between the Republic and the Hasmonean family. Josephus only makes a passing reference to Simon's alliance with Rome.[64] He quotes a *senatus consultum* (*Ant.* 14.145–48) that is similar to the letter of the consul Lucius mentioned in 1 Macc 14:16–24.[65] Goldstein suggests that the Romans in 1 Macc 14:24 also recognized Demetrius II as king of the Seleucid Empire.[66] This would indicate that the Senate at this time knew that Tryphon had murdered Antiochus VI. According to Diodorus Siculus, the Roman Senate had refused to accept Tryphon's gift of a golden statue of the god Victory because they considered him a usurper and a murderer.[67] This suggests that Tryphon's assassination of the young Antiochus VI prompted the Romans to acknowledge Demetrius II as monarch of the Seleucid Empire. Because the Roman Senate recently had favored Simon's delegation, Demetrius II recognized him as high priest so as not to offend the Romans.

---

63. Goldstein 1976, 478, 493; Schürer et al. 1973–87, 1:89–90; VanderKam 2004, 272.

64. *Ant.* 13.227. See also 1 Macc 15:16–24.

65. The consul of this letter must be Lucius Caecilius Metellus who held the office in 142 B.C.E. since he is the only such consul between 143 and 137 B.C.E. with the *praenomen* Lucius. See Broughton 1952a, 471–84, esp. 474. For a skeptical position that this embassy never took place, see further Fischer 1970, 96–101. Goldstein (1976, 493) proposes that 1 Maccabees is not in chronological order and that the passage in 15:15–24 is misplaced and belongs to ch. 14.

66. Goldstein 1976, 478.

67. Diod. Sic. 33.28a.

Because the *Antiquities* and 1 Maccabees offer different chronologies for the first years of the reign of Simon, it is important to compare their contents in order to reconstruct the most probable chronological sequence of events between the Hasmoneans and the Seleucid rulers at the time he declared independence. Table 1 shows the order of events in each of these books:

Table 1. *Chronological Listing of the Events for the Reign of Simon in Antiquities and 1 Maccabees*[68]

Event	Josephus, Antiquities	1 Maccabees
Capture of Demetrius II by the Parthians	13.184–86	14:1–3
Capture and murder of Jonathan by Tryphon	13.187–209	12:39–48
Simon elected as leader	13.201–203	13:1–11
Simon's relationship with Demetrius II and his proclamation of independence from the Seleucids	13.213–14	13:41–42
Tryphon murders Antiochus VI	13.218–19	13:31–32
Antiochus VII Sidetes kills Tryphon	13.223–24	

Josephus places the capture of Demetrius II by the Parthians (*Ant.* 13.184–86) immediately before Tryphon seized and murdered Jonathan (*Ant.* 13.187–209). According to his account, Tryphon took advantage of the absence of Demetrius II to capture and kill Jonathan, murder Antiochus VI, and assume the throne.[69] The death of Jonathan prompted the Jews to elect Simon as their leader (*Ant.* 13.201–203). Simon then proclaimed independence from the Seleucid rulers (*Ant.* 13.213–14). The new Seleucid king, Antiochus VII Sidetes, later murdered Tryphon (*Ant.* 13.223–24). According to Josephus's chronology, the unexpected imprisonment of Demetrius II was ultimately responsible for all these events; it led to Simon's proclamation of independence and the birth of the Hasmonean state.

68. Josephus excludes the items listed in this chart from the *War*, with the exception of a brief reference to the Jonathan's murder in *War* 1.49.

69. According to Josephus, Tryphon captured Jonathan and took him to Addida (*Ant.* 13.203), to the area of Jerusalem (*Ant.* 13.207), to Adora in Idumaea (*Ant.* 13.207), and to Coele-Syria. Tryphon then killed Jonathan at Galaaditis (*Ant.* 13.208–9), and returned to Antioch (*Ant.* 13.209). App. (*Syr.* 68) merely states that Antiochus VI died during an operation. See further Livy, *Per.* 55.

The account of 1 Maccabees offers a slightly different chronology. It places Tryphon's capture and murder of Jonathan (1 Macc 12:39–48) before the assassination of Antiochus VI (1 Macc 13:31–32). About this time, Simon declared independence from the Seleucid Empire (1 Macc 13:41–42).[70] However, after all these events the Parthians captured Demetrius II in the Seleucid year 172 (= 141/40 B.C.E.; 1 Macc 14:1–3). The author of 1 Maccabees believes the Parthian campaign of Demetrius II had nothing to do with the creation of Simon's state. According to the chronology of this book, it took place after Simon's proclamation of statehood. According to 1 Maccabees, Demetrius II and Tryphon were still fighting one another when Simon broke free from the Seleucid Empire.[71]

The writer of 1 Maccabees includes a paean to Simon (1 Macc 14:1–49) to highlight his growing political power. To emphasize further this theme, the author includes a section that describes how Simon boldly resisted the demand of the new Seleucid monarch, Antiochus VII Sidetes, that the Jews give up territory he claimed belonged to him (1 Macc 15:1–36). Sidetes also acknowledged the legitimacy of the Hasmonean state and granted Simon economic control over Jerusalem and the temple, remission from taxes, forgiveness of past debts, and the right to mint his own currency. The author implies that Sidetes had no choice but to recognize Simon as high priest and ethnarch of the Jews, as well as the leader of an independent Jewish state, because he had not yet gained control over the Seleucid Empire and needed Hasmonean military support to do so. But what is unclear from 1 Maccabees is what, if any, role Tryphon played in affairs at this time.

Unlike Josephus, the author of 1 Maccabees does not include an account of Tryphon's death. He merely comments that in the Seleucid year 174 (= 139/8 B.C.E.) Sidetes besieged Tryphon at Dor (1 Macc 15:10–14, 25).[72] The writer then mentions that Tryphon escaped by ship

70. The author of 1 Maccabees (13:34–40) introduces this proclamation with a list of earlier concessions that Demetrius II had granted to Simon.

71. The author inserts a brief account of the murder of Antiochus VI in 1 Macc 13:31–32 that interrupts his descriptions of Simon's request to Demetrius II, the Seleucid monarch's concessions to the Jews, and the subsequent declaration of Jewish independence. The placement of this story suggest that the author of 1 Maccabees assumed that the death of Antiochus VI preceded the capture of Demetrius II.

72. Sling bullets found at the site, including one with the inscription "for the victory of Tryphon," date to this siege. See further, Gera 1985. For a different reading of this inscription, see Fischer 1992. Recent petrographic examination of 217 stone-balls from Dor, which were used in artillery engines (stone-throwers), has revealed that they were made from rocks taken from the coastal plain north of the Gulf of

to the Phoenician city of Orthosia (1 Macc 15:37). Goldstein comments that the account of Tryphon's death in Josephus is similar to the passage in 1 Maccabees that mentions his flight to Orthosia. He suggests that Josephus's omission of Orthosia in his narrative of Tryphon's demise shows this section was missing in the scroll of 1 Maccabees he consulted to write his *Antiquities*.[73] However, because neither 1 Maccabees nor Josephus provide a full account of Tryphon's actions, it is probable that neither had access to a complete history of this time. Josephus was apparently uncertain of the chronology for this period. He briefly mentions that Tryphon fled from Dor to Apamea, where he was besieged, captured, and put to death (*Ant.* 13.224).[74] But if the chronology of his murder in the *Antiquities* is preferred, then it appears that the capture of Demetrius II motivated Tryphon to kill Jonathan and prompted Simon to issue his proclamation of independence in the Seleucid year 170 (= 143/2 B.C.E.). The key to understanding this decree is determining the date when Tryphon murdered the young Antiochus VI, and the subsequent reactions to it in the Hasmonean and the Seleucid Empires.

Josephus and several non-Jewish writers place the murder of Antiochus VI after the capture of Demetrius II.[75] Livy and Diodorus Siculus date the rebellion of Tryphon later in the consular year 138 B.C.E.[76] However, the coins of Antiochus VI date from 144–142/1.[77] This numismatic evidence suggests that the final year of the reign of Antiochus VI, and the date of his murder by Tryphon, occurred sometime in 142–141 B.C.E.[78] It shows

Haifa. This evidence shows that Sidetes docked his navy near present-day Haifa where his troops manufactured these stone-balls and subsequently brought them to Dor. See further, Shatzman 1995.

73. Goldstein 1976, 519. The verbal similarities in the two works make it probable that Josephus used a copy of 1 Maccabees that did not include a complete account of the death of Tryphon.

74. App. *Syr.* 68; Just. *Epit.* 36.1.8; Frontin. *Str.* 2.13.3. According to Strabo (*Geogr.* 14.5.2) he committed suicide.

75. App. *Syr.* 68; Just. *Epit.* 36.1.7.

76. Livy, *Per.* 55; Diod. Sic. 33.28.

77. Hoover 2009, 202–3. Tryphon minted these coins in the name of Antiochus VI.

78. See further, Ehling 2008, 178–81; Grainger 1997, 28, 69–70. A Babylonian astronomical diary dated to 140 B.C.E. mentions the arrival of a "general" of Antiochus VI in Babylon accompanied by soldiers who spoke to the Greeks there. It appears that Tryphon attempted to gain support from the Greek community in Babylon in the name of Antiochus VI. Assuming that Tryphon murdered Antiochus VI shortly after this general left for Babylon, it is probable that the news of his death had not reached Babylon when this text was written. For this text, see Sachs and Hunger 1996,

that the murder of Antiochus VI by Tryphon took place approximately one and half years after Simon's appointment as leader of the Jews.

A notice in an Astronomical Diary from Babylon suggests that the Parthians may have captured Demetrius II at approximately the same time as the death of Tryphon. It dates the defeat and capture of Demetrius II in IV.174 S.E. (= 7/8 July–4/5 August 138, B.C.E.).[79] This date is supported by the Armenian version of the *Chronicle* of Eusebius, which records that Demetrius II marched against Arsaces (= Mithridates I) in the Olympic Year 160.2 (= July 139–June 138 B.C.E.) and was captured the following year (138–7 B.C.E.).[80] The numismatic evidence shows that the coins minted in the name of Tryphon, which were issued for four years, cease in S.E. 174 (= 139–138 B.C.E.). Tryphon died no earlier than 138 B.C.E., and most probably in 137 B.C.E. This evidence contradicts the narrative of Josephus, who places the death of Tryphon well after the capture of Demetrius II.[81] It supports the basic chronology of 1 Maccabees, which appears to place Tryphon's passing closer to the capture and exile of Demetrius II in 138 B.C.E.[82] Yet, there is evidence that Tryphon's rebellion played a major and unappreciated role in the creation of the Hasmonean state.

The extant textual sources and numismatic evidence suggest that the events of 145 B.C.E. led to the creation of the Hasmonean state. When Demetrius II, with the help of mercenaries from Crete, took power in Antioch in that year he attempted to dissolve the Seleucid army there. The garrison at Apamea mutinied. Its commander, Tryphon, seized its weapons and proclaimed the young Antiochus VI king. Tryphon made the city of Chalcis his headquarters and defeated Demetrius II in battle. He issued new currency in the name of Antiochus VI, and later in his own name, as king.[83]

No. 30 A₁, A² , Obv. ´22´, 25´. See further Van der Spek 1997–98, 171–72. The year 140 B.C.E., during which no coins were minted in the name of Antiochus VI, suggests that he was either murdered in that year or earlier.

79. Just. (*Epit.* 36.1.4–6) writes that the Parthians captured Demetrius II and exiled him to Hyrcania. This is contradicted by the cuneiform record, which shows that he was imprisoned in Media. See Sachs and Hunger 1996, 137A. For the capture and exile of Demetrius II, see Assar 2006b, 47–48; Dąbrowa 1992; Ehling 2008, 185–86. Cf. Grabbe 1991, 66.

80. Citation from Aucher 1818, 349.

81. *Ant.* 13.184–87, 223–24.

82. 1 Macc 12:39–53, 13:31–14:3.

83. Josephus states that Antiochus VI reigned for four years (*Ant.* 13.218) and Tryphon ruled as king for three years (*Ant.* 13.244). The numismatic evidence shows

The mint marks of the coins issued in the name of Demetrius II in Antioch may provide some evidence to support the thesis that the rebellion of Tryphon was largely responsible for Simon's proclamation of independence. The symbols of most of the mint officials from Antioch also appear on the coins of Antiochus VI that were manufactured in Apamea.[84] This suggests that many officials left the mint at Antioch and moved to Apamea to help Tryphon seize power.[85] Diodorus Siculus states that at this time Demetrius II confiscated much property in Antioch. The subsequent rioting drove many out of the city.[86] The numismatic evidence suggests that this action of Demetrius II appears to have caused many cities to support Tryphon's bid for the throne. The following places struck coins in the name of Antiochus VI: Apamea, Antioch in Seleucia and Pieria, Tarsus and Mallus in Cilicia, Byblos in Phoenicia, and Ptolemais in Coele-Syria. Coins of Tryphon are known from the following cities: Antioch, Mallus, Byblos, Ascalon, and Akko. These locations indicate that Tryphon had widespread support throughout the Seleucid Empire when he ruled on behalf of Antiochus VI and later on his own. This suggests that the opposition to Demetrius II was greater than our extant sources indicate. It may have had its roots in the previously existing Hellenistic settlements in the Seleucid Empire that remained loyal to Tryphon because of their shared cultural heritage.

Although neither Josephus nor 1 Maccabees describe the ethnic composition of Tryphon's supporters, it appears that many were of Greek and Macedonian descent. The city of Apamea played a major role in his rebellion. Tryphon also received help from the regions of Apollonia,

that Tryphon declared Antiochus VI king at Apamea in S.E. 168 (= 144 B.C.E.). Antiochus VI reigned from that year until S.E. 171 (= 142–41 B.C.E.), which is approximately two and a half calendar years. Coins were issued in Antioch with his name from 143 to 142/1 B.C.E. Tryphon's reign lasted nearly four complete years, from 142/1 B.C.E. to the turn of 138/7 B.C.E. Although he minted coins from S.E. 171 (= 142–141 B.C.E.) to S.E. 174 (139–138 B.C.E.), it is probable that his reign extended partly into 137 B.C.E. The numismatic evidence suggests that Tryphon controlled Antioch from 142/1 to 138/7 B.C.E. See Houghton 1992; Fischer 1972; Seyrig 1950, 16–17.

84. Houghton 1992, 134–39.

85. Strabo (*Geogr.* 16.2.10) says that Tryphon was born in Casinia, a fortress of the Apameian country. Ath. (8.333c) merely writes that he was from Apameia. His many relatives and partisans there apparently supported his claim to the throne.

86. Diod. Sic. 33.4.4.

Megara, Cassiana, and Larissa.[87] Apamea was one of the most important Macedonian military settlements in northern Syria. Strabo notes that Larissa had a large number of military colonists from Thessaly; many had served in the Seleucid cavalry.[88] Bar-Kochva suggests that the remaining cities that supported Tryphon, two of which are named after places in Greece and Macedonia, may have been military settlements as well.[89] It appears that many ethnic Greeks in the Seleucid Empire revolted against Demetrius III and took control of some of his most important cities.

The concessions that Demetrius II granted to Simon exceeded those any Seleucid monarch had given to a Jewish leader: they were almost a declaration of Judean independence. He gave them in a desperate effort to convince the Jews to oppose Tryphon. In his letter to Simon, Demetrius II even allowed him to build fortresses, gave him a waiver from past taxes, and exempted him from all duties collected in Jerusalem for the Seleucid treasury, and allowed him to enroll Jewish soldiers in the royal bodyguard. It is surprising that Demetrius II recognized the assumption of Simon to the office of high priest because he had received prior Seleucid approval to hold this position. Demetrius II apparently believed he was so politically weak at this time that he needed Hasmonean support to protect him from his enemies. He also may have feared that many of his subjects of Greek descent posed a threat to his kingdom. Demetrius II likely concluded that he had no choice but to recognize Simon as the religious and political head of an independent state as long as he and the Jews continued to oppose Tryphon. Nevertheless, the public declaration of Hasmonean support by Demetrius II, which took place in 145 B.C.E., should be viewed as a sign of Seleucid weakness since it was a proclamation that he had given up any claim to Judea. The dilemma Demetrius II now faced was that the Hasmonean state was powerful enough to threaten the security of the Seleucid Empire. He began to worry more about Simon than about the threat Tryphon still posed to his kingdom.

---

87. Strab. *Geogr.* 16.2.10. These cities all appear to have had large pagan populations, and may have had substantial numbers of ethnic Greeks. Apollonia (Arsuf) was located near Joppa. See Plin. *HN* 5.69. The name of the Seleucid city of Megara is similar to the name of the city Megara in Greece. It is plausible that the town was founded by colonists from Greece. See further G. Cohen 2006, 119–20.

88. Diod. Sic. 33.4a. See further Bickerman 1938, 88–93; 1988, 81–129.

89. Bar-Kochva 1989, 423–24. He also proposes that the Royal Guard of Demetrius II consisted of highly paid Macedonian soldiers.

Simon's Military Conquests and the Early Expansion
of the Hasmonean State

Demetrius III was correct to fear Simon at this time. After Simon secured his position as Judea's leader and high priest, he set out to expand his realm by attacking Judea's principal Seleucid strongholds. He first campaigned against Gezer, which was ideally situated to use as a base for expeditions in the coastal plain.[90] According to 1 Macc 9:52 the site already possessed a Seleucid garrison. He resettled the city with observant Jews and stationed Hyrcanus there as commander of all his forces.

The decision of Simon to place Hyrcanus as commander of his military was instrumental in preserving the independence of the Hasmonean state. The Hasmonean family's adoption of the organizational structures and weapons of the neighboring Hellenistic armies is perhaps the principal reason for Simon's military successes. It also helps to explain the concessions Demetrius II and Sidetes granted him: the Hasmoneans were too formidable a military power for the Syrians to oppose at this time. The texts support this assertion. According to 1 Macc 13:43, Simon constructed a large shooting tower and breaching device known as a *helepolis*.[91] Simon besieged the Akra in Jerusalem and forced its inhabitants to surrender.[92]

---

90. 1 Macc 13:43. A graffiti found at Gezer from this time contains the plea: "Pamphras, may he bring down (fire) on the palace of Simon." See Seger 1977, 390.

91. According to tradition, Demetrius Poliorcetes invented this machine at the end of the fourth century B.C.E. It consisted of a tower with catapults and battering rams, and was manned by over two hundred soldiers. See Diod. Sic. 20.92.1–2; Plut. *Dem.* 21; Judas appears to have used artillery machines during his unsuccessful attempt to take the Akra. See 1 Macc 6:20; *Ant.* 12.363. The presence of siege equipment in the Hasmonean army shows that four years after the beginning of the revolt against Antiochus IV Epiphanes, the army of Judas was able to use this form of Hellenistic warfare. This suggests that the Hasmoneans, from the early days of Mattathias's rebellion against the Seleucid Empire, adopted Hellenistic weaponry and tactics. For this evidence, see further Shatzman 1991, 24. The discovery of a Hellenistic gladius in Jericho may provide additional evidence that the Hasmoneans were not only trained in Greek military tactics, but that they also had adopted Hellenistic weapons as well. See Stiebel 2004.

92. The traditional date of the siege of the Akra is from 143 to 141 B.C.E. Simon expelled its inhabitants and instituted an annual celebration of this event (1 Macc 13:49–52; 14:7, 36), which is also mentioned in the *Megillat Ta'anit* (23 Iyyar). See Sievers 1990, 113–15; Goldstein 1976, 483; Zeitlin 1922, 84. Despite numerous efforts to uncover the Akra's location and determine its size, archaeologists are unsure of where it stood or what it looked like. Ben-Dov (1985, 65–71) believes it was located

Dąbrowa notes that the extant sources are silent about the response of Demetrius II to Simon's extensive territorial conquests.[93] This is surprising given that Simon's military activities were directed towards Gentiles. However, it appears that Demetrius II had no choice but to ignore them because he needed Simon as an ally. The Hasmonean army was so powerful that both Demetrius II and Tryphon made alliances with Jonathan to stay in power. It appears that Demetrius II later regretted the concessions he had granted to Simon and the Hasmoneans. It is plausible that he realized that his earlier relationship with the Hasmoneans had made them rulers of an independent state in lands Syria's rulers claimed belonged to the Seleucid Empire. The Hasmoneans were now a major threat to the territorial integrity of the Seleucid Empire.

Despite Simon's achievements, it was his son, Hyrcanus, who actually created a true Hellenistic state. He broke free from Syrian domination and undertook an unprecedented series of military campaigns to annex portions of the Seleucid Empire. Hyrcanus, more than any other Hasmonean ruler, epitomized the religious zeal of his ancestor Mattathias. He directed his military might against the Seleucid Empire, and used violence against what he deemed to be a heretical form of Judaism within his border. It is to his amazing life that we now turn in our quest to uncover the story of the Hasmonean state, beginning with Hyrcanus's acquisition of the military skills necessary to rule that he acquired while serving his father before attempting to sort out Josephus's confusing chronology of his reign.

south of the Hulda Gate and that Simon demolished it to its foundations and built houses atop it. This would account for the lack of any visible archaeological remains of this massive structure.

93. Dąbrowa 2010a, 59; 2010b, 8–11.

Chapter 3

JOHN HYRCANUS:
HIS ROLE DURING SIMON'S REIGN
AND HIS CONSOLIDATION OF POLITICAL
AND SECULAR POWERS

His Family Background[1]

John Hyrcanus was one of Simon's three sons.[2] If the author of 1 Maccabees lists them according to their ages, then he was the second in order of
birth.[3] His Hebrew name is Yehohanan (יהוחנן). It is sometimes translated
as Jonathan, but most frequently as John.[4] Josephus calls him Hyrcanus.[5]

1. For the major historical sources for the life of John Hyrcanus, see 1 Macc
16:23–24; *War* 1.55–69; *Ant.* 13.230–300; Atkinson 2012c, 67–86; 2013e.
2. According to 1 Macc 2:3 he was also called "Thassi" (θασσί). In *Ant.* 12.266
he is referred to as Thatis (θάτις). There are several variant forms of this name in the
manuscripts of the *Antiquities*. See further Niese 1892, 117. Its origin and meaning
are uncertain. Simon is sometimes designated as Simon III to distinguish him from
the two previous high priests named Simon.
3. According to 2 Macc 2:2–5, the five sons of Mattathias were named John,
Simon, Judas, Eleazar, and Jonathan. The list in 1 Macc 2:22–23 replaces John with
Joseph. 1 Macc 16:2 states that "Judas and John" are Simon's "two eldest sons" while
v. 14 mentions an additional brother named Mattathias. Josephus (*Ant.* 13.229) refers
to Hyrcanus as Simon's third son. His elder brother, Judas, was presumably named
after their famous uncle and freedom fighter, the legendary Judas (a.k.a. Maccabeus,
"the Hammer"). Simon likely named his third son, Mattathias, after his father, whose
defiance of the Seleucid edict banning Judaism started the uprising commonly known
as the Maccabean rebellion.
4. The LXX translates this biblical name into Greek as Ιωάναν. See Koehler,
Baumgartner, Richardson, and Stamm 2001, 396. The author of 1 Maccabees (13:53;
16:1–10, 18–24) uses this Greek form of the name. The Hebrew name "John" (יהוחנן)
is found on coins that Hyrcanus minted in Judea. See Meshorer 2011, 30–31, 44–45,
257–56. Hyrcanus (יוחנן) is likely mentioned in *4QpapHistorical Text C* (4Q331 1 i
7). See Fitzmyer 2000a, 277.
5. *War* 1.54–55; *Ant.* 13.228.

Some ancient writers believed this Greek name was given to him to commemorate his conquest of Hyrcania.[6] Josephus does not record how old he was when he became high priest, but we can estimate that he assumed this office when he was approximately twenty-six years of age.[7] If this proposal is correct, then a simple calculation reveals that he was born in 161 B.C.E.[8] His place of birth was presumably Modein, which was

6. The name Hyrcanus etymologically means "one from Hyrcania," which is a region on the Black Sea. Several ancient writers believed this name is a sobriquet that was given to him to commemorate his conquest of the Hyrcanians. See Euseb. *Chron.* (in Schöene 1999, 2:130–31); Syn. *Chron.* 1.548; Jer. *Olympiad CLXV* (in Schöene 1999, 2:131); Sulpicius Severus, *Chron.* 26.2. Hyrcanus is not a classical name. It was used by Jews in antiquity and is attested earlier than the Hasmonean period. See *Ant.* 12.186–236; 2 Macc 3:11. See further, Ilan (1987, 1–2). It became quite popular since Josephus and Herod of Chalcis named their sons Hyrcanus. See *Life* 5; *War* 2.221; *Ant.* 20.104. For all known examples of the name Hyrcanus, see Machiela 2010. Machiela (2009, 142) proposes that the name Herqanosh (חרקנוש) in *1QapGen*[ar] (20.8, 21) is equivalent to Ὑρχανός. He believes the name supports a Ptolemaic setting for this composition, which he suggests provides additional information to support his thesis that it is of Egyptian origin. He does not believe the Hyrcanus in this text is a historical person. However, it is plausible that persons in Egypt or elsewhere were named Hyrcanus because they, or their ancestors, were of Hyrcanian descent.

7. Josephus (*Ant.* 13.228) calls him a "youth" (νεανίσκος) at the time of his father's assassination. This is the common Greek word for a "youth" or "young man." See Liddell and Scott et al. 1968, 1164; Muraoka 2009, 472. If the ages and Greek terms for the various stages of life provided in Philo's *Op. Mund.* (36.105) reflects historical reality, then a male is considered a νεανίσκος until he reached his twenty-eighth birthday. This would mean that Hyrcanus was no older than twenty-eight years of age when his father, Simon, was murdered. Josephus does not record Simon's age at the time of his death, but merely states that he reigned for thirty-one years (*Ant.* 13.299). In a latter passage (*Ant.* 20.240–41) he writes that Hyrcanus died "in old age" (τελευτᾷ γηραιὸς). According to Philo, a γῆρας was a person over fifty-six years of age. If we take Philo's lowest figure for this period of life and assume that Hyrcanus was fifty-seven years of age at the time of his death, we can estimate his approximate age when he became high priest by subtracting the length of his reign from this figure. The result is twenty-six years of age, which is within Philo's range for a νεανίσκος. In his *War* (1.68) Josephus writes that Hyrcanus ruled for "thirty-three years." Because the Latin version of *Heg.* (*Hist.* 1.1.10) reads *trigesimo et primo anno* and supports the *Antiquities*, the figure in the *War* is a mistake. I use Philo's division of the life cycle in this chapter to provide a plausible range of ages for important moments in the life of Hyrcanus.

8. This figure is based on Philo's statement that old age begins at fifty-seven and that a person is considered a youth from twenty-one to twenty-seven years of age. If these proposed dates are correct, they reveal that Hyrcanus was born approximately

the ancestral home of his family and the location were several of them were buried.[9]

The author of 1 Maccabees has little to say about Hyrcanus and ends his book with a brief description of his elevation to his father's position as the nation's political and religious leader. Josephus describes him as the most pious and competent of all the Hasmonean rulers.[10] Because Josephus admired Hyrcanus more than any other Hasmonean, he often exaggerates his achievements.[11] For this reason, Josephus's accounts must be read carefully since he rearranges his sources to highlight the military accomplishments of Hyrcanus, and to portray his reign as a sort of Hasmonean "Golden Age" during which God blessed the nation with an unprecedented military expansion.[12] But this great period was unexpected, for Hyrcanus was likely not his father's intended heir. Rather, he came to the throne through a great tragedy.

Hyrcanus as High Priest and Political Ruler

Simon's wife and two of his sons, Mattathias and Judas, accompanied him to Jericho on a tour to survey his realm. Hyrcanus was presumably occupied with his duties as the general of the Hasmonean forces stationed at Gezer. The royal entourage stopped in the fortress of Dok, near Jericho, to visit Simon's son-in-law, Ptolemy, son of Abubus.[13] The details of the

three years after Judas rededicated the temple on 25th Kislev, in the Seleucid year 148 (December 164 B.C.E.). See 1 Macc 4:52; Collins 1993, 354. This date assumes that Jerusalem followed the Seleucid Babylonian calendar, including its intercalations. Because this is uncertain, others date this event to 162 B.C.E. See Sievers 1990, 46; Schürer et al. 1973–87, 1:165.

9. 1 Macc 2:70; 13:24–30; *War* 1.36.

10. 1 Macc 16–11:24. For Josephus's praise of Hyrcanus, see *War* 1.54–69; *Ant.* 13.230–300.

11. Thoma 1994.

12. Josephus's admiration of Hyrcanus was so great that he apparently named his son after him. See *Life* 5. S. Schwartz (1990b, 11) disagrees and suggests that Josephus chose this name to flatter Julius Hyrcanus, the son of Queen Berenice and Herod of Chalcis (*War* 2.221; *Ant.* 20.104). This thesis does not exclude the possibility that Julius Hyrcanus was also named after John Hyrcanus.

13. 1 Macc 16:11 mentions Ptolemy's position and the name of his father. Goldstein (1976, 524) proposes that Ptolemy's name and his office (*strategos*) are Greek. This may indicate that Simon's regime by this time had come to use Greek titles. The names of Judah's commanders and delegates to Rome also had Greek names, which provide additional evidence to support this thesis. See further Regev 2013, 22. The Syriac version of 1 Maccabees suggests that Ptolemy's family name, Habub, is Semitic.

murder of Simon by Ptolemy are uncertain because of our conflicting sources.[14] What is clear is that Ptolemy had his men kill Simon and his entourage at a lavish banquet he put on in his honor: the deed was committed while the guests were intoxicated.

Josephus and 1 Maccabees agree that Hyrcanus was not present at Dok, and that Ptolemy sent assassins to Gezer to kill him. The author of 1 Maccabees insists that Ptolemy murdered Simon and his sons, but says nothing about his spouse. However, Josephus claims that Ptolemy captured Simon's wife and sons.[15] According to 1 Maccabees, Ptolemy sent letters to the Seleucid king Antiochus VII Sidetes offering to hand over Judea's cities and taxes. He also tried to bribe Simon's troops to join his revolt, and sent men to seize Jerusalem and take control of the Temple Mount. Josephus does not mention Ptolemy's dispatches, but merely states that he led a failed attempt to capture Jerusalem.[16] Both sources agree that Hyrcanus was warned that Ptolemy's men wanted to murder him. Hyrcanus fled to Jerusalem, where his father's supporters gave him shelter.

Despite Ptolemy's unsuccessful effort to eliminate the Hasmonean family, Judea's political situation remained stable. Few of its citizens supported Ptolemy. But it cannot be ruled out that some disaffected elements of Judea's ruling elites assisted him. Nevertheless, if Ptolemy and his partisans hoped to block the creation of a Hasmonean dynasty in which rule would automatically pass to a descendant of Mattathias they were mistaken. Hyrcanus appears to have received widespread support among the population; he became the first son since Onias III to succeed his father as high priest. The position remained a hereditary office and a possession of the Hasmonean family until 35 B.C.E. when Herod executed Aristobulus III.[17] Unfortunately our extant sources offer conflicting dates when he took power. Fortunately, papyrological discoveries from Egypt now clarify the contradictory figures in the surviving documents, and show that our present chronology of the Hasmonean rulers from Simon's death to the beginning of the reign of Alexander Jannaeus is in error.

This name appears in an inscription from Palmyra in Syria. See Goldstein 1976, 524; Sievers 1990, 131. His family may have come from the Transjordan region since he fled there after he killed Simon. See *War* 1.60; *Ant.* 13.235.

14. For this event, see 1 Macc 16:11–22; *War* 1.54; *Ant.* 13.228–29.

15. 1 Macc 16:16; *War* 1.54; *Ant.* 13.228.

16. 1 Macc 16:18–20; *War* 1.54–55; *Ant.* 13.228–29.

17. The Hasmoneans held the office of high priest continuously during this period with the exception of the two-year gap from 37 to 35 B.C.E. See VanderKam 2004, 285.

Problems and Sources for Reconstructing the Reign of Hyrcanus

Josephus used a variety of sources to write his account of the reign of Hyrcanus, which may explain some of the errors in his chronology. To complicate matters, he consulted works that used different dating systems, which sometimes caused him to misplace events in his narratives. The majority of writings he used are unknown. In addition to oral materials about the Hasmoneans, he apparently had access to the lost history of Hyrcanus mentioned in 1 Macc 16:23–24.[18] This book resembled 1 Maccabees and could have provided Josephus with considerable historical material. Josephus may have used the lost book on the kings of Judah by Eupolemus to document the early reign of Hyrcanus.[19] For the period between Antiochus IV Epiphanes to the accession of Archelaus (6 C.E.), Josephus primarily used Nicolaus of Damascus. As Herod the Great's court historian, Nicolaus is not the most reliable source for Hasmonean history. He often portrays the Hasmoneans negatively and emphasizes their internecine strife. He does this because some members of the Hasmonean family, especially Hyrcanus II, opposed his patron, Herod the Great.[20] Josephus also used the writings of several Roman historians. Unfortunately, most of these Gentile authors obtained their materials second-hand and seldom preserve reliable information about Hyrcanus.[21]

18. The supposed sixteenth-century C.E. reference to this book by Sixtus Senesis refers to an edition of Josephus and not to this lost work. See further, Schürer et al. 1973–87, 1:20; 2:185–86.

19. The work of Eupolemus is dated to the middle of the second century B.C.E. If we are correct in placing the birth of Hyrcanus to approximately 161 B.C.E., Eupolemus could have included material about his early life since he documents Hasmonean expansion and would have been his contemporary. Keddie (2013) dates the writing of the work of Eupolemus to the time of Hyrcanus, but suggests that it reflects events of 141 B.C.E. Although Eupolemus is identified as the ambassador who led the embassy to Rome, the unusual syntax could indicate that his father actually undertook this mission to Italy. For this thesis, see Zollschan 2004. If this view is correct, Eupolemus could have received much of his information about the early Hasmoneans and their relationship with the Roman Republic from his father. Fortunately, the resolution of this debate does not affect the present study.

20. M. Stern 1974–80, 1:229–31; Schürer et al. 1973–87, 1:28–32; Wacholder 1962, 52–58, 65–70. For Nicolaus's pro-Herodian bias, see T. Landau 2006, 20–30.

21. In addition to Nicolaus of Damascus and Thucydides, the following are some of major historians that influenced Josephus: Polybius of Megalopolis (middle second century B.C.E.); Curtius Rufus (first century C.E.); Strabo of Amaseia (first century B.C.E.); and Diodorus Siculus (first century B.C.E.). See further Schürer et al. 1973–87, 1:200–25; Bilde 1988, 27–32.

Most studies on the Hasmonean dynasty do not recognize that the sources offer conflicting dates for the beginning of the reign of Hyrcanus. According to the author of 1 Macc 16:14, Ptolemy murdered Simon "in the year 177 in the eleventh month, which is the month of Shebat." This year, which marks the beginning of Hyrcanus's tenure, is traditionally dated to 134 B.C.E. However, Bickerman and others have proposed the author of 1 Maccabees dated events of Seleucid interest according to the Macedonian era, and used the Babylonian era to document Jewish history.[22] Subsequent commentators of 1 Maccabees have generally followed this thesis. Determining which calendar an author used is the problem.

According to the Seleucid calendar, the eleventh month of Shebat in the year 177 correlates to April 135–134 B.C.E. Based on this interpretation, the beginning of the reign of Hyrcanus is usually dated to 134 B.C.E.[23] But if the author of 1 Maccabees dated the death of Simon according to the Macedonian calendar, then the Seleucid year 177 correlates to October 136–135 B.C.E. Egyptian documents show that the writer of 1 Maccabees used the Macedonian dating system since these texts reveal that Jannaeus was in power in 104 B.C.E.[24] Consequently, the traditional dates for the Hasmonean rulers from Hyrcanus to Jannaeus must be adjusted to begin

22. Bickerman 1937, 155–68; Goldstein 1976, 21–25, 40–43; Grabbe 1991. Cf. Bringmann 1983, 15–28.

23. Goldstein 1976, 524; Grabbe 1991, 59–60; Niese 1892, 216–28; Klausner 1972b, 211; VanderKam 2004, 285. The Macedonians, and most Greeks, adopted a calendar in which the civil year coincided with the regnal year. In this calendar the Seleucid Era is based on the numbering of the satrapal years of Seleucus I. He counted his reign from the beginning of the first calendar year after his conquest of Babylon in April, 311 B.C.E. When he later became *Basileus*, he kept this system, but adjusted it for the Macedonians by pushing back the calculation of the beginning of his kingship by a year to autumn 312 B.C.E. when the Macedonian regnal year commenced. This means that the Macedonian calendar placed the beginning of the second year of the Seleucid era in autumn 311 B.C.E., while according to the Babylonian calendar it started in April 310 B.C.E. The two calendars coincide from April to October, but in the winter the Macedonian era is always greater by one year than the Babylonian era. It appears that many Jewish authors, unlike the Babylonians, numbered the Seleucid era as a regnal year that began from Nisan 312 rather than Nisan 311. This error means that a writer could cite a year based on a date before Seleucus I conquered Babylon. Goldstein (1876, 21–25, 40–43) suggests that that author of 1 Maccabees drew on at least two sources: a non-Jewish work that dated events according to the Macedonian Seleucid era and Jewish records that dated events according to the Babylonian Seleucid era. See further Bickerman 1944.

24. *P. dem. BM* inv. 69008 + *P. dem. Berl.* Inv. 13381. For these texts, see Van 'T Dack et al. 1989, 50–61.

one year earlier. This means that Simon died in 135 B.C.E., which is also the year Hyrcanus took power.[25] This year may also provide an explanation as to why his first military campaign at Dok was unsuccessful.

The Siege of Dok

Hyrcanus began his reign with a military campaign to seek revenge against his father's assassin. He besieged Ptolemy in the fortress of Dok near Jericho.[26] Siege works dating to this time confirm Josephus's account that a lengthy battle took place there.[27] Ptolemy's revolt was a failure since he was unable to secure help from his supporters in Jerusalem or elsewhere in Judea. According to the author of 1 Maccabees, he was also unable to bribe any officers in the Hasmonean army to support his attempted coup.[28] Dąbrowa suggests this indicates that only the troops Ptolemy commanded as governor of Jericho backed him.[29]

According to Josephus, when the Hasmonean army approached Dok, Ptolemy tortured the mother and brothers of Hyrcanus atop its walls. However, according to 1 Macc 16:16 Ptolemy murdered Simon along with two of his sons at Jericho.[30] The author of this book does not mention Simon's wife. Goldstein suggests that Josephus is mistaken, and Ptolemy only took the mother of Hyrcanus hostage.[31] If Ptolemy imprisoned Simon's sons at Dok, this would mean that Hyrcanus assumed civil and religious powers while they were in custody. Because there is no hint of opposition to his succession, it is perhaps more probable that Ptolemy only took the mother of Hyrcanus captive. His brothers were presumably dead, leaving him the only heir. Whether Josephus, or one of his sources, inserted Hyrcanus's siblings in the story is unknown. However, the origin of this account does not matter because our text is the work of Josephus. He clearly placed it here to show that the decision of Ptolemy to torture the mother and siblings of Hyrcanus made him unfit to replace

25. For the evidence in support of this date, see further G. Cohen 1989.

26. 1 Macc 16:11–24 refers to the fortress as Dok. Josephus calls it Dagon, which may have been the site's pagan name. It is to be identified with the fort of Taurus or Threx. See further, Shatzman 1991, 51–52.

27. H. Eshel 2008, 74. The construction of Dok is dated to 167 B.C.E. See further Garbrecht and Peleg 1994, 164; Amit 2002; Netzer 2001, 70–72. Little is known of the site because it has not been excavated.

28. 1 Macc 16:19.

29. Dąbrowa 2010a, 67.

30. *War* 1.54; *Ant.* 13.228.

31. Goldstein 1976, 525.

the Hasmoneans. But Josephus's account of the siege of his brothers at Dok raises some unsettling questions concerning Hyrcanus's conduct there: Josephus insists he abandoned his siblings and his mother knowing Ptolemy would murder them.

Josephus writes that Hyrcanus panicked when he saw Ptolemy's partisans torturing his mother and brothers atop Dok's walls. In his narrative he includes a moving plea by the mother of Hyrcanus in which she urged him to seek revenge against Ptolemy. His account is reminiscent of the speech an unnamed mother gave to her seven sons during the persecution of Antiochus IV Epiphanes, which undoubtedly served as its model.[32] But what is unique is Josephus's version of how the siege ended. He claims that Hyrcanus had to abandon his blockade of Dok, and leave his mother and brothers behind, because of the arrival of the Sabbatical Year during which Jews were not allowed to wage war. Because this is such an unusual story, it is not surprising that some scholars have challenged its veracity to argue that no Sabbatical Year occurred at this time. But overlooked chronological evidence indicates otherwise.

Scripture suggests the Sabbatical Year prohibitions were sometimes ignored. Yet, Josephus insists Hyrcanus observed them. He was not alone. Enough farmers followed the Sabbatical Year rules that it created conditions of economic hardship throughout the country every seventh year. To compensate for the inevitable economic downturn during a Sabbatical Year, the government was forced to stimulate the economy and provide aide to relieve famine.[33] Josephus tells his readers that the Sabbatical Year was like the Sabbath: God prohibited fighting during both.[34] Because the Sabbatical Year arrived while Hyrcanus was trying to rescue his mother, Josephus believed he had no choice but to end his siege and leave her in God's hands. But there is a difficulty with his account—the Hasmoneans had long fought their enemies on the Sabbath.

In the early years of the Jewish rebellion against Antiochus IV Epiphanes, the Syrian forces killed Jews who refused to fight on the Sabbath. Mattathias quickly realized this religious prohibition put the Jews at a great military disadvantage. He made a significant religious innovation when he ordered his men to attack the Seleucid forces on the Sabbath.[35]

32. 2 Macc 7:21–23; *War* 1.58–59; *Ant.* 13.231–33.

33. For violations of the Sabbatical Year, see Jer 34. For Sabbatical Year regulations, see Exod 20:8–11; 21:2–4; 23:9–12; Lev 25:8–17, 23–28; Deut 15:12–15; de Vaux 1961a, 173–75. For economic stimulus during the Sabbatical Year, as suggested by increased coin production, see Pfann 2006.

34. *Ant.* 13.234.

35. For the historicity of this story, see Borchardt 2015.

Because the Hasmoneans since Mattathias had fought their enemies on the Sabbath, there was no need for Hyrcanus to curtail his siege.[36] For this reason, Sievers, Bickerman, and Schürer are skeptical that a Sabbatical Year took place during Hyrcanus's blockade of Dok.[37] Because papyrological evidence shows the reign of Hyrcanus actually began in 135 B.C.E., there is no reason to doubt the claim of Josephus that Hyrcanus fought Ptolemy and Sidetes during a Sabbatical Year since one occurred from October 135 B.C.E. to October 134 B.C.E.[38]

Although Josephus claims Hyrcanus had to abandon his siege of Dok because of the Sabbatical Year, it is more probable that he departed when he received news of the unexpected arrival of the Seleucid army in Judea.[39] His retreat left Ptolemy free to do as he wished. According to Josephus, he killed the mother and the siblings of Hyrcanus and fled to the Hellenistic metropolis of Philadelphia, east of the Jordan River. Ptolemy received sanctuary there from a local despot named Zeno.[40] Since Josephus does not mention that Hyrcanus avenged his family's death, Ptolemy was presumably never punished for his crimes. It is here that Josephus's story takes an unexpected turn.

The Siege of Jerusalem by Antiochus VII Sidetes

Josephus reports that Sidetes invaded the Hasmonean state and besieged Jerusalem shortly after Hyrcanus became his country's political leader and high priest. Based on our chronological examination of Hyrcanus's siege of Dok, Sidetes's incursion must have taken place sometime after the beginning of the Sabbatical Year of October 135 B.C.E. This is partially supported by Josephus's text. In *Ant.* 14.236 he writes that Sidetes invaded Judea in the fourth year of his reign and the first year of the reign of

36. Johns 1963; Weiss 1998. Although 1QM 2.6–9 states that the eschatological war is to be interrupted during the Sabbatical Year, there is no evidence that the Hasmoneans observed such a prohibition.

37. Sievers 1990, 136 n. 3; Bickerman 1937, 157 n. 2; Schürer et al. 1973–87, 1:19. Bar-Kochva (1989, 545–46) suggests Josephus used Nicolaus of Damascus as his source for this story. He proposes that Nicolaus did not understand the Sabbatical Year, and confused some of its regulations with the prohibitions pertaining to the Sabbath. On this possibility, see further Grabbe 1991, 60–63. Zeitlin (1918) believes the text of Josephus's account of the siege was corrupted by scribes during its transmission and it did not occur during a Sabbatical Year.

38. Pfann 2006, 110; Wacholder 1973, 163–65, 188; 1983, 125–27.

39. For this suggestion, see Werner 1877, 25–27.

40. *War* 1.60; *Ant.* 13.235

Hyrcanus "in the hundred and sixty-second Olympiad." The first two dates correspond to 135/4 B.C.E., while the 162nd Olympiad began in July 132 B.C.E.[41] Porphyry claims Sidetes subdued the Jews in the third year of the 162nd Olympiad, which correlates to 129 B.C.E.[42] Josephus also mentions the setting of the Pleiades, which occurs in November, took place during the siege.[43] He records this information because this celestial event coincided with the rainstorm that alleviated Jerusalem's water shortage. Schürer notes that because the blockade was in progress the following October when the Festival of Tabernacles arrived, the siege lasted more than a year.[44]

Sidetes surrounded Jerusalem with a rampart, seven camps, and a ditch to prevent supplies from reaching its inhabitants. He then constructed a hundred mobile siege towers, each three stories in height, to batter Jerusalem's vulnerable northern wall that lacked a natural protective ravine. Hyrcanus responded by sending raiding parties outside the city to attack the Syrian siege engines. His men inflicted great causalities on Sidetes's forces, and temporarily damaged their siege equipment.[45] Then, the unexpected occurred.

Josephus reports that a downpour alleviated Jerusalem's water shortage. Nevertheless, the city had insufficient provisions to feed its population. In desperation, Hyrcanus ejected the noncombatants from the city to extend his supplies. Sidetes proved equally heartless: he refused to allow these civilians to pass through his siege line. Jerusalem's population defied Hyrcanus's orders and allowed them back inside.[46] How the siege subsequently ended is difficult to reconstruct.

Josephus preserves a detailed account of Sidetes's cordon of Jerusalem in his *Antiquities* that is reminiscent of the version of Diodorus Siculus. The similar content, language, and details between these two writers

---

41. Josephus uses the same phrase to record Olympiad and consular datings elsewhere in the *Antiquities* (*Ant.* 14.4, 66, 389, 487). Because in two instances (*Ant.* 14.4, 389) these synchronisms do not fit the events they describe, Sievers (2013, 4–7) suggests that Josephus used a source that provided this chronological data.

42. *FHG* 3.712–13. For these correlations, see Bickerman 1968, 150.

43. *Ant.* 13.237. See, Plin. *HN* 2.47.125.

44. Atkinson 2012c, 75–78; Schürer et al. 1973–87, 1:202–3; *Ant.* 13.241.

45. A cache of weapons excavated in the Jerusalem citadel has been dated to this siege. It includes numerous ballista stones, arrowheads, and iron spear butts. Two lead sling bullets found there with impressions of a winged device are similar to those discovered at Dor that were produced by Tryphon. See Sivan and Solar 1994, 173–77.

46. *Ant.* 13.241.

suggest they used a common source.[47] Unfortunately, Diodorus Siculus does not describe the end of the siege. To figure out how it concluded, we must turn to Josephus and (Pseudo) Plutarch. Both these writers appear to have used a work that recounted its termination.[48] They state that Hyrcanus asked Sidetes for a seven-day truce so the Jews could celebrate the Festival of Tabernacles. Sidetes agreed and gave Hyrcanus bulls and vessels of gold and silver filled with spices. Josephus ironically claims that Sidetes became known as "the Pious" (Εὐσεβῆ) because of his favorable treatment of the Jews.[49] Josephus claims he then sent envoys to Sidetes requesting that he allow him to keep the traditional form of Jewish government.[50] Sidetes offered Hyrcanus the same conditions he earlier had demanded of Simon, namely the surrender of arms, tribute in exchange for Joppa and other areas outside of Judea, and the partial restoration of the Akra.[51] Hyrcanus refused to accept the last condition since his father had expelled its Seleucid soldiers from the city. In lieu of this request, he offered three hundred hostages and five hundred talents.[52] Sidetes razed Jerusalem's walls, and withdrew from Judea.[53] Josephus also mentions that Hyrcanus made a friendly alliance (φιλία καὶ συμμαχία) with Sidetes. Hyrcanus even

47. Diod. Sic. 34.35.1.1–5. Diodorus Siculus used Posidonius. It is unlikely that Josephus consulted Posidonius directly. Rather, he may have read Posidonius through quotations of his work that were preserved in the writing of Nicolaus of Damascus. See further, M. Stern 1974–80, 1:184.

48. (Pseudo) Plutarch, *Mor.* 184 E–F; M. Stern 1974–80, 1:563–64.

49. *Ant.* 7.393; 13.244. The accounts of Diod. Sic. (34/35.1.5) and (Pseudo) Plut. (*Mor.* 184 E–F) emphasize the respect of Sidetes for Judaism. The former states that he rejected the advice of anti-Semites in his army to abolish Judaism. Porph. (*FHG* 712), however, claims that Sidetes killed many of the leading Jews. Sievers (1990, 137–38) believes this statement is untrustworthy since Hyrcanus survived the siege and remained as high priest. It is possible that Josephus, or his source, knew that Sidetes had rejected the advice of his men to act like Antiochus IV Epiphanes and left the temple intact. The Jewish community may have called him "Pious" in gratitude for his decision to spare the sanctuary.

50. *Ant.* 13.245.

51. *Ant.* 13.246–47.

52. The statement (*Ant.* 13.247) that a brother of Hyrcanus was among the hostages is certainly an error by either Josephus or one of his sources. Josephus earlier implied that Ptolemy had murdered the two siblings of Hyrcanus (*Ant.* 13.228).

53. 1 Macc 16:23 lists the construction of Jerusalem's walls by Hyrcanus as one of the major achievements of his reign. Josephus claims (*Ant.* 13.248) that only the top of the city wall (στεφάνην τῆς πόλεως), or perhaps its battlements, was destroyed. Diod. Sic. (34/35.1.5) and Porph. (*FHG* 712–13) contradict him and provide a more realistic account. They state that Jerusalem's wall was demolished. Josephus took

hosted him and his troops in Jerusalem, and lavishly supplied them with their needs.[54]

In the *Antiquities*, Josephus makes the startling claim that Hyrcanus robbed David's tomb and used the funds to pay Sidetes to end the siege.[55] Elsewhere in this book he states that Hyrcanus removed three thousand talents of silver from David's tomb, and used this sum to become the first Jewish king to hire foreign troops.[56] Yet, Josephus also condemns Hyrcanus three times for his desecration of David's tomb.[57] Syncellus, however, includes his plundering of David's tomb among his greatest achievements.[58] He, or his source, considered this incident important since it gave Hyrcanus the funds he needed to hire a mercenary force that he used to conquer extensive territory and expand the Hasmonean state.[59] Because Josephus implies that Hyrcanus used some of David's wealth to pay the Seleucid army and entertain them in Jerusalem, it is apparent that he became a Seleucid vassal to preserve the Hasmoneans state.[60] In exchange for his submission, and a considerable payment, Sidetes allowed the Jews to retain their traditional form of government.

The differences between Josephus's accounts of the siege of Sidetes and its aftermath provides some insight regarding his historical methodology, especially his use of Nicolaus of Damascus. Josephus apparently abbreviated his account of the siege in his *War* from Nicolas's book,

his information from Nicolaus, who may have used the word "crown" as a figure of speech to stress the importance of Jerusalem's wall for its security. For this understanding, see Bar-Kochva 1989, 162–63. Cf. *Pss. Sol.* 8:17.

54. *Ant.* 13.249. See also (Pseudo) Plut. (*Mor.* 184E–F).

55. *Ant.* 7.393.

56. *Ant.* 13.249. Dąbrowa (2010a, 81–82) believes that Hyrcanus had concealed some of his father's financial resources inside the traditional tomb of David. He further proposes that Josephus combined two events that took place at separate times. The first is the payment of money to Sidetes by Hyrcanus that he obtained from his father's treasury. The second is the use of the remaining funds by Hyrcanus to hire mercenaries.

57. *Ant.* 7.393; 13.249; 16.179.

58. *Chron.* 548.20.

59. Syncellus claims that Hyrcanus removed 30,000 talents from David's tomb. In the same paragraph he contradicts himself and writes that Hyrcanus removed 3,000 talents. These discrepancies may indicate that he combined material from different sources, or it could be the result of a scribal error. He also claims that Solomon's treasure had been placed in David's tomb. Syncellus implies that Hyrcanus did not remove the entire treasure since he mentions that a portion of it survived until the reign of Herod the Great.

60. *Ant.* 13.249. See further Bickerman 1938, 135–37, 189–90.

which he cites as a source for this period. There is no doubt that Nicolaus of Damascus documented the later participation of Hyrcanus in the Parthian campaign of Sidetes since Josephus quotes from his account of it in the *Antiquities*. Because the passage he copied from Nicolaus refers to Hyrcanus as a "Jew" (Ὑρκανοῦ τοῦ Ἰουδαίου), it likely came from a section on Seleucid history.[61] As with all his accounts, the final product should be considered the work of Josephus. However, there may be another reason for Josephus's claim that Sidetes abruptly ended his siege and returned home—the threat of Roman intervention.

Diplomatic Relations between the Roman Republic and the Hasmonean State

The Hasmoneans had long sought relations with the Roman Republic. The writer of 1 Maccabees records several important diplomatic efforts by the Hasmoneans. One took place during the early period of Simon's high priesthood in 142 B.C.E.[62] There is also a letter of "Lucius, consul of the Romans" to Ptolemy VIII Euergetes I, preserved in 1 Macc 15:16–21 whose authenticity is disputed.[63] But there is a problem with this text: its content appears to be reproduced in the *senatus consultum* dated to the "ninth year of the Hyrcanus the high priest and ethnarch in the month of Panemus" (47 B.C.E.) issued by "Lucius Valerius, son of Lucius, the praetor" found in Josephus's *Ant.* 14.145–48. The date in this passage places this embassy during the reign of Hyrcanus II. The chronological problem becomes more acute for the reign of Hyrcanus because Josephus likely misdated several decrees that recount his diplomatic efforts. The passage in *Ant.* 14.145–48 is one of them.

---

61. *Ant.* 13.251. Nicolaus may have copied this material from a work of Posidonius of Apamea. See Bar-Kochva 1989, 561; M. Stern 1974–80, 1:240. Büchler (1896) proposes that Josephus in *Ant.* 12.236–44 relied on both 1 Maccabees and Nicolaus of Damascus. He also suggests that Josephus in *Ant.* 13.236–44 used an anonymous author, who in turn consulted Polybius and Posidonius. Berthelot (2003, 133–41) has put forward a rather complicated stemma of Josephus's likely sources to explain his conflicting accounts of the events associated with the siege. Such efforts are hypothetical given our limited data. However, even if we can isolate Josephus's sources the extant work is his composition and the resulting confusion in his books must be attributed to him.

62. 1 Macc 14:16–18, 24, 40.

63. See Schürer et al. 1973–87, 1:194–95; Sievers 1990, 116–19.

Menahem Stern's analysis of the senatorial decrees in the *Antiquities* may resolve the chronological confusion in the accounts of Josephus for the reign of John Hyrcanus.[64] In his detailed analysis of these treaties, he has convincingly demonstrated that John Hyrcanus sent three embassies to Rome: Josephus correctly dated the delegation recorded in *Ant.* 13.259–66 to the time of John Hyrcanus, but misdated the others (*Ant.* 14.145–48, 247–55) to the reign of Hyrcanus II. Let us look at each of them according to Stern's ordering to see what they tell us about John Hyrcanus's use of diplomacy.

Josephus's account of the first delegation in *Ant.* 14.145–48 contains a *senatus consultum* that renewed the friendship between the Romans and the Jews. Josephus misdates it to the time of Julius Caesar and Hyrcanus II. But Lucius Valerius, who issued this document, was consul in 131 B.C.E. and *praetor* in 134 B.C.E. The year 134 B.C.E. is the latest possible date when the consul of 131 B.C.E. could have been praetor and almost coincides with the beginning of the reign of John Hyrcanus. News of this treaty likely forced Sidetes to end his siege of Jerusalem and allow John Hyrcanus to retain power. The possibility of Roman intervention was no mere threat, for the Roman general Popillius Laenas in 168 B.C.E. presented Antiochus IV Epiphanes with a decree from the Senate that required him to abandon his invasion of Egypt or be regarded as an enemy of Rome.[65]

Josephus correctly dates the second decree recorded in *Ant.* 13.259–66 to the reign of John Hyrcanus. Stern dates it after the 129 B.C.E. death of Sidetes, between 128 and 127 B.C.E., based on its historical content and Roman names.[66] The timing of this delegation coincides with the events mentioned in the succeeding section of the *Antiquities* that recounts how Alexander II Zabinas seized the throne from Demetrius II.[67] It cannot date

---

64. M. Stern 1961. In this section I use the full name John Hyrcanus here, and Hyrcanus II for his son, to avoid any confusion between the two.

65. A passage in the *Periochae* (57) of Livy describes how the ambassadors of Sidetes gave Scipio Aemilianus presents in 134 B.C.E. while he was besieging Numantia. This mission shows that the Romans were in contact with Sidetes at the time he besieged Jerusalem. It provides some indirect support of the reconstruction of events offered here, since the Romans could have sent ambassadors to the Seleucid Empire, or to the officials of Sidetes in Numantia, at that time with a warning to Sidetes not to interfere in Hasmonean affairs. For Popillius Laenas's encounter with Antiochus IV Epiphanes, see Polyb. 29.27.1–8; Diod. Sic. 31.2; Livy, *History* 45.12.1–8; App. *Syr.* 66.350–52; Just. *Epist.* 34.3.1–3. Cf. Dan 11:29.

66. See M. Stern 1961, 7–12; Bar-Kochva 1996, 291–92.

67. *Ant.* 13.267–69.

prior to 128 B.C.E., for at that time Demetrius II was trying to invade Egypt and the Seleucid Empire still controlled the southern Judean coast.[68] This senatorial decree makes better sense if it describes the request of John Hyrcanus for the restoration of territories previously granted to the Jews by Sidetes, which had subsequently been taken away from him. Fear of possible Roman incursions apparently kept subsequent Seleucid monarchs from attempting to annex the Hasmonean state. As new Seleucid rulers came to power, the Roman Republic continued to issue decrees warning them to stay from Hasmoneans lands. One such proclamation helped John Hyrcanus later when a new civil war threatened the stability of the Seleucid Empire.

Josephus mistakenly inserts the third Roman decree of *Ant.* 14.247–55 into a pronouncement by the people of Pergamum honoring Hyrcanus II and the Jews. This text mentions a "King Antiochus, son of Antiochus." This document can only refer to the son of Antiochus VII Sidetes, Antiochus IX Cyzicenus.[69] The events in this document coincide with Josephus's account of the civil war between Antiochus VIII Grypus and Antiochus IX Cyzicenus.[70] Because the Hasmoneans were no threat to the Romans, their annexation of Seleucid territory only weakened a potential rival of the Republic.

Stern's placement of the three senatorial decrees to the reign of John Hyrcanus best explains their contents and sheds considerable light on Hasmonean diplomacy. They suggest that the Roman Republic played a role in the expansionist program of John Hyrcanus by allowing him to take territory from the Seleucid Empire. But there is one additional issue that must be raised concerning the inclusion of these three senatorial decrees in the *Antiquities*. How did Josephus obtain them?

H. R. Moehring argues that Josephus could not have read any of the senatorial treaties he quotes in the *Antiquities* during his time in Rome since eight thousand bronze tablets that contained copies of them were lost during the fire of December 69 C.E.[71] If correct, this would cast doubt on Josephus's veracity and suggest that he possibly fabricated the contents of the treaties he cites. It is plausible that the basic contents of these treaties were known to the Jewish community and that Josephus

---

68. See Euseb. *Chron.* (in Schöene 1999, 1:257–58).

69. For this evidence, see Bar-Kochva 1996, 292; Bevan 1902, 256, 303; Fischer 1970, 73–82; Giovannini and Müller 1971; Gruen 1984, 751; Kasher 1990, 124; Schürer et al. 1973–87, 1:207. M. Stern (1961, 12–19) dates it to the year 113–112 B.C.E.

70. See *Ant.* 13.270–74.

71. Suet. *Vesp.* 8.5; Moehring 1975, 131.

merely reproduced what he had heard about them orally. However, it is very possible that Josephus saw copies of them. An overlooked source may support this thesis.

All the Roman treaties known to us from inscriptions mention that its text was to be engraved on a bronze tablet, which was a metal believed to have the magical ability to ward off evil, and placed in the city of Rome. They were mounted in many locations, such as the Temple of Dius Fides on the Quirinal, the Temple of Diana on the Aventine, the Atrium Libertatis near the Forum of Julius Caesar, and other shrines where the gods could protect them.[72] Temples were jam-packed with them; many had to be mounted in high and inaccessible locations due to lack of space. This overcrowding was necessary because the Romans believed that as long as these bronze plaques were displayed on temple walls the treaties inscribed on them remained valid. According to 1 Macc 8:22, the 161 B.C.E. treaty between Rome and Mattathias's son Judas was inscribed on a bronze tablet. A twelfth-century C.E. guidebook to Rome, the *Mirabili Urbis Romae*, mentions that it was still in the church of San Basilio, which was located in the ruins of the Temple of Mars Ultor in the Forum of Augustus.[73] It apparently was a tourist attraction. Josephus, therefore, should not be necessarily be doubted when he cites Roman documents dating to the first century B.C.E. since not all these tablets were destroyed in the fire of 69 C.E.

The Parthian Campaign of Antiochus VII Sidetes

Despite assurances of Roman support, Hyrcanus was so weak at this time that he had no choice but to become a Seleucid vassal. Numismatic evidence shows that Hyrcanus minted coins in Jerusalem for Sidetes in the Seleucid years 181, 182, and 183 (= 131–129 B.C.E.) with the inscription ΒΑΣΙΛΕΩΣ ΑΝΤΙΟΧΟΥ ΕΘΕΡΓΕΤΟΥ. They depict a lily on the other side, which may have been the heraldic flower of Israel. If so, this may testify to the effort of Hyrcanus to emphasize his status as high priest, and avoid offensive images, even though he was a Seleucid subject.[74]

---

72. See Zollschan 2012, 233; Zeev 1998, 384.

73. For this tablet, see Zollschan 2012, 233–35.

74. See further Hendin 2007–2008, 83–87; Kushnir-Stein 2000–2002; Hoover 1994, 42–51; Houghton 1983, 84, nos. 831–34 and plate 49. The existence of Hyrcanus coins has been the subject of a long debate. Recent archaeological finds conclusively demonstrate that he also minted coins with the name יהוחנן. For the most recent treatment of this issue, which supersedes all earlier works, see Meshorer 2011, 25–27.

Although Josephus claims Hyrcanus hosted Sidetes in Jerusalem after the Syrian siege of the city, it is perhaps more probable that the Seleucid monarch travelled to Jerusalem just before his Parthian campaign. He ostensibly undertook this visit to inspect Jewish troops, discuss military strategy with Hyrcanus, and organize the logistics for this costly undertaking. The Romans would have welcomed this conflict, for it pitted two of their adversaries against one another.

The *Antiquities* is the only extant source that mentions the participation of Hyrcanus in Sidetes's invasion of Parthia.[75] Josephus identifies Nicolaus of Damascus as one of his sources he used to document this campaign.[76] The few extant Parthian records for the period prior to and following the invasion of Sidetes makes it difficult to corroborate the details of Josephus's account. The first-century B.C.E. historian Pompeius Trogus, a third-generation Roman of Gallic origin, wrote an extensive history of the Hellenistic period that included a lengthy section on the history of Parthia. His work unfortunately survives in an epitome by Justin that has been dated as early as 144 C.E. to as late as 395 C.E. Justin states that he intentionally removed approximately thirty-five years of Parthian history between the reigns of Mithridates II (123–88 B.C.E.) and Orodes II (ca. 56–38 B.C.E.) from the original work of Pompeius Trogus.[77] Largely because of his omission, this period has been called the Parthian "Dark Age."[78] Justin fortunately includes some material about this time that that we can use in conjunction with a few classical references and coins to offer a reconstruction of this war and suggest why it took place when it did.[79]

---

75. In *War* 1.62 Josephus merely alludes to the death of Sidetes during this campaign, and states that his demise gave Hyrcanus an opportunity to annex additional foreign lands without any fear of Seleucid intervention.

76. *Ant.* 13.250.

77. Pompeius Trogus, Sallust, Livy, and Tacitus belonged to the ancient canon of the four great Latin historians. See *Hist. Aug.* (Aurel. 2.1); (Probus 2.7). For possible dates of Justin's edition, see further Yardley and Develin 1997, 1–10.

78. Assar 2006b, 112.

79. Ael. *De natura animalium* 10.34; App. *Syr.* 59, 68; App. *B. Civ.* 11.68; Euseb. *Chron.* (in Schöene 1999, 1:255–56); Ioannes Antiochenus, "Excerpta de insidiis" (*FHG* 4.561); Livy, *Per.* 59.13; Oros. 5.190.310; (Pseudo) Plut. *Mor.* 184E–F. For additional sources, some of which are of lesser quality but may preserve ancient traditions, see Atkinson 2012c, 78–82; Fischer 1970, 29–31.

The Parthian monarch Mithridates I died of an illness in 132 B.C.E. His son Phraates II (= Arsaces VII 132–127 B.C.E.) succeeded him to the throne.[80] He appears to have followed his father's policy of attacking the Seleucid Empire. It is probable that he decided to take advantage of Sidetes's protracted siege of Jerusalem to annex additional Seleucid territory. This threat of a Parthian invasion appears to have forced Sidetes to make peace with Hyrcanus and compel the Hasmonean army to join his expedition.

The Parthian campaign of Sidetes was a dangerous undertaking. According to Diodorus Siculus, he set out in spring when the snow was still melting. Phraates II supposedly sent envoys to discuss terms of peace. Sidetes demanded the release of his brother, the withdrawal from territory he claimed as his own, and tribute as restitution for past Parthian crimes against the Seleucid Empire. Phraates II became angry at these demands. Diodorus Siculus claims the companions of Sidetes pleaded with him to take refuge in the mountains to neutralize the threat of the Parthian cavalry.[81] Sidetes was apparently so overconfident of success that he took an excessive number of noncombatants with him to Parthia.[82] This made him more vulnerable since it slowed down the march of his army in hostile terrain. Nevertheless, Sidetes initially did quite well. According to Justin, he won three battles and forced the Parthians to flee towards Iran.[83] His men began to call him "the Great."[84] This title was intended to recall his namesake, Antiochus III, who had retaken Parthia and Bactria. These initial victories convinced Sidetes to reject any negotiation with the Parthians and continue his invasion since he was thus far winning.

---

80. The last dated reference to Mithridates I is contained in an Astronomical Dairy dated to 132 B.C.E. See Sachs and Hunger 1996, 220–34, No. –132C+D_1+D_2+E. Just. (*Epit.* 41.6.9) mentions that he died of old age.

81. Diod. Sic. 34/35.15–16.

82. A son and daughter of Sidetes by Cleopatra Thea, Seleucus and Ladocie, accompanied the army. Both were captured. The fate of the son is unknown; the daughter became part of the royal harem. Some scholars mistakenly identify one or both as children of Cleopatra Thea by her former spouse Demetrius II. See further, Just. *Epit.* 38.10; Bevan 1902, 245; Dąbrowa 1992, 49–50; Grainger 1997, 47–48; Whitehorne 1994, 157.

83. Just. *Epist.* 38.10.6.

84. Antiochus VII Sidetes is called "Megas S(oter?) Euergetes Kallinikos" in an inscription from Ptolemais. See Y. Landau 1961. This is the only extant testimony of his epithets "Soter" and "Kallinikos." See also Grainger 1997, 30. The title "Megas Euergetes" appears on a gold stater minted by Sidetes. See Ehling 2008, 204–5; Houghton 1989.

This forced the Parthians to take an extreme measure to repel him. Justin states that Phraates released the imprisoned monarch Demetrius II (he was also Sidetes's brother) in the hope that he would return to Syria and start a civil war for the throne that would force Sidetes to leave Parthia.[85] This ploy was unsuccessful; Sidetes continued his march and reached Babylon before late summer in S.E.B. 182 (= July/August 130 B.C.E.).[86] He minted a bronze coin there in S.E.M. 183 (= 129 B.C.E.) to celebrate his victory. He remained in the city from approximately July 130 B.C.E.–October 129 B.C.E.[87]

It is uncertain how the expedition ended. Justin mentions that Sidetes quartered his troops throughout Parthia for the winter, and compelled the local population to furnish them with supplies. It is probable these were local ethnic Greeks living in settlements under Parthian rule that he forced to help him. According to Justin's account, the offensive behavior of the Seleucid troops caused the locals to revolt. Unable to obtain provisions, Sidetes was forced to disperse his men throughout the countryside. This made communications between his units nearly impossible. The Parthians took advantage of Sidetes's desperate situation and launched their final assault. Coins struck in the name of Sidetes in Syria, dated 128 B.C.E., suggest he was killed in the autumn of 129 B.C.E. The news of his death did not reach the Seleucid Empire until after the turn of the next year, when the last coins bearing his name were minted.[88] It is uncertain how he died. Diodorus Siculus merely states that Phraates II killed 300,000 of Sidetes's men.[89] Justin mentions that he also captured some Seleucid soldiers and forced them to serve as conscripts in his army to fight the Scythians. He claims that Phraates II later perished during a fight against

85. Just. *Epit.* 38.10.7.

86. See Assar 2006b, 103.

87. A dozen undated silver tetradrachms commemorate his initial victory over the Parthians. For these coins and their respective dates, see Assar 2006b, 113–14.

88. Just. *Epit.* 38.10.8–9. Euseb. (*Chron.* in Schöene 1999, 1:255) confused the dates of the death of Sidetes with his siege of Jerusalem and claims that he subdued the Jews in the third year of the 162nd Olympiad (= 129/29 B.C.E.). App. (*B. Civ.* 11.68) claims that Sidetes committed suicide after the Parthians defeated him. Julius Obsequens (in Kapp 1772, 101–102) dates the death of Sidetes to A.U.C. (*ab urbe condita*) 624 (= 130 B.C.E.). The prologue to ch. 36 of Justin mistakenly claims that Sidetes killed Hyrcanus. Because this contradicts the content of Justin's book, this error should be attributed to the anonymous writer of the prologue. The latest coins of Sidetes do not necessarily imply that he was alive when they were minted since news of his death took time to reach Syria

89. Diod. Sic. 37.17.1.

hostile tribes because some of these men defected during the battle.[90] This information, if reliable, shows that the Parthians did not decimate the army of Sidetes; many Seleucid soldiers were taken captive. A large number also escaped and made it home.

There may be some physical evidence of some of the survivors of Sidetes's failed invasion. Coins from Merv (ancient Mergiana) of Artabanus I (= Arsaces IX; 127–23 B.C.E.) contain the legend ΒΑΣΙΛΕΩΣ ΑΡΣΑΚΟΥ ΦΙΛΑΔΕΛΦΟΥ ΦΙΛΕΛΛΗΝΟΣ. Additional coins of Mithridates II (= Arsaces XI; 123–87 B.C.E.) found at Merv also contain the word ΦΙΛΕΛΛΗΝΟΣ. Loginov and Nikitn suggests that the unusual phenomenon of two kings suddenly becoming philhellenic in a remote northeastern province of Iran is best explained by the presence of Greeks there, who were considered a threat. They believe these Greeks were the surviving soldiers of Sidetes's army that Phraates II had captured. Their exile to such a remote location, and their apparent harsh treatment, is what apparently led them to rebel against Phraates II.[91] They purportedly defected during a battle to join forces with invading nomads and kill Phraates II.[92] According to Diodorus Siculus, as many as 300,000 Parthians died in the engagement. Mithridates II subsequently had to campaign in the western portion of Seleucid Empire, particularly Babylon, where Arabs began to take advantage of the insurrection of these Greek soldiers to wage their own revolt.[93]

It is certain that Sidetes's disastrous expedition, and the fate of many of his men left behind in Parthia, was widely known in antiquity. Some of Josephus's critics may have wondered why he omitted the defeat of Sidetes by the Parthians in the *War*, especially since only Hyrcanus survived with his army intact. How was this possible? Josephus decided to explain it in his *Antiquities*. He is the only extant writer to include an account of Hyrcanus's participation in the Sidetes's invasion of Parthia. He was so worried his readers would doubt the veracity of his account of how Hyrcanus and his men survived that he took the unusual step of identifying his source. He states that, according to Nicolas of Damascus

90. Just. *Epit.* 42.1.1–5.

91. Loginov and Nikitin 1996, 40. A letter Mithridates II sent in 119 B.C.E. to the Greek citizens of Babylon for support in his war against the Guti provides additional evidence that large numbers of Greeks resided in the Parthian Empire at this time. The survivors of Sidetes's army may have joined with these Greeks to revolt against the Parthians. See Sachs and Hunger 1996, 326–27, no. 118a.

92. Diod. Sic. 34/35.17.1

93. See further Olbrycht 2010, 146–47.

and other writers, the fortuitous arrival of a religious holiday again saved Hyrcanus from a catastrophe. This time it was the Festival of Pentecost:

> On this we have the testimony of these things, also of Nicolaus of Damascus, who writes as follows, "After defeating Indates, the Parthian general, and setting up a victory monument at the Lycus River, Antiochus remained there two days at the request of the Jew Hyrcanus because of a festival of his ancestors during which Jews are forbidden to travel." Nor does he speak falsely in saying this; for the Festival of Pentecost had come round, following the Sabbath, and we are not permitted to travel either on the Sabbath or on a festival.[94]

This enigmatic account implies that Sidetes and his army had to leave Hyrcanus and the Jews behind to delay the Parthians. Although it is possible Sidetes was killed before Hyrcanus and his men could rejoin the expedition, it is perhaps more probable that Hyrcanus simply abandoned Sidetes. This would explain the mysterious disappearance of the Hasmonean army from the story. Josephus does not explain the further actions of Hyrcanus in Parthia. He merely writes that as soon as he received a report that Sidetes had died in battle, he took advantage of the absence of the Seleucid army to begin a successful series of conquests beyond the Jordan River, in Samaria, and in Idumea to add an unprecedented amount of territory to the Hasmonean state. But a close reading of the *Antiquities*, when combined with the classical sources and numismatic evidence, suggests that Josephus has provided an abbreviated, and highly misleading, account of Hyrcanus's subsequent military conquests. He may have done so to avoid mentioning Hyrcanus's use of religion to betray Sidetes.[95] It is doubtful that Hyrcanus planned to rejoin the expedition. He likely abandoned Sidetes and his men in hostile territory. Josephus focuses on Hyrcanus's unprecedented territorial acquisitions following the death of Sidetes to imply that God blessed him and to overlook this betrayal. But there is a problem with Josephus's accounts of these conquests.

Chronological Inconsistencies in the Writings of Josephus

Josephus's account of the period between 129–104 B.C.E. is chronologically incorrect. Although most scholars use it as the basis for their reconstructions of Hasmonean history, it has virtually no archaeological

94. *Ant.* 13.250–52.
95. *Ant.* 13.254–58.

support.[96] Josephus claims Hyrcanus conquered many Syrian cities immediately after the 129 B.C.E. death of Sidetes. However, the archaeological evidence shows that the towns he claims Hyrcanus subjugated at this time were continuously occupied from 129 B.C.E. to 112/111 B.C.E. They were not destroyed until 112/111 B.C.E. These include such strategic locations as Marisa,[97] Mount Gerizim, and Shechem.[98] Imports of Rhodian amphorae cease around 112/111 B.C.E. at Marisa, Shechem, and Scythopolis. This provides firm evidence of trade disruption at that time.[99] The dates of the destruction layers, occupational gaps, and evidence for an interruption in trade goods from these and other sites match Josephus's lists of the cities Hyrcanus conquered. However, they demonstrate that Hyrcanus did not capture them before 112/111 B.C.E. more than fifteen years after the death of Sidetes.[100] But the archaeological evidence reveals that Hyrcanus did not seek to dominate all the territories he captured.

Josephus claims the Hasmoneans treated Idumea differently than other regions. He writes that Hyrcanus allowed the Idumeans to remain in their country as long as they practiced circumcision and followed Jewish law.[101] Strabo disagrees; he claims the Jews did not force the Idumeans to practice their religion.[102] Yet, a passage from the *History of King Herod* preserved by Ptolemy the Historian claims that Hyrcanus compelled the Idumeans to adopt circumcision.[103] What do the data from the material culture show?

There is no archaeological evidence of a widespread destruction of Idumea. None of the potsherds or amphorae found in Marisa show any

96. Atkinson 2011.

97. Dated tomb inscriptions from Marisa are almost continuous from 196/195 B.C.E. to 112/111 B.C.E. Coins from Ascalon and Tel Beer Sheba cease at the same time. For this evidence, see Barag 1992/93; R. Barkay 1992/93, plates 3–5); Oren and Rappaport 1984; Shatzman 1991, 97. There is also a numismatic gap at Tel Beer Sheba in Idumea between 112/111 B.C.E. and 4/3 B.C.E. The evidence suggests that Tel Beer Sheba was abandoned as a result of the conquests of Hyrcanus sometime around 112/111 B.C.E. See Kushnir-Stein and Gitler 1992/93, 15, 18.

98. Barag 1992/93, 6–7; Shatzman 1991, 60–61; Magen 2008a, 178–79; 2008b, 25–28; Plummer 2010, 1183.

99. Finkielsztejn 1998, 38–41.

100. See further Atkinson 2012c, 182–86; Bar-Kochva 1989, 560–62; Barag 1992/93.

101. *Ant.* 13.257. In *War* 1.63 Josephus merely states that Hyrcanus "took numerous cities in Idumean including Adora and Marisa."

102. Strabo, *Geogr.* 16.2.34.

103. Ptolemy the Historian (in M. Stern 1974–80, 1:356). This author is likely Ptolemy of Ascalon, who lived at the end of the first century B.C.E.

sign of burning; much of the visible damage at the site was due to building collapse after its abandonment. A lead weight with a date and an inscription attests to the existence of an *agoranomos* of the city in 108/7 B.C.E. The ritual baths found there may provide some indirect confirmation of Josephus's claim that its inhabitants followed Jewish law.[104] Occupation levels at Idumean sites such as Tel 'Ira and Tal Halif also show no visible signs of destruction. This evidence indicates that Hyrcanus took much of the region peacefully.

The archaeological findings reveal that Jerusalem and its environs were economically isolated from Idumea, the Negev, the coastal region, and the Transjordan. The ceramic remains from Jerusalem and other Jewish sites within and outside Judea consist almost exclusively of a limited repertoire of locally manufactured household pottery. In contrast, other regions contain a wealth of foreign imports. The uniformity of Jewish pottery in this area at this time suggests that the Hasmoneans promoted a policy of economic independence in the areas under their control.[105] They expanded their territory to the south gradually. The lack of any clear evidence of fortresses in Idumea lends additional support for this reconstruction, and reveals that the region south of Judea was annexed without any significant conflict. But the situation was very different in Samaria.

The Samaritans

Josephus recounts the history of the Samaritans in *Ant.* 9.288–91. This passage has generated considerable scholarly discussion concerning the ethnicity and the religious practices of the people who inhabited Samaria. In his *War* and his *Antiquities* he claims that Hyrcanus defeated the "Cuthaeans," who inhabited the region of Samaria and erected a temple there that was modeled after the Jerusalem sanctuary. Josephus based his understanding of this region's inhabitants on 2 Kgs 17. He uses the word "Cutheans" (Χουθαίων) for the syncretistic population that was comprised of the region's indigenous inhabitants as well as foreigners the Assyrians had brought there.[106] Egger believes that the residents of Samaria in the first century B.C.E. were considered descendants of settlers brought to the region by the Assyrians. She does not believe Josephus includes the

104. Finkielsztejn 1998, 40, 47; Shatzman 2007, 267–68.

105. Berlin 1977, esp. 29–30.

106. *War* 1.63; *Ant.* 13.256. Three limestone capitals discovered at Mt. Gerizim similar to other proto-Aeolic capitals found in Judea, Samaria, and the Galilee may have been taken from a nearby Israelite sanctuary and reused in the original Samaritan shrine. For this possibility, see further Stern and Magen 2002.

Samaritans of Mt. Gerizim in *Ant.* 9.288–91 when he describes Χουθαῖοι and Σαμαρεῖται. Egger argues that Josephus believed the Samaritan community originated when Jews/Israelites settled in Samaria and Shechem in the fourth century B.C.E. (*Ant.* 11.303, 340).[107]

Plummer proposes that because hostility to the Samaritans is evident in Josephus's writings, he must have had the Gerizim community in mind. But he believes the word Σαμαρεῖται does not necessarily mean "Samaritans" in Josephus's books. Rather, Plummer suggests he uses τό Χουθαίων γένος to describe those who lived around the temple on Mt. Gerizim that Hyrcanus conquered.[108] Plummer also proposes that Josephus (*Ant.* 11.302) not only claims the Σαμαρεῖς are descended from the Cutheans, but also that he also uses the names Σαμαρεῖται, Σαμαρεῖς, and Χουθαῖοι synonymously regardless of what these terms meant in his sources and describes the inhabitants of this region to his Roman audience as opportunists: they profess they are Jews when it suits them, but in reality they belong to a different people (foreigners brought in by the Assyrians).[109]

Josephus's different terms for the Samaritans appear to include both residents of Samaria, who consider Mt. Gerizim as the only legitimate place of worship, as well as those who believe that it is actually Jerusalem where God wanted his sanctuary built. The decisive event that led to the alienation of the Samaritans from the Jerusalem temple priests appears to have been the 112–111 B.C.E. destruction of the temple atop Mt. Gerizim by Hyrcanus. Up to this time, the inhabitants of this region were not monolithic in their religious beliefs.[110] Hanan Eshel comments that sources from the third century B.C.E. even refer to the Samaritans as "Judeans." He suggests this shows that the formation of Samaritan identity was a long and gradual process.[111] The Samaritans only appear to have emerged as a distinctive religious and ethnic community during the Hellenistic period following the building of the Samaritan temple atop Mt. Gerizim and Hasmonean opposition to it.

In his *War* Josephus writes that Hyrcanus sent his sons, Aristobulus and Antigonus, to besiege Samaria. Its inhabitants called upon Antiochus IX Cyzicenus (115–95 B.C.E.) for help.[112] Cyzicenus came to their aide.

---

107. Egger 1986, 48–59, 176–213.

108. *War* 1.63; *Ant.* 13.255–56.

109. Plummer 2009, 65–80.

110. See further Plummer 2010, 1082–84; Magen 2008a, 178–79; 2008b, 25–28.

111. H. Eshel 2012.

112. *War* 1.64–65. The Greek here reads Ἀσπόνδιον, which Niese (1894, 16) and Thackeray (1927, 32) emend to Ἀσπένδιον. Aspendius is the unofficial surname of Antiochus VIII Epiphanes Philopator Callinicus Grypus (ca. 123/2–113 B.C.E.). A

Hyrcanus's sons defeated him and expelled him from the region. Aristobulus and Antigonus then captured Samaria, razed it to the ground, and enslaved many of its inhabitants. Josephus includes a second story of Samaria's destruction in a later section of his *Antiquities*.[113] In this story he states that Hyrcanus sent his sons to attack the Samaritans because of their alliance with the Seleucid rulers, and their hostile actions against territory he had colonized in Samaria.[114] It was this event that caused the Samaritans to request help from Antiochus IX Cyzicenus. After the sons of Hyrcanus defeated and expelled him from the region, he returned with additional forces supplied by Ptolemy IX Soter. Hyrcanus's men repelled both armies and captured Samaria after a siege of over one year. According to Josephus, the Hasmonean troops destroyed the city.[115] For Josephus, the Samaritans deserved their punishment for bringing a Seleucid ruler to territory that rightfully belonged to the Hasmonean state. If there was any doubt, he emphasizes Hyrcanus's unprecedented piety: he was closer to God than all of the Hasmoneans!

few manuscripts read Antigonus instead of Antiochus. Josephus here mistakenly refers to Antiochus VIII Grypus. He corrected this error in *Ant.* 13.276, where he writes that the Samaritans called in Antiochus Cyzicenus, who was Grypus's brother and rival. See further Sievers 2001b, 35.

113. *Ant.* 13.275–79. The earlier story in *Ant.* 13.254–56 should be placed here along with *War* 1.63. Except for the spelling of Gerizim, the passages in *War* 1.63 (Ἀργαριζεὶν) and *Ant.* 13.255 (Γαριζεὶν) are identical. Because the former name is a contraction of הר and גרזים (הגרזים), which is the Samaritan form, it has been suggested that Josephus (or his source) used a Samaritan tradition. To support this thesis, Egger (1986, 295–96) proposes that the Samaritans did not use the term "Cutheans" for themselves, but used it to refer to the Sidonians/Phoenicians in Shechem and its vicinity. Plummer (2009, 205–6), however, remarks that there is insufficient evidence to assume that either passage is based on a Samaritan source, and it is unlikely Josephus would have needed such a document to write his account of the conquests of Hyrcanus.

114. *Ant.* 13.275. I accept the emendation of Samaria instead of Marisa in this passage since it is improbable that the Samaritans controlled an Idumean city. See also Niese 1892, 202. The text presumably states that the Samaritans harassed settlers who had moved to the region of Samaria as part of the expansionist policy of Hyrcanus. See Egger 1986, 102–21.

115. *War* 1.64–65. Dąbrowa (2007, 455) proposes that the siege began about 112/111 B.C.E. and ended in the autumn of 110 B.C.E. or sometime in 109 B.C.E. A Greek inscription (Tushingham 1972, 63) from Samaria may provide additional support for Josephus's account of the capture of this city by the sons of Hyrcanus.

The *War* includes a series of apocryphal stories that highlight Hyrcanus's gift of prophecy.[116] Josephus apparently intended these accounts to provide evidence of the close contact Hyrcanus had with God. However, he does so for a brutal reason. He implies that Hyrcanus's vicious treatment of the Samaritans, and his destruction of their temple, was divinely sanctioned. However, the *Antiquities* contains a very different account of the campaign of Hyrcanus against the Samaritans. Josephus in this book alludes to his earlier tale of how Manasseh, the brother of the high priest, married the daughter of Sanballat, the governor of Samaria. Jaddua, the high priest, and a large segment of Jerusalem's population opposed the union. Manasses left Jerusalem to serve as high priest in Samaria. According to Josephus, many priests from Jerusalem followed him there.[117]

The Samaritans constructed their shrine during the power vacuum that was created in the Middle East between the fall of the Persian Empire and the conquests of Alexander the Great. His arrival in the region complicated affairs for both Jews and Samaritans.[118] Quintus Curtius Rufus, Eusebius, Jerome, and Syncellus all claim that the Samaritans revolted against Alexander the Great while he was in in Egypt in 331 B.C.E.[119] Alexander subsequently turned Samaria into a Macedonian military colony. Archaeologists have discovered skeletons of men, women, and children in the Wadi ed-Daliyeh, along with pottery, clothing, and papyrus documents that date from 375–335 B.C.E.[120] These provide physical confirmation that Alexander retaliated against the Samaritans who had participated in this revolt. If the testimony of Pseudo-Hecateus is factual, the Jews may have played an active role in suppressing the Samaritan uprising.[121]

---

116. *War* 1.67–69.

117. *Ant.* 11.322–24; 13.256.

118. *Ant.* 11.317–24. For the basic authenticity of Josephus's account of the activities of Alexander the Great in the East, see Egger (1986, 65–84). When the Syrians persecuted the Jews, the Samaritans sought to separate themselves from the Jews. They appealed to the Seleucid rulers and complained they were being treated like Jews although they were Sidonians by origin (*Ant.* 12.257–58). Mor (1989, 15) suggests that the Samaritans, by calling themselves Sidonians of Shechem, wanted to emphasize their embracement of Hellenistic culture and demonstrate they were not Jews.

119. For these sources, see further the discussions in Tcherikover 1959, 47–48; VanderKam 2004, 78–79.

120. For this material, see further Leith 2010.

121. Pseudo-Hecateus, *apud* Josephus, *Apion* 43. Cf. Curt. 4.8.34.9–11. For the possibility that Jews helped suppress the Samaritan revolt, see further Kasher 2005, 211–13.

In his *Antiquities*, Josephus emphasizes the history of the Jews to portray the Samaritans as apostates. His account of Alexander the Great's visit to the Jerusalem temple is intended to show that this shrine is superior to all others. Even Alexander recognized the importance of the Jewish religion, Josephus claims, and offered sacrifice in the Jerusalem temple according to the high priest's direction.[122] This account is undoubtedly shaped by Josephus's later situation in Rome. It is an implicit message to the Roman emperor of his day that foreign rulers have long favored the Jews and respected their religion. Josephus did not regard the Samaritans with such favor, or associate them with the Romans. Rather, he appears to have regarded them as apostate Jews like those Mattathias and his sons had killed. Hyrcanus had every right to conquer them for their theological betrayal: they rejected Jerusalem as the only lawful place for sacrifice! In addition, they had long been hostile to the Jews. The lineage of their priests only compounded the tense history between the Jews and the Samaritans that went back to the time of Alexander the Great.

During the chaos of the Syrian wars the Samaritans captured three districts that had been given to the Jews by Alexander the Great. They were encouraged to do this by the Ptolemies. Hyrcanus sought to regain these lands and subdue the Samaritans not merely for territorial gain, but primarily for reasons of religion and nationalism. The Samaritan temple and its high priests since Manasseh traced their descent through the Zadokite family, which many Jews considered the legitimate high priestly line.[123] Hyrcanus could not tolerate the existence of a competing shrine so close to Jerusalem, especially after the Samaritans had received military support from the Seleucid Empire.[124] The Samaritans, and other forms of "Judaism" such as the community of Heliopolis, constituted a threat to Josephus's presentation of a Judaism centered in Jerusalem. In his *Antiquities* he shows much more animosity toward the Samaritans than in his *War* that cannot be attributed to his use of sources. This suggests some change in his attitude towards the Samaritans.[125] Be that as it may, none of his accounts condemn Hyrcanus for his treatment of the Samaritans and his destruction of their temple.

122. *Ant.* 11.336.

123. Later Samaritan traditions claim that the Samaritans, not the Jews, were the true heirs of the Aaronide high priesthood through Phinehas. See Babota 2014, 280–81.

124. See Mor 1989, 17–18.

125. Mor 1989, 13. See also *Apion* 1.1; 2.193. Hjelm (2005) suggests Josephus may have used the name Sidonian to portray the Samaritans as Gentiles since the biblical tradition associates the Sidonians with the worst forms of idol worship.

Josephus is not the only ancient Jewish author to express hostility towards the Samaritans. Several Hellenistic Jewish writers used Gen 34 to espouse anti-Samaritan sentiments. Among these are Theodotus, *T. Levi* 6–7, *Jub.* 30, Jud 9, Pseudo-Philo's *L.A.B.* 8:7, and Philo (*De mig.* 224; *De mut.* 193–95 and 199–200).[126] These texts suggest that many Jews were hostile towards the Samaritans, and that some were not reluctant to use Scripture to sanction violence against them. Theodotus is among our best witnesses to this hatred.

The work of Theodotus is an anti-Samaritan polemic composition that may shed additional light on Jewish relations with this community.[127] Its author insists on circumcision and a strict adherence to the prohibition of intermarriage with Gentiles. There is no need to accept Robert Bull's proposal that Theodotus was written before the mid-second B.C.E., prior to 150 B.C.E., because its description of Samaria matches the fortification wall he uncovered during his excavations there.[128] Because he believes this structure went out of use in the first half of the second century B.C.E., he dates the poem's composition prior to this time. But there is no evidence that Theodotus actually refers to this wall. Bull's dating, moreover, is primarily based on the chronology of Josephus and not on the stratigraphy of the site. This led him to believe that Hyrcanus conquered Samaria twice, in 129 B.C.E. and 107 B.C.E. The archaeological evidence demonstrates that he only campaigned in the region in 112/111 B.C.E.[129]

The dates of the destruction levels at Shechem and the temple on Mount Gerizim may settle the chronological debate over the number of campaigns Hyrcanus undertook against the Samaritans. As previously discussed, the archaeological evidence shows that the latest coins from both Shechem and Samaria date to 112/111 B.C.E., which supports the

---

126. For extensive discussions of the anti-Samaritan polemic in these texts, see Collins 1999, 57–60; 1980; Nickelsburg 1981, 121–25; Plummer 1982, 177–88.

127. In his arguments in support of the traditional view that this work was written by a Jew to oppose the Samaritans, Jacobson (2013, 724) emphasizes the anti-Samaritan polemic in the composition and comments that Theodotus turned the Shechemites into doublets of the inhabitants of Sodom to resolve the ethical problem of Hyrcanus's treatment of the Samaritans.

128. Bull 1967.

129. The *Megillat Ta'anit* may contain a reference to Jews celebrating the destruction of the Samaritan heartland by Hyrcanus when it bans mourning on the "Day of Gerizim" (יום הר גרזים). The notation in the Scholion mistakenly attributes this destruction to Alexander the Great. For the text, see Lichtenstein 1931–32, 339–40; Noam 2003, 46, 100–103; Zeitlin 1922, 67 #9.

revised chronology previously presented for the conquests of Hyrcanus.[130]
The findings from the Mt. Gerizim sanctuary are less certain. Bull's
excavations at Tell er-Ras uncovered a Greek temple (Building A)
dedicated to Zeus and Roman coins from Antoninus Pius (138–161 C.E.)
to Volusianus (251–53 C.E.). Underneath Building A he found a large
podium of unhewn stones built atop bedrock, with pottery from the third
century B.C.E. Bull identified these remains as portions of the Samaritan
Temple, and the half-cube of unhewn stones as its altar.[131]

The new excavations of Samaria led by Yitzhak Magen have demonstrated there was no Samaritan temple beneath the Roman temple to Zeus
that is located on Tell er-Ras. The archaeological evidence also shows no
signs of Hellenistic construction atop the tell. The pottery sherds found
there actually came from fill that was brought there from the Hellenistic
city some twenty meters away. Building B at the site also contains no
trace of the Samaritan temple. The findings of Magen suggest that the
temple was located on the main peak, where he uncovered evidence of
fortifications, residential quarters, and olive-presses from the second
century B.C.E. Magen believes the fragmentary Hebrew inscriptions, and
a broad entrance with stairs he found at the site, belonged to the Samaritan
temple and its holy precinct. He proposes that a *temenos* was built in the
Persian era and expanded during the Hellenistic period, and surrounded by
a large city. The temple, according to his reconstruction, was constructed in
the *temenos* in the fifth century B.C.E. and rebuilt in the Hellenistic period.
Although there is still no definitive physical evidence of the Samaritan
temple, the coins from the site cease around 112/111 B.C.E. and suggest
that Hyrcanus destroyed whatever type of shrine was there at that time.
The date of the end of occupation at Samaria provides additional evidence
to support the revised chronology for the military conquests of Hyrcanus.[132]
Other findings provide additional evidence of the site's importance, and of
Hyrcanus's hostility towards it.

130. Atkinson 2011, 8–11; 2012c, 78–82; Barag 1992/93, 7–8; G. Wright 1957,
27; Reisner, Fisher, and Lyon 1924, 1:263 n. 31; Plummer 2009, 200–10.

131. Bull 2008; Bull and Wright 1965.

132. Magen 2008a, 178–79; 2008b, 25–28; 2010, 26–35, 70; Plummer 1989,
168–69, 172. Berlin (1977, 10–11) observes a notable absence of imported or luxury
goods at Shechem and Mt. Gerizim even though the Samaritans had contact with
other countries.

Two inscriptions found in Delos show that the Samaritan community there sent offerings εἰς ἱερὸν Ἀργαριζείν.[133] The imprecise dating of these inscriptions unfortunately does not necessarily prove that the Samaritans in the Diaspora sent offerings to Samaria only while a temple stood there. It is feasible that some form of cult was performed atop the mountain even if there was no physical structure. By the beginning of the second century B.C.E. Mt. Gerizim was enclosed by a wall. Sheep bones found within this enclosure may be the remnants of sacrifices.[134] But there is no conclusive archaeological evidence for the existence of a physical temple, although the literary sources suggest that some type of shrine once existed atop the mountain. It is possible that any remains are under the Theotokos Church.[135] The large podium (Building B) found at the site could have been the foundation of temple, though it is equally probable that it was the base of an altar. Although it is theoretically possible that Hyrcanus destroyed some Samaritan shrine atop Mt. Gerizim in 128 B.C.E., the absence of any firm archaeological evidence from the site, and the lack of destruction levels at nearby Shechem from this time, suggests that he did not conquer any cities in Samaria until approximately 112/111 B.C.E.

The Qumran text 4Q372 (*4QApocJos*[b]) provides some indirect evidence for hostilities towards the Samaritans at this time that may help us to understand why Hyrcanus wanted to destroy their shrine.[136] It contains an anti-Samaritan polemic directed against the Shechem community and its cultic center at Mt. Gerizim when it denounces those who make a high place atop a mountain to provoke Israel.[137] The editors of this document, Schuller and Bernstein, comment that the author has slightly changed several biblical texts to transform what is a common prophetic indictment

133. The inscriptions that mention a Samaritan sanctuary are dated to ca. 250–175 B.C.E. (Menippos Inscription) and ca. 150–50 B.C.E. (Serapion Inscription). See further, Plummer (2009, 16–17). Although it is possible these inscriptions do not refer to a temple, but merely to "holy Argarizin," the phrase εἰς ἱερὸν Ἀργαριζείν suggests otherwise. The expression ἱερὸν Ἀργαριζείν in Pseudo-Eupolemus (fragment 1, par. 15) may also indicate that the Delos inscriptions refer to an actual temple.

134. See Berlin 1977, 10–11.

135. See further, Plummer 1989, 172–75.

136. This document is found in three scrolls from Qumran (4Q371, 4Q372, and 4Q373. For the texts, see Schuller and Bernstein 2001. Schuller (2006, 315) proposes the text predates the attack of Hyrcanus on Shechem, and that its anti-Samaritan hostility may suggest a pre-Maccabean date of composition. Tov's (2010, 20, 47) latest inventory of the Dead Sea Scrolls designates 4Q371, 4Q372, and 4Q373 as *Narrative and Poetic Composition*[a-b] and 2Q22 as *apocrDavid? (Narrative and Poetic Composition)*.

137. 4Q372 1 11–12. Cf. 4Q371 1 10–11.

into a specific reference to the Samaritans on Mt. Gerizim. Concerning the anti-Samaritan polemic in this document, they comment that 4Q372 1 demonstrates that identity and legitimacy among rival Jewish groups was a contentious issue long before Josephus.[138] The content of the writings of Theodotus also suggests that many Judeans despised the Samaritans. His paraphrase of the biblical story of Dinah's rape in Gen 34 appears to show a clear anti-Samaritan bias. In his version of this biblical tale, Jacob refuses to give his daughter Dinah in marriage to Shechem unless the inhabitants of the city of Shechem "become Jews by being circumcised" (περιτεμνομένους 'Ιουδαῖσαι) so they can intermarry with the Israelites.[139] Theodotus even expands this biblical narrative to justify the attack of Simeon and Levi against Shechem. He implies God sanctioned it! His account of this incident, as well as the content of 4Q372, appears to reflect tensions that existed during the reign of Hyrcanus when the Judeans increasingly emphasized nationalism and forced the neighboring peoples to adhere to Jewish law.

The Samaritan Pentateuch, and texts that reflect this version, suggest that the campaign of Hyrcanus against Samaria created a permanent religious division between the Samaritans and the Jewish community in Jerusalem. The document *4QTestimonia* (4Q175), which was copied at the end of the second century B.C.E. or the beginning of the first century B.C.E., contains a harmonistic version of Exodus that displays the same amount of editorial changes from the proto-Masoretic Text as the Samaritan Pentateuch.[140] Its date suggests that the primary version of the Samaritan Pentateuch was undertaken by the second century B.C.E., presumably prior to the 112/111 B.C.E. destruction of Mt. Gerizim by Hyrcanus.[141] The Masoretic Text may provide additional evidence in support of this thesis. The special, or "sectarian," Samaritan readings were traditionally thought to comprise twenty-one changes in the Deuteronomic formula from "the place that Yhwh your God *will* choose (יבחר)" to "the place that Yhwh your God *has* chosen (בחר)."[142] However, Adrian Schenker's textual study of these passages, and all extant variants and versions, suggests that בחר was the

---

138. Schuller and Bernstein (2001, 171 n. 4) also state that the definitive "break" between the Samaritans, the Jerusalem Temple, and the Jerusalem priesthood occurred only after the Samaria campaign of Hyrcanus.

139. Fragment 4, line 15. For the basis of this translation, see further Holladay 1989, 176 n. 82; S. Cohen 2001, 188–89, 261. See also Esth 8:17 (LXX).

140. The same scribe produced 1QS and 4Q175. See A. Steudel 2000, 936–38.

141. For this evidence, see further Eshel and Eshel 2003; Schorch 2005.

142. Deut 12:5, 11, 14, 18, 21, 26; 14:23, 24, 25; 15:20; 16:2, 6, 7, 11, 15, 16; 17:8, 10; 18:6; 26:2; 31:11.

original reading in the Hebrew *Vorlage* of the LXX, and that the Masoretic Text is a theologically motivated correction.[143] This suggests that the Samaritan Pentateuch is based on a text type that was in use during the last two centuries B.C.E.

During the second or first century B.C.E. the Samaritans apparently made a small number of theologically motivated changes in a few select places of the Tanakh, primarily the insertion of "Mt. Gerizim" in place of "Mt. Ebal," to stress their belief in the sanctity of Mt. Gerizim. A fragment of Deut 27:4b–6, presumably from Qumran and dated to around the middle of the first century B.C.E., contains the reading "on Mt. Gerizim" (בהרגרזים).[144] This evidence suggests the Hasmoneans, especially during the time of Hyrcanus, considered any challenge to the holiness of Jerusalem, and to the validity of their version of the Tanakh, an intolerable situation. This disagreement over the correct place to worship, as demonstrated by the textual and archaeological evidence, led Hyrcanus to attack and destroy Samaria and its shrine.[145]

Conclusion

In his *War* Josephus depicts Hyrcanus as the Hasmonean ruler most favored by God. He consistently portrays him as a successful administrator, a pious high priest, and a great military leader. Nevertheless, his terse account of the last days of Hyrcanus suggests that he ended his reign during a time of great turmoil. In *War* 1.67 Josephus mentions that towards the final period of his life he faced social unrest and rebellions that forced him to wage war against rebels to restore law and order. Although Josephus provides no information about this rebellion or its organizers, he

143. Schenker 2008.

144. See Charlesworth 2015. The Samaritan version emphasizes Mt. Gerizim in the following places: Exod 13:11a; Deut 11:29b; 27:2b–3a, 4a, 5–7, and 11:30. For a discussion of this evidence, and additional biblical passages, see further, Plummer 2009. For the manuscript variants, with an opposing interpretation favoring the primacy of the Masoretic Text, see McCarthy 2007, 84.

145. If the tubs discovered in the Hellenistic city on Mt. Gerizim destroyed by Hyrcanus were also used for ritual purification, this would provide evidence that Jews and Samaritans adopted many of the same purity rituals. This similarity between the daily lives of the Judeans and the Samaritans, as evident by the remains uncovered by archaeologists, may have increased tensions between the two groups in the time of Hyrcanus when the Hasmoneans appear to have begun to force a common form of Judaism upon the inhabitants in territories under their control. See further, Zangenberg 2013, esp. 541–45.

writes that it was aimed against the ruling family and suggests Hyrcanus subdued it with much violence.[146]

In his *Antiquities* Josephus expands his favorable portrayal of Hyrcanus as a ruler blessed by God (*Ant.* 13.300) to recount his manipulation of his Seleucid rivals, his military conquests, and his frequent diplomatic missions with Rome, to portray his reign as a successful period of senatorial self-rule.[147] Josephus also inserts a lengthy account of the Pharisees to explain the transition from this illustrious period to the destructive reign of his son, Aristobulus. It was Aristobulus who changed the Hasmonean state into a monarchy. However, his short reign is to a great extent a continuation of the narrative of Hyrcanus: God had warned him that Jannaeus was his rightful successor.[148] But to understand Jannaeus, we must first go beyond Josephus to recount the tragic rule of his brother, Aristobulus.

---

146. For this rebellion, see further Dąbrowa 2010a, 78–79. This disturbance appears unconnected with the opposition from the Pharisees documented in *Ant.* 13.288–99.

147. Description from Mason 2009, 197.

148. *Ant.* 13.322.

Chapter 4

JUDAH ARISTOBULUS:
THE CREATION OF THE HASMONEAN MONARCHY

His Family and His Royal Title[1]

Judah Aristobulus should never have been the ruler or the high priest of the Hasmonean state: he took power against the wish of his father, John Hyrcanus. He was not perceived as charismatic like his predecessors, Mattathias, Judah, Jonathan, Simon, or Hyrcanus.[2] Rather, Josephus presents his reign as a series of intrigues and violence. Because of the brevity of his time in power, it is difficult to reconstruct what took place when he governed his late father's kingdom. Josephus complicates matters since his narratives of Aristobulus's reign are largely novels that contain little historical fact. Nevertheless, Aristobulus is an important figure in Second Temple period history because he created the Hasmonean monarchy.

Aristobulus was one of John Hyrcanus's five sons.[3] Josephus states that the Greek name of Judah was Aristobulus (Ἰούδᾳ τῳ καί Ἀριστοβούλῳ).[4] He is the first known member of his family to have this Greek name.[5]

---

1. For the major historical sources for the life of Judah Aristobulus, see *Ant.* 13.301–19; *War* 1.70–84; Atkinson 2012c, 91–102; 2014a. Judah Aristobulus is sometimes referred to as Judah Aristobulus I to distinguish him from the youngest son of Jannaeus, who is commonly referred to as Aristobulus II.

2. Regev 2013, 118–20.

3. *Ant.* 13.299. According to Josephus, Aristobulus and Antigonus were the two eldest sons (*Ant.* 13.322). Antigonus was the younger of the two (*Ant.* 13.302). Jannaeus (*Ant.* 13.320; *War* 1.85) and Absalom (*Ant.* 13.323; 14.71) are the only other named offspring of Hyrcanus. Josephus mentions another brother whose name he does not record. See *Ant.* 13.323; *War* 1.85.

4. *Ant.* 20.240.

5. Meshorer (2011, 45). He is called Aristobulus in the *Chronicles* of Eusebius (in Schöene 1999, 1:129) and Jerome (in Schöene 1999, 2:131 [169th Olympiad]). His nephew, a fourth-generation Hasmonean, was also named Aristobulus. The name was also in use in the sixth generation when it was given to Jonathan Aristobulus, the son

Aristobulus minted coins with the inscription "Judah the High Priest and the Congregation of the Jews" (יהודה הכוהן הגדל וחבר היהודים).[6] Recent doubts have been raised concerning the testimony of Josephus that he was the first Hasmonean monarch since his coins do not contain the title "king."[7] The inscriptions on the coins of Aristobulus are nearly identical to those minted by his father and his brother, Jannaeus. It appears that the same engraver produced many of them.[8] However, Jannaeus appears to have faced some opposition to his use of the title "king" on his currency. He overstruck many of these coins to replace "king" with "high priest."[9] Because the designation "king" was still problematic during the reign of Jannaeus, the absence of any royal designation on the currency of Aristobulus during his short reign does not indicate that he was never an actual monarch.

The Succession Process

The account of Aristobulus in the *War* and the *Antiquities* is largely a drama that focuses on the dysfunctional aspects of the Hasmonean family. According to Josephus, he was not his father's successor. Although Hyrcanus loved Aristobulus and Antigonus more than his other sons, God wanted neither to govern the Hasmonean state! God told Hyrcanus that Jannaeus would be his heir.[10] This undoubtedly apocryphal tale was likely created to explain the unexpected rise of Jannaeus to power. But, despite this divine revelation that Jannaeus was God's choice, Hyrcanus picked his wife as his successor.[11] Despite her importance in Hasmonean history, Josephus does not tell us her name.[12]

of Herod and his Hasmonean wife, Mariamne. See *Ant.* 15.342; 18.133; 20.13. See further, Ilan 1987, 2–5, 19–21.

6. Although there was a longstanding debate as to whether these coins were minted by him or Aristobulus II, recent numismatic discoveries have demonstrated that Aristobulus minted coins with the name "Judah." See Barag and Qedar 1980, 8–21, and plates 3–9; Meshorer 2011, 27–29; Seyrig 1958.

7. Rappaport 2012, 393.

8. Hendin 2009/2010b, 36.

9. Hendin and Shachar 2008.

10. *Ant.* 13.322.

11. *Ant.* 13.302; *War* 1.71. Marcus (1966, 379 n. c) makes the unsubstantiated claim that Hyrcanus did not appoint his wife as the next ruler, and that Josephus mistakenly attributed a story about Jannaeus to Aristobulus.

12. Josephus seldom names women, including his own wives, in his accounts. Of the thirty-nine women mentions by name, twenty appear in sections that appear to be

The decision of Hyrcanus to name his wife as his political successor was unprecedented in Jewish history. Scripture records the reign of only a single female monarch, Athaliah.[13] It is doubtful that Hyrcanus or his subjects would have cited her as a precedent since the biblical authors denounced her for her usurpation of the Davidic throne and her paganism. Her gender, moreover, excluded her as a lawful monarch.[14] But there is no reason to doubt the claim of Josephus that Hyrcanus gave his wife political power. It is the unusual nature of his account that makes this story plausible. It is difficult to believe he would have fabricated a tale in which his hero, Hyrcanus, willingly appointed his spouse as his political successor unless there was some truth to it.

The choice of Hyrcanus to designate his wife as his political successor was novel for Judea, but not in the region. Female rule was common in Egypt and Syria.[15] It is possible that these neighboring Hellenistic kingdoms influenced Hyrcanus to appoint his wife to succeed him. But the Hasmonean state and its neighbors differed when it came to religious authority. Although Hellenistic women could function as priests, they could only hold secular power in Judaism since Scripture explicitly bans them from the priesthood.[16] Hyrcanus, therefore, clearly intended someone else in his family to serve as high priest during her reign. Josephus does not tell us which son he chose, but some clues point towards Jannaeus. This decision was likely made public, and would account for Aristobulus's bad treatment of Jannaeus. It would also explain why Jannaeus eventually succeeded his surviving siblings to become high priest. It is also possible that Hyrcanus and his spouse feared that Aristobulus, and perhaps Antigonus as well, would kill Jannaeus. If the story that Hyrcanus sent Jannaeus to live in the Galilee is factual, he and his spouse may have sent him there to protect him from his elder siblings.[17]

dependent on Nicolaus of Damascus. With a single exception of Acme (*War* 1.641; *Ant.* 17.134), these women are of royal blood. See Ilan 1996.

13. See 2 Kgs 11:1–20; 2 Chr 22:10–23:21; *Ant.* 9.140–56. Because Josephus does not denounce the wife of Hyrcanus as an unlawful ruler like Athaliah, he presumably accepted her right to hold political power. For Josephus's unflattering portrayal of Athaliah, which influenced his depiction of the wife of Hyrcanus, see Atkinson 2012c, 87–90; Begg 1996.

14. Jer 33:17.

15. For numerous examples of female rulers in Egypt and Syria, see Atkinson 2012c, 103–28; Macurdy 1932.

16. See further de Vaux 1961b, 345–403.

17. *Ant.* 13.322.

With his mother and siblings out of the way, Aristobulus, along with his brother Antigonus, were free to do as they wished. Josephus writes that Aristobulus transformed the Hasmonean state into a kingdom ruled by a monarch. The claim of Josephus that Aristobulus was the first Hasmonean king conflicts with the testimony of Strabo, who writes that "Alexander was first to declare himself king instead of priest (πρῶτος ἀνθ᾽ ἱερέως ἀνέδειξεν ἑαυτὸν βασιλέα Ἀλέξανδρος).[18] Since no Hasmonean relinquished the office of high priest to adopt the title "king," the account of Josephus is to be preferred.

Aristobulus is largely absent in the ancient sources. George Syncellus does not even mention his reign in his *Chronicle*. This omission is surprising since he used Eusebius's *Chronicle*, which states that Aristobulus was the first to wear the royal diadem and that he held the offices of king and high priest.[19] The short reign of Aristobulus apparently led either Strabo or one of his sources to assume that he had never reigned as king, and that Jannaeus was responsible for the creation of the Hasmonean monarchy.

Aristobulus's combination of the high priesthood and the kingship was unique in Jewish history. However, it has a precedent in the *Aramaic Levi* texts from Qumran.[20] The author of this work claims "the kingdom of priesthood is greater than the kingdom."[21] It appears the Hasmoneans believed that holding the high priesthood was a prerequisite to kingship. Since they considered themselves rightful high priests, they also held that they were the nation's lawful monarchs.[22] Although the date of *Aramaic Levi* is disputed, James Kugel believes it is doubtful that such a claim would have been written about Levi before the rise of the Hasmonean dynasty. He suggests that the work dates no earlier than the second half of the second century B.C.E.[23] The Hasmoneans used the tradition reflected in this book to propose that kingship was not limited to the tribe of Judah (Gen 49:10), as Levi made clear to his descendants in this document. This gradually became a common belief as reflected in the accounts of Josephus and Justin.[24]

---

18. *Geogr.* 16.2.40. Because Strabo next mentions this ruler's sons, Hyrcanus II and Aristobulus II, there is no doubt this passage refers to Jannaeus.

19. Euseb. *Chron.* (in Schöene 1999, 1:129). The same information is found in Jerome, *Chronicle* (in Schöene 1999, 2:131 [169th Olympiad]) and the *Excerpta Latina Barbari* (in Schöene 1999, 2:223 [46a]).

20. 1Q21 7 2; 4Q213 2 10–18.

21. 1Q21 1 2.

22. For this understanding, see Regev 2013, 171–72.

23. Kugel 2007.

24. *Ant.* 14.78; Just. *Epit.* 36.2. Cf. *Ant.* 14.404.

The creation of a non-Davidic monarchy by Aristobulus was not only unprecedented, but its beginning is uncertain. Josephus gives two different dates for the start of his reign in the *War* and *Antiquities*. He appears to have determined the length of the tenure of Aristobulus in light of his understanding of biblical chronology. In *War* 1.70 he writes that Aristobulus became king "471 years and three months" after the return of the Jews from the Babylonian captivity. In *Ant.* 13.301 he gives the figure of "481 years and three months" after the end of the Babylonian captivity. Both numbers are too large and represent an early interpretation of the seventy weeks of years, or 490 years, in Dan 9:24–27. If the one-year reign of Aristobulus is added to this figure, then *Antiquities* places the beginning of the reign of Jannaeus at the start of the 70th heptad (years 483–490). This number is similar to Eusebius's *Praeparatio evangelica* (8.2.394b–d), which calculates the length of time from Cyrus to the death of Jannaeus as 482 years.[25] The interpretation of Daniel in Josephus is similar to *4QApocryphon of Jeremiah C^e* (4Q390), which also uses Dan 9:24–27 to date the last historical epoch to the period of the Hasmonean revolt.[26]

The figures in all these texts appear to presuppose the Danielic chronology. This suggests that Josephus or a Jewish source he used derived the lengths of the reigns of some of the Hasmonean rulers from Scripture, especially the periodization of Daniel. For this reason, none of these documents can be used for historical reconstruction. The calculations in these texts are nevertheless significant since they reflect widespread ancient understandings about the importance of the Hasmonean period, and the belief that its creation marked the beginning of the final age of history as foretold by the biblical prophets. The date of the beginning of the reign of Jannaeus, which is based on Egyptian papyrological evidence written during the "War of Scepters" (103–101 B.C.E.), shows that none of our extant works provides an accurate chronology for the early Hasmonean monarchy. The Egyptian evidence revels that Aristobulus became king in 105 B.C.E.[27] But who sat beside his throne?

25. The notes in Loeb editions of *War* 1.70 (Thackeray 1927, 34–35) and *Ant.* 13.301 (Marcus 1966, 379) recognize that Josephus's figures are incorrect. For discussions of this chronology in Josephus, see Atkinson 2016, 52–54; Grabbe 1997, 600–601.

26. For 4Q390 and its use of sabbatical chronology, see further Atkinson 2016; Dimant 2001, 113–16, 235–53; H. Eshel 2008, 25–27; Werman 2006. The text 4Q559, the only extant chronograph from Qumran, matches no known chronology (Wise 1997) and should make us cautious in assuming that we can reconstruct ancient chronologies with confidence.

27. G. Cohen 1989, 119. This dating is discussed in detail in Chapter 5.

The Wife of Aristobulus: Salina or Salome/Shelamzion?

The account of the reign of Aristobulus in the *War* and the *Antiquities* is largely a novel that is of little historical value. One of its major characters is his wife, whose identity remains the subject of a longstanding academic debate. Josephus does not tell us her name in his *War* but merely states that after the death of Aristobulus, "The woman (γυνὴ) released his brothers raising Alexander to kingship."[28] He provides more information about her in his *Antiquities* when he writes that the wife of Aristobulus, Salina (Σαλίνα), also known as Alexandra (Ἀλεξάνδρα), released her late husband's brothers from prison and appointed Jannaeus as king.[29] This passage is unusual for three reasons. First, Josephus departs from his customary practice of referring to the Hasmoneans by their Greek names and includes their Semitic names. Second, this paragraph is unique because Josephus states that the wife of Aristobulus selected the next king and high priest. Third, it is one of the few sections in which Josephus names a woman. These three features indicate that Josephus likely copied this paragraph from a lost history of the Hasmonean family.

Many scholars assume that Salina Alexandra was the wife of Judah Aristobulus, and that after his death she married Jannaeus. She is, therefore, often identified as the woman commonly referred to as Shelamzion (Salome) Alexandra who was married to Jannaeus, and, after his death, became his political successor and monarch. Josephus never tells us the Semitic name of this ruler; he only refers to her by her Greek name, "Alexandra" (Ἀλεξάνδρα).[30] And he never says that she married her late brother-in-law after the death of her husband. The apparent source of the confusion regarding the identity of the wife of Aristobulus goes back to the ancient Christian scholars who copied and transmitted Josephus's books. They were puzzled by the presence of two women with similar names in his narratives. Under the assumption that they were the same person, they often changed the name Salina Alexandra to Salome Alexandra in their manuscripts. Many scholars continue to accept this emendation, and

---

28. *War* 1.85. Marcus (1966, 42–43) translates "the woman" (ἡ γυνὴ) as "the widow of Aristobulus" based on *Ant.* 13.320. He also makes the unsubstantiated claim in his note on this passage: "Though Josephus never expressly says so, it appears certain that, besides the throne, she gave Alexander Jannaeus her hand in marriage."

29. *Ant* 13.320. For reasons discussed below, I consider the name "Salome" (Σαλώμη) found in some manuscripts a later scribal change to the text. See further Niese 1892, 210; Marcus 1966, 388.

30. Ilan 2006, 52–55. Ilan (1987, 3) suggests that this name was given to her after she married Jannaeus. There is no evidence for this proposal.

therefore believe that Salome Alexandra was the wife of Aristobulus.[31] It is commonly assumed that after the death of Aristobulus she wed her brother-in-law, Jannaeus, as required by the biblical rules of levirate marriage.[32]

There are four reasons why the Hasmonean ruler Alexandra could not have engaged in a levirate marriage.[33] First, no ancient text mentions such a union: there is absolutely no evidence that she wed her brother-in-law, Jannaeus. Second, during the Second Temple period marriage to a widow, a divorced woman, or a prostitute was believed to disqualify a man from serving as high priest. Philo comments on this issue that a high priest cannot marry an ordinary virgin, but only a virgin daughter of another priest. However, Philo states that ordinary priests were permitted to marry the daughters of non-priests.[34] Because Alexandra's husband, Jannaeus, was high priest she could not have been a widow. If she had been married to Aristobulus, then Jannaeus would have been ineligible to hold this office since he would not have married a virgin. Third, Josephus always refers to Hyrcanus II as the son of Alexandra and Alexander Jannaeus. If she had entered into a levirate marriage, Hyrcanus II would have been the legal son of Aristobulus and Alexandra. Fourth, Josephus tells us that Aristobulus was married to Salina Alexandra: he never claims she was the spouse of Alexander Jannaeus. For these reasons, and because of the absence of any ancient testimony that the wife of Aristobulus later married her brother-in-law, we should abandon the theory that Jannaeus engaged in a levirate marriage. The best interpretation of the extant evidence is that Salina Alexandra and the Hasmonean monarch Alexandra are two different women. The tenure of Salina Alexandra's husband was quite brief and violent. Let us turn to the only significant accomplishment Josephus records for Aristobulus's reign, his conquest of the Itureans. The main issue regarding this campaign is whether it actually occurred.

Aristobulus and the Itureans

Things did not go well for Aristobulus once he eliminated all opposition to his rule. Josephus records the following incident that took place during the Festival of Tabernacles. Aristobulus was ill and unable to attend. Antigonus had returned from an unspecified successful campaign and appeared in the temple during the festival wearing his armor and accompanied by some

---

31. See further Atkinson 2008, 62; 2012c, 60–64; Ilan 1993.

32. Deut 25:5–6. This theory first appears in J. Müller 1711, 12–14.

33. Atkinson 2012c, 60–64.

34. *Spec. Leg.* 1.110–11. Klausner (1972c, 225–26) suggests, without evidence, that the Hasmoneans did not observe the biblical marriage laws.

of his soldiers.[35] Because Aristobulus reigned for approximately one year, this was the only celebration of the Festival of Tabernacles to have taken place during his brief time in power. His inability to officiate at this holiday suggests that he was incapacitated for much of his rule. This provided an opportunity for his opponents to undermine him. Foremost among his enemies was apparently his sibling and trusted confident, Antigonus.

Josephus does not mention where the campaign of Antigonus took place. The *War* may provide a clue. In this book he states that Antigonus procured for himself some fine armor and military decorations in the Galilee.[36] In his *Antiquities* Josephus provides some information about Aristobulus that he obtained from Timagenes, through a citation in Strabo. According to Timagenes, Aristobulus was a "kindly person" and "compelled" (ἀναγκάσας) the Itureans to "be circumcised and to live in accordance with the laws of the Jews."[37] Since the Itureans resided in the Galilee and the Golan, Antigonus presumably acquired the weapons mentioned in the *War* during his invasion of their territory in the north. Since this is the only recorded military campaign during the reign of Aristobulus, we can presume that Antigonus returned from fighting the Itureans in some unspecified location in the Galilee just before the Tabernacles incident. But who lived there?

Determining the ethnicity of the Galilee's inhabitants is complicated because we have little written evidence about the region from this period. The extensive surveys and excavations in the Galilee, especially Zvi Gal's investigation of the Lower Galilee, reveals that the Upper and the Lower Galilee were largely destroyed and depopulated following the Assyrian campaigns of 733/732 B.C.E. Extensive portions of these regions were deserted during the seventh and sixth centuries B.C.E.[38] This absence of Galilean settlements effectively refutes the thesis that an independent Israelite village culture lived there continuously from the Iron Age to the Roman periods.[39] Yet, this does not necessarily mean that the Galilee did not have a Jewish presence when Aristobulus became king.

Archaeological excavations in the Galilee have uncovered numerous modest sites from the Persian and Late Hellenistic periods. Most appear to have been agricultural settlements since there is no evidence of industrial activities at these communities.[40] The Upper Galilee, the Huleh Valley,

---

35. *Ant.* 13.304.
36. *War* 1.76. This information is missing in the parallel in *Ant.* 13.308.
37. *Ant.* 13.318.
38. Gal 1992, 54–62. See also Myers 2010, 26–29.
39. See further Cromhout 2005, 212–13.
40. See further Berlin 1977, 12–14; Reed 2000, 35–39.

and the Coastal Plain share a common pottery of Phoenician origin known as "spatter painted ware."[41] Because the evidence for the Early Hellenistic period in the Galilee is sparse, it is difficult to determine the ethnicity of the inhabitants in this region who used this pottery. However, the finds there reveal they were poor. The locally made utilitarian pottery of the area's residents shows they did not have extensive trade with Phoenicia or the neighboring regions. The emergence of a village culture in the Upper Galilee during the Persian and early Hellenistic periods may provide additional evidence for Jewish migration there. It is plausible that there may have been a need for new settlements and military outposts in the area following the Hasmonean expansion northwards.

The belief that there was a large-scale Judaization of the Galilee has no archaeological support.[42] Simon's campaign (ca. 164 B.C.E.) to the Galilee to assist Jews there (1 Macc 5:14–23) suggests that there was already a significant Jewish presence in the region.[43] The battle of Ptolemy Soter against the Jewish population of Asochis (Talmudic Sikhnin), five miles north of Sepphoris, around 103 or 102 B.C.E. on the Sabbath provides additional evidence for some Jewish settlements in the Galilee.[44] The accounts of 1 Maccabees (11:63–74) and Josephus (*Ant.* 13.158–62) likewise testify to a Jewish presence in the Upper Galilee when they mention that Demetrius II encamped at Kadesh to draw Jonathan to the Galilee. He did this because he expected Jonathan to go there to protect "his own people" from the Seleucid rulers.[45]

41. Aviam 1993; Berlin 1997, 75–88.

42. Schürer et al. (1973–87, 1:142, 216–18, 561–73) is the most explicit, and perhaps widely cited work that accepts the thesis that the Hasmoneans engaged in the conquest and Judaizing of the northern territories.

43. The description of the region in 1 Macc 5:14–17 refers to it as "Galilee of the Gentiles" (Γαλιλαίαν ἀλλοφύλων). The author distinguishes its pagan inhabitants from the family of Mattathias, who were in distress in the Galilee (ῥῦσαι τοὺς ἀδελφοὺς σου ἐν τῇ Γαλιλαίᾳ). This group presumably practiced the same religion as Judas and Simon. For this reason, Judas urged his brother, Simon, to rescue them from their pagan oppressors.

44. *Life* 207, 233, 384. For the identification of this site, see Grootkerk 2000, map 15, no. 41.

45. Josephus appears to regard the Galileans as *Ioudaioi* (*War* 1.309; *Ant.* 12.421; 13.336–37; 14.120). His accounts suggest that the *Ioudaioi* began to dominate the Galilee during the reign of Jonathan, and not at the time of the supposed Iturean conquest of Aristobulus. During the reign of Demetrius II the toparchy of Judea included Samaria, the Galilee, and portions of Peraea (*Ant.* 13.50; 13.154). Josephus claims in *Ant.* 13.154 that Jonathan considered the Galileans to be "of his own people" (τοὺς γὰρ Γαλιλαίους ὄντας αὐτοῦ).

There is a notable increase in the number of settlements across the Galilee, and portions of the Golan, during the Late Hellenistic period after the Hasmoneans began to rule portions of Judea. These include several excavated sites whose earliest architecture dates to the Late Hellenistic period or the first century B.C.E. This list includes the Galilean cities of Capernaum, Hammath Tiberias, Horvat Arbel, Yodefat, Khirbet Shema', Meiron, Nazareth, Sepphoris, and the Golan towns of Qatzrin and Gamla.[46] Numismatic finds from the Galilee and the Golan are especially important for demonstrating a Jewish presence in these regions before the Hasmoneans annexed these areas. During the first century B.C.E. Hasmonean coins proliferate there, especially those minted by Jannaeus.[47] This is especially true of the Golan region. At the site of Gamla archaeologists have uncovered 310 coins of Hyrcanus, 30 of Aristobulus (the largest collection to date), and the greatest hitherto recorded find of Jannaeus coins from a single site. The coins of Jannaeus from Gamla comprise most of the coins found there. They are especially abundant from the middle of the first century C.E. to the time of the First Jewish Revolt. The late date of circulation for these coins suggests that the site's occupants preferred to use Hasmonean currency during the Roman period.[48]

Phoenician coins have also been found in the Galilee and the Golan, especially those minted in Tyre. Several scholars suggest these coins show that the Galilee and the Golan were closely connected with Tyre and the Phoenician coast. The Phoenician coins found in the Galilee and the Golan tend to be larger denominations (didrachmas and tetradrachms). In contrast, the Hasmonean currency in these regions is represented by the smallest denominations (prutot). The difference between the values of these coins suggests that the Tyrian coins, because they represent larger denominations, were reserved for trade, the Jerusalem temple economy, and for use among the wealthy. The Hasmonean coins, because they comprise the bulk of the lower denomination coins, were used for local purchases and played a greater role in the lives of the masses. This evidence suggests that the Galilee's population, despite some possible evidence of contact

46. Meyers, Strange, and Meyers 1981, 155; Reed 2000, 40–42.

47. More coins of Jannaeus have been found throughout ancient Palestine than any other Jewish coins. See further, Berlin 1977, 37–43; Reed 2000, 41–42; Kasher 1990, 142; Shachar 2004.

48. Leibner 2009, 324; Syon 1992/93. Syon notes that Gamla's western quarter yielded the greatest number of Herodian and other first-century C.E. coins. Yet, 75% (1,885) of the coins from this single area are Jannaeus coins. The Seleucid coins make up only 9.7% of Gamla's currency while Roman coins comprise 4.85%. For these issues, see further Syon 2004, 27, 38, 97–100, 118.

with Phoenicia, was primarily connected by trade and ideology with the Hasmonean state and the Jerusalem temple.[49] This is especially true of the ceramics from the lower Galilee and the Golan. By the first century B.C.E. the residents of these settlements stopped purchasing products from the coastal areas and made vessels in shapes that are common in Judea. This evidence suggests that some Judeans had moved to these regions by this time. The appearance of *miqva'ot* throughout the Galilee and the Golan shows that these newcomers adopted a lifestyle that emphasized ritual purity, which separated them from then region's pagan population.[50]

Numismatic data provide further evidence to support the thesis that there was a Jewish presence in the Galilee and the Golan before the supposed annexation of these areas to the Hasmonean state during the reign of Aristobulus. This comes from bronze coins of Antiochus VII Sidetes found in the Galilee and the Golan that were minted in Jerusalem.[51] These coins depict a lily—an apparent concession to Jewish religious sensitivities—and an anchor surrounded by the inscription "of King Antiochus the Benefactor" (ΒΑΣΙΛΕΩΣ ΑΝΤΙΟΧΟΥ ΕΓΕΡΓΕΤΟΥ).[52] They were minted from 133/2 to 131 B.C.E., which is the period after Sidetes made peace with Hyrcanus until just before the Seleucid monarch's 130 B.C.E. death in Parthia.[53] They are found at several sites in the Galilee and the Golan, including Gush Halav, Gamla, Yodefat, Shihin (Asochis), Arbel, Bet She'an, and Tel Basul. Josephus reveals that the first five of these sites were already inhabited by Jews in the early Roman period. Although Hyrcanus conquered Bet She'an (Nysa-Scythopolis), 2 Macc 12:29–31 shows it had a sizeable Jewish population earlier. Because Soter attacked Asochis on the Sabbath when he overran the kingdom of Jannaeus, a Jewish population must have settled there before he invaded the region during the War of Scepters.

---

49. For this evidence, see Hanson 1980, 53–54; Barag 1982/83; Syon 1992/93, 42–44; Raynor and Meshorer 1988; Reed 2000, 42; Meyers 1976. Meyers believes the numismatic evidence shows strong geographical, administrative, and cultural ties between Jews in the Galilee and the Golan. Syon (2004, 116) observes that many coins found at Gamla were minted in Jerusalem.

50. Berlin 2006, 17–18, 142–43; 2011, 69–106; Tessaro 1995.

51. The find spots of these coins are primarily in Jerusalem and the surrounding area, which makes it almost certain they were actually minted there. For this evidence, see Ariel 1982, 280–81; 1990, 111–12; Hendin 2009/2010b, 36.

52. For the evidence these were minted in Jerusalem, see Hoover 2003, 32–34.

53. Houghton 1983, 83–84.

The coins of Sidetes found in the Galilee and the Golan may provide some information about the relationship between these two areas with Judea. His currency is rarely found in these regions. The Jewish coins used in these areas tend to be lower denominations that were intended for local circulation. Such currency normally did not travel far from its place of production. The coins were manufactured for local use and would not have been acceptable currency elsewhere. Danny Syon proposes that the Sidetes coins found in the Galilee were brought there by Jews who had returned from the yearly pilgrimage to the temple, which demonstrates there was an established Jewish presence at the Galilee and the Golan before the reign of Sidetes.[54] The discovery of many sites in the Galilee containing chalk vessels, stepped plastered pools, ossuaries, and the notable absence of pork bones in the settlements there, provides additional evidence of Jewish occupation. These findings are not limited to the Hasmonean period, but continue into the first century C.E. and show that this Jewish presence remained in the region after the Hasmonean period. The archaeological finds from first-century B.C.E. Galilee match those in Judea and provide additional support for the thesis that Jews settled in the Galilee and portions of the Golan before the Hasmonean annexation of these regions.[55] But were any of these Jews formerly Itureans?

It is plausible that some Jews were once Itureans.[56] However, it is difficult to reconcile the accounts of the Iturean conquest of Aristobulus with the archaeological evidence. The Iturean culture appears to have originated in the mountainous interior of Lebanon. Their capital was located at Chalcis in the Beq'a. The Iturean kingdom of Chalcis extended north of Damascus, and included Baalbek/Heilopolis.[57] In 332 B.C.E. Alexander the Great fought the Itureans in the anti-Lebanon mountains

54. Syon 2006.

55. See further, Cromhout 2005, 217–22; Reed 2000, 39–55.

56. The Itureans were Arabs. They created a distinctive culture in the Lebanon Mountains and adjacent regions, but shared the Arabic language with other Arab groups. See further Klein 2013, 601–2; Kropp 2013. Strabo, *Geogr.* 16.2.10. Restö (2003, 408) comments that although the Itureans were Arabs, the ancient sources make a distinction between the two because of their different cultures.

57. Freyne 2001, 190–93; Dentzer 1985, 399–403; Will 1983, 141–46. Strabo (*Geogr.* 16.2.10) locates the Itureans and other Arab groups in the mountainous regions between the Lebanon and Anti-Lebanon ranges and Damascus. The only numismatic evidence of possible Iturean presence in the Hermon region is a coin of Ptolemy, the son of Mennaeus, discovered at Bir An-Sobah. See Dar 1993, 131–32. Because coins do not necessarily indicate the ethnicity of their owners, this coin may have been brought to the site as a result of trade by a non-Iturean.

when they tried to prevent his men from felling trees there for his siege of Tyre.[58] It has been suggested that the Itureans and the Arabs opposed Alexander the Great because the Persian crown allowed them to remain in this region in exchange for their loyalty.[59] By the later second century B.C.E. the Itureans expanded their territory southwards. But there is no evidence they lived in the Galilee.[60] The center of their power was the Valley of Massys, which includes the cities of Chalcis and Heliopolis, and the two flanking ranges of the Lebanon and the Anti-Lebanon Mountains.[61] The Itureans were greatly exposed to Hellenism.[62] This is clearly evident in their shrines.

The Iturean site of Niha in Syria contains two temples. One dates to the mid-second century C.E. and contains a mixture of local and Roman styles and has numerous Latin and Greek inscriptions.[63] The Har Senaim complex, located a few kilometers from Banias near Mt. Hermon, dates to the Hellenistic (second to first century B.C.E.) and the early Roman periods. It contains decorated columns, cornices, architraves, eagle statues, a relief of Helios, and Greek inscriptions.[64] The Itureans apparently settled around Mt. Hermon because many in the region already regarded it as an ancient sacred site.[65] The material culture of the Itureans suggests they assimilated the religious beliefs and architectural styles of their neighbors, which makes it difficult to distinguish their material culture from other nearby groups.

---

58. Arr. *Anab.* 2.20.4–5.

59. See further Eph'al 1982, 201–206.

60. Berlin 1977, 37; Reed 2000, 39.

61. Myers 2010, 82–101.

62. The name "Chalcis," which was an Iturean center, recalls the name of several cities in Greece as well as the Chalcidic peninsula. Stephanos claims that it was founded by "Monikos the Arab." Because Ptolemy, the son of Mennaeus, was a philhellene and named his son Ptolemaios (Strabo, *Georg.* 16.2.10; *War* 1.185), Cohen suggests that he was an Arab sheik who founded Chalcis and gave it a Greek name as a sign of his philhellenism. He also comments that a Roman inscription from nearby Heliopolis refers to a Macedonian quarter, which suggests there was a Hellenistic settlement at the site. This evidence provides additional support for the thesis that at least some Itureans were Hellenized. See further, G. Cohen 2006, 239–42, 254; Regev 2013, 274–78.

63. Krencker and Zschietzschmann 1938, 1:101–21.

64. Dar 1993, 28–92; Dar and Kokkinos 1992.

65. For the sanctity of Mt. Hermon as reflected in ancient texts, particularly the traditions associated with the sacred geography of *1 En.* 6–16, see further Bautch 2003, 59–66.

Josephus suggests that several Iturean leaders opposed Hasmonean expansion in the Galilee and the Golan.[66] Ptolemy, son of Mennaeus, attempted to block Jewish settlement in these regions. Zenodorus urged his followers to raid commercial caravans and rob the territory of Damascus. The Iturean region was never fully incorporated into the Hasmonean state. Herod later fought to pacify the Itureans and settled large numbers of Jews and Idumeans in their territory. Both Pompey and Octavian demolished some of the Iturean strongholds, which suggest they continued to pose a threat to the region's stability as late as the early Roman period.[67] But the major Iturean population centers, and locales from which some Itureans opposed the Hasmoneans, were beyond the control of Aristobulus and no threat to him. It is also clear that the region of the Northern Golan, Mt. Hermon, and the Lebanese Beq'a remained outside the border of the territory under Hasmonean control, and that the population of these areas remained Iturean-pagan.[68]

If Antigonus fought the Itureans, he did so somewhere near the border of Iturean territory in the Golan Heights. The most probable location is near the slopes of Mount Hermon where many Itureans resided. Approximately sixty settlements identified with the Itureans have been discovered there that appear to be characteristic of a pastoral group. They consist of simple single-room buildings of fieldstone construction with livestock enclosures. Many were used seasonally, but two of the Hermon settlements are large enough to be classified as villages. The inhabitants of these sites used a distinctive light brownish-pink color pottery known as "Golan Ware," which is heavily tempered with grit, grog, and chaff. The most common vessel of this type is a large, heavy-bottomed, storage jar with a short narrow mouth and toe that could be inserted into a floor for support.[69] These archaeological findings match the ancient descriptions of the Itureans as an agricultural and herding society.[70] The similarities between the material culture and the literary records strongly suggest that Itureans inhabited these Hermon sites.

Shimon Dar's survey of the Mt. Hermon region also reveals that some Itureans lived in permanent villages there. He found nine temples dating to the Hellenistic period, three open-air cult sites, and many *massevot* placed

---

66. *War* 1.115; *Ant.* 13.418.

67. A. Jones 1931.

68. Leibner 2009, 315–28.

69. Berlin 1977, 36–37; Dar 1993, 18, 168–99, 200, 210, 242–43; Freyne 2001; Hartel 1987.

70. *Ant.* 15.344; 16:271; Strabo, *Geogr.* 16.2.20.

around houses.[71] These settlements and their pottery have been found across the Hermon and Lebanon Ranges as well as the Northern Golan. This evidence suggests that these sites were inhabited by a distinctive semi-nomadic pastoral culture in the early stages of sedentarization. The remains of Iturean occupation from Mt. Hermon and the Upper Golan suggests that it was a dimorphic society, namely one that was both partly settled and partly nomadic. These lifestyles apparently were not in conflict with one another.

There is no archaeological evidence to support the claim of Josephus that Aristobulus forcibly converted the Itureans. None of the sites associated with the Itureans shows any evidence of attack or destruction. Local pagan cult traditions persisted uninterrupted throughout the Hasmonean period.[72] There is no archaeological evidence of Jewish practices at these sites. The Hasmoneans acquired the area over time through a gradual and organized colonization, and not conquest. If there was any military activity there during the reign of Aristobulus it was at most a minor engagement that left no discernible trace in the archaeological record.

The lack of any evidence to support the report of Josephus that Aristobulus conquered the Itureans, and forcibly circumcised them, raises the question of whether the Hasmoneans attempted to Judaize their newly conquered territories. Although 1 Macc 2:46 suggests that Mattathias adopted this practice, this passage refers to implementation of circumcision among Jews who had abandoned it. However, Joseph Sievers suggests this text is not historical. He believes it is an effort by the author to attribute to Mattathias events that occurred later, but which were considered of paramount importance to subsequent Hasmonean rulers. Sievers believes the policy of forced circumcision appears only during the reigns of those Hasmoneans who maintained large units of mercenaries. This suggests that the traditions about forced conversion by the Hasmoneans reflects later beliefs about the importance of purity, and the conviction that all the inhabitants of Hasmonean territory should be Jewish.[73]

In his *Geography*, Strabo provides some additional information about the incorporation of the Idumeans into the Hasmonean state that may clarify the accounts of the Itureans in the writings of Josephus. Strabo claims the Idumeans joined the Judeans and shared many of their customs.[74] A similar tradition of a friendly alliance between the Judeans and the Idumeans may be preserved in a tradition recorded by Alexander Polyhistor. He claims

71. Dar 1993, esp. 28–133, 171–79; 1988.
72. Berlin 1977, 37; Meyers and Chancey 2012, 33–34.
73. Sievers 1990, 86, 143.
74. Strabo, *Georg.* 16.2.34.

that the name Judaea "derives from the children of Semiramis Judea and Idumaea."[75] Although Polyhistor uses imaginary etymologies to explain geographic names and the origins of various peoples, his account seems to presuppose the peaceful amalgamation of the Judeans and the Idumeans into a single nation. However, Ptolemy the Historian contradicts these writers and sates that Idumeans were not Jews, but Phoenicians and Syrians who had been subjugated (κρτηθέντες) by the Jews and forced (ἀναγκασθέντες) to undergo circumcision.[76] Ptolemy presumably refers to John Hyrcanus.[77] Josephus may preserve some information that supports a close relationship between the Idumeans and the Jews. He writes that Herod appointed the Idumaea Costobar as the region's governor. Costobar was nevertheless reluctant to carry out Herod's order and force the Idumeans to abandon their ancestral religion.[78] This suggests that many Idumeans, despite their relationship with the Hasmoneans, never fully embraced Judaism.

Like the Itureans, most Idumeans appear to have remained distinct from Jews. However, both groups practiced circumcision before they came into contact with the Hasmoneans.[79] Yet, Cohen observes that many ancient texts also state that the Arabs practiced circumcision. He believes that the Itureans, because they were Arabs, likewise circumcised their males. In light of this evidence, he proposes we should favor the account of Strabo (drawing on Timagenes) over Josephus. He suggests that later Jews were uncomfortable with the idea that the Hasmonean state had expanded through voluntary associations with pagan groups. Because Josephus wanted to portray the incorporation of the Itureans and the Idumeans as involuntary, he, or one of his sources, apparently fabricated the accounts of their forced conversions. Since subsequent generations of Iturean kings governed Lebanon as independent rulers, it is doubtful that Aristobulus could have annexed much, if any, Iturean territory.[80]

75. Cited in M. Stern 1974–80, 1:164, no 53. This excerpt may have come from his work Περὶ Ἰουδαίων. See *FGH* 237.

76. Translation from M. Stern 1974–80, 1:356, no 146. Ptolemy the Historian may be the grammaticus Ptolemy of Ascalon (late first century B.C.E.). See further Schürer et al. 1973–87, 1:27–28.

77. *Ant.* 13.257; 15.254. Cf. *War* 1.63; Strabo, *Geogr.* 16.2.34.

78. *Ant.* 15.253–55.

79. Herodotus 2.104.3; *Ant.* 8.262; *War* 1.168–71. M. Smith (1996, 273) proposes that *Ant.* 13.257–58 can be translated to state that the Idumeans actually practiced circumcision. For the thesis that the Idumeans and the Edomites adopted a variant form of circumcision, and that the Hasmoneans compelled the former to adopt the Jewish manner of circumcision, see Steiner 1999.

80. *Ant.* 13.322, 337. Kasher 1988, 79–85; VanderKam 2004, 317.

There is little historical or archaeological evidence to determine when the Itureans in the Mt. Hermon region came under Hasmonean control. A coin of Hyrcanus found in the upper cult enclosure at the Iturean settlement of Har Senaim may relate to the activity of the Hasmoneans in the Hermon region. Dar suggests that Hasmonean influence there reached its peak during the reign of Aristobulus when some Itureans may have converted to Judaism.[81] However, the Hasmoneans came into contact with the Itureans earlier. Jonathan waged campaigns in Iturean territory.[82] It is possible that he and Simon cooperated with the Phoenician coastal cities against the Itureans; both hoped to take advantage of the weakness of the Seleucid Empire to gain additional territory and expand their trade networks.[83] The presence of a synagogue adjacent to an Iturean temple at Kharuvi'a suggests that at least a few Jews either settled in Iturean territories, or that some of the region's population later converted to Judaism.[84]

Numismatic evidence sheds some additional light on this period. Iturean coins were struck between 73 and 25 B.C.E.[85] The coins of Ptolemy, son of Mennaeus, are mainly dated according to the Seleucid era.[86] But three bear Pompeian-era dates starting in 64/63 B.C.E. This evidence, coupled with the archaeological and ceramic remains, suggests that some of the Itureans were closely associated with the Seleucid rulers, and later with the Romans. This would have made it difficult for the Hasmoneans to have annexed their territory since it would have posed a direct threat to the Seleucid Empire and Roman sovereignty.

There is no evidence of a forced Judaization of the Galilee during the reign of Aristobulus. It appears doubtful that the Itureans willingly allied with the Hasmonean state. Strabo portrays them as robbers who frequently interrupted the region's trade. We find later descriptions of the Iturean leader Zenodorus raiding commercial caravans.[87] It is doubtful that Aristobulus sent troops into the Galilee to convert its inhabitants.

---

81. Dar 1993, 83.

82. 1 Macc 11:62; 12:25.

83. The Iturean culture shows much Phoenician influence. Coins minted in the Phoenician coastal towns of Tyre and Sidon were also discovered at Har Senaim. See Dar 1993, 83; Grainger 1991, 150–57.

84. Kasher 1988, 84–85.

85. Myers 2010, 102–14.

86. Herman 2006; Gitler and Kushnir-Stein 2009, 171.

87. Strabo, *Geogr.* 16.2.18; *Ant.* 15.344–46; *War* 1.398–400. Syn. (*Chron.* 355) records that the Itureans and the Nabateans joined forces to oppose Jannaeus. Josephus reports (*Ant.* 13.418; *War* 1.115) that Salome Alexandra sent her son, Aristobulus II, to Damascus to foil the expansionist policy of the Iturean ruler Ptolemy, son of Mennaeus.

Freyne suggests that if the campaign of Antigonus is based on a historical reality it should be associated with the destruction of Philoteria. He also raises the possibility that Antigonus, like his brother Jannaeus, lived in the Galilee. Freyne believes that Antigonus merely returned to Jerusalem for the Festival of Tabernacles with weapons as a display of his independence, which his brother subsequently considered a threat to his authority.[88] Because the Hasmonean ruler Shelamzion Alexandra campaigned against the Itureans, it is doubtful they ever became part of the Hasmonean state or Antigonus conquered them.[89] Jewish expansion in Iturean territory appears to have been a gradual process. It was never completed since the Itureans remained in the Golan after the campaigns of Pompey and the Roman annexation of the Seleucid Empire and continued to fight for their independence.[90] The health of Aristobulus guaranteed that little effort would be made to expand the Hasmonean state there.

The Physical Decline of Aristobulus

The account of the death of Aristobulus in the *Antiquities* is of limited historical value. It is somewhat reminiscent of Artapanus's *On the Jews*. This composition is not a straightforward historical or ethnographic narrative, but a work that focuses on the adventures of Jewish figures in Egypt. Josephus adopts many novelistic features in his account of the death of Aristobulus. He incorporates several dramatic incidents that are intended to teach moral lessons and to portray Aristobulus unfavorably. Josephus wants the reader to conclude that his premature death was God's punishment for his murder of his mother and his brother. His unexpected passing was also the fulfillment of Hyrcanus's dream that God chose Jannaeus as his heir.

According to Josephus, Aristobulus became estranged after Aristobulus paraded about the temple courts in his military uniform. Josephus writes that "evil men" (ὁι πονηροὶ) told Aristobulus that Antigonus was preparing to use troops to murder him.[91] Aristobulus gradually began to believe these charges and barricaded himself in the Baris, which was protected by defensive towers and a moat.[92] The decision of Aristobulus to reside in this fortified citadel instead of the Hasmonean royal palace suggests that he feared for his life.

88. Freyne 1980, 42–43.
89. *Ant.* 13.418; cf. *War* 1.115.
90. See further Chapter 7.
91. *War* 1.74; *Ant.* 13.305.
92. Abel 1947, 249–51; Bahat 1996, 45; Ben-Dov 1985, 65–67; Ritmeyer 1992.

Josephus attributed the death of Antigonus to fate.[93] He writes that an Essene elder named Judah, whose prophecies had never been false, predicted the day and location where Antigonus would die.[94] But when Antigonus was spotted in the temple on his way to the Baris, Judah realized that he was wrong. There was insufficient time for Antigonus to travel the nearly sixty-five miles to Strato's Tower, which was the spot where he was supposed to perish that day. Soon afterwards Judah and his followers received word that Antigonus had been killed in the underground passage to the Baris that was called "Strato's Tower." Josephus writes that Judah's prophecy had been correct: Judah the Essene had merely assumed that the location was Strato's Tower on the coast.

Josephus also emphasizes envy in his account of Antigonus's death. Earlier, he wrote that the Pharisees and their popular supporters hated Hyrcanus and his sons.[95] Envy also caused the rift between Hyrcanus and the Pharisees. He even writes of Antigonus's passing: "Now his death clearly proves that there is nothing more powerful than envy and slander, nor anything that more easily disrupts goodwill and the ties of nature than these influences."[96] Because this passage and the deathbed speech of Jannaeus contain many identical words, both are almost certainly the creation of Josephus.[97] Although Josephus undoubtedly used sources, we should attribute the engaging account of Aristobulus's demise to him.

The Death of Aristobulus

The concluding portion of the account of the death of Aristobulus is clearly a romance. Josephus writes that when Aristobulus heard the news of the death of Antigonus, he was overcome with remorse for the murder of his

93. Josephus in his *War* and *Antiquities* portrays fate as a force that holds sway over the lives of men, entire nations, cities, and which predetermines destiny. See further, Varneda 1986, 46–50.

94. In *War* 2.159 Josephus writes that the Essenes rarely fail in their predictions. He emphasizes this by using ἀστοχέω, which occurs only here and in *War* 4.116 and 5.61. For Essenes in Josephus's books, see further Atkinson 2012b; Atkinson and Magness 2010.

95. *Ant* 13.288; *War* 1.67.

96. *Ant.* 13.310.

97. *Ant.* 13.400–2. Mason (1991, 216–45, 248–51) notes that the anti-Pharisaic and pro-Hasmonean tone of several passages (*War* 1.110–14; *Ant.* 17.41–45; *Life* 1–2, 189–98; and *Ant.* 13.288; 16:187). He suggests that the μῖσθός φθόνος theme (*War* 2.82; 4.566; *Ant.* 2.10; 6.193; 13.288, 296; 20.29) and the use of vocabulary in these sections are typically Josephan.

brother. He lost his mind because of his guilty deed; he was overcome with pain in his intestines, and he vomited blood.[98] Then, according to Josephus, a rather ominous event occurred. He claims that one of the servants came and cleaned up the blood and, as he was leaving, he slipped and knocked over the container on the very spot where the stains made by the blood of the murdered Antigonus were visible. Josephus writes that this was no mere accident, but had been caused by "divine power" (δαιμόνιον).[99] After he was told about this accident, Aristobulus became inconsolable. He cried out that he was not destined to escape God's wrath, but that retribution continued to pursue him for his murder of his brother.[100] He then died of his illness after a reign of approximately one year.[101]

Josephus provides a few valuable clues about the character of Aristobulus. He writes that he was known by the title "Philhellene" (Φιλέλλην). He also states that Strabo, citing Timagenes, wrote that he was as a "kindly person" and conferred many benefits on his country.[102] Although Josephus does not explain why he was known as Philhellene, because there are several examples of non-Greek princes and kings who were praised by the Greeks, the claim of Josephus that pagans honored him is plausible.[103]

Josephus extends his account of the rule of Aristobulus to the beginning of the reign of his brother, Jannaeus. He does this by inserting a story about how God supposedly forewarned Hyrcanus that Jannaeus would be his true successor.[104] Given this prophecy, the reign of Aristobulus could have only ended in tragedy regardless of his character or his deeds. Josephus's story about the downfall of the first Hasmonean king also accounts for the unexpected rise to power of Jannaeus, and the unprecedented length of his reign. It is to this amazing Hasmonean monarch that we now turn who, more than any person in his family, exemplified the military might of his famed grandfather, Mattathias.

98. *Ant.* 13.314. Also, *War* 2.81.

99. *Ant.* 13.314. Josephus portrays demons as spirits of evil men that have the power to kill their helpless victims (*War* 2.185). He also links the concept of "divine power" with God's providence over men that can both help or harm humans (*War* 2.457; 3.341, 485; 4.217, 622; 5.502; 6.59, 252, 296; 7.318; *Ant.* 13.314; 16.210). See further D. Schwartz 2013, 73–74.

100. *War* 2.83–84; *Ant.* 13.316–18.

101. *War* 2.84; *Ant.* 13.318.

102. *Ant.* 13.318–19.

103. For examples, see Kasher 1990, 135 n. 52.

104. *Ant.* 13.322.

Chapter 5

ALEXANDER JANNAEUS:
A PERIOD OF CONQUEST AND EXPANSION

Alexander Jannaeus in the Works of Josephus[1]

The account of the reign of Alexander Jannaeus in the *War* and the *Antiquities* is quite lengthy. It is a well-crafted narrative that presents a rather schematic, and often misleading, portrayal of his accomplishments.[2] In his *War* Josephus tends to focus on personalities. He always introduces major characters with a description of their physical and moral qualities, as well as their character flaws.[3] This is particularly true of Jannaeus. In his *Antiquities* Josephus greatly expands his earlier account of the Hasmonean monarchy in his *War* to describe the personality of Jannaeus and to highlight his moral failings.

Josephus was clearly influenced by his narrative of John Hyrcanus when he wrote his accounts of Jannaeus. He was convinced that the successes of Jannaeus were proof that God had blessed Hyrcanus. Josephus adopts the same basic narrative structure to recount the reign of Jannaeus that he used in his account of Hyrcanus to highlight the similarities between them. He groups together events that often happened at different times. He divides the foreign campaigns of Jannaeus into three major sections. He intersperses between these wars accounts of three invasions—Ptolemy IX Soter, Demetrius III, and Antiochus XII Dionysus—and two reports of civil wars between the Ptolemies and the Seleucids. Josephus also includes two reports of how Jannaeus faces internal revolts against his rule.[4] He not

---

1. For the major historical sources for the life of Alexander Jannaeus, see *Ant.* 13.301–19; *War* 1.70–84; Sync. *Chron.* 555.8–17; Atkinson 2012c, 129–40; 2014a, 1–19.

2. See further Atkinson 2011, 8–11.

3. Varneda 1986, 69–74, 135–39.

4. Both books follow this basic sequence. Only the *Antiquities* contains detailed accounts of the two invasions. *War*: Invasion of Soter (*War* 1.86); Campaign (*War*

only completes his father's expansion of the Hasmonean state, but he does so despite potential threats from his Jewish opponents.

Of all the Hasmonean rulers, the study of the reign of Jannaeus benefits most from going beyond Josephus's *War* and *Antiquities*. Archaeological findings, the Dead Sea Scrolls, classical texts, papyrological discoveries, numismatics, and rabbinic literature reveal a plethora of new information about Jannaeus not found in any contemporary study of the Hasmoneans. Although the writings of the rabbis must be used with caution, archaeological evidence suggests they preserve some reliable traditions about him. But this material will only be used when plausible arguments can be made for its historicity. The rabbinic literature is particularly important for determining whether Jannaeus is his actual name.

The Name and Title of Jannaeus: Texts and Numismatics

Josephus uses the name Alexander for the third son of Hyrcanus. He is the first known member of his family with this name. The name Ἀλεξανδρός later became the most common Greek name among the Hasmonean family. Although its origin is unknown, it is possible that Jannaeus, or perhaps an earlier member of his family, was named after Alexander the Great.[5] His currency sheds additional light on his reign and also provides some insight concerning his use of the title "king."

The coins of Jannaeus are the most common Jewish currency found at archaeological sites in the lands that made up the Hasmonean state. They represent over 87% of all coins discovered in Jerusalem, and 39% of the coins found throughout ancient Palestine from the Hasmonean, the Herodian, and the Byzantine periods.[6] Gamla includes the largest hitherto recorded discovery of Jannaeus coins from a single location. They are regularly found throughout the site in loci dating from the middle of the

---

1.87); Revolt (*War* 1.88); Campaign (*War* 1.89–90); Revolts (*War* 1.91–98); Invasion of Demetrius III (*War* 1.92–95); Campaign (*War* 1.99–106). *Antiquities*: Campaign (*Ant.* 13.324–29); Invasion of Soter (*Ant.* 13.330–55); Seleucid Civil Wars (*Ant.* 13.365–71); Revolt (*Ant.* 13.372–73); Campaign (*Ant.* 13.374–78); Revolts (*Ant.* 13.379–83); Invasion of Demetrius III (*Ant.* 13.377–78); Seleucid Civil Wars (*Ant.* 13.384–86); Invasions of Antiochus Dionysus and Aretas III (*Ant.* 13.387–92); Campaign (*Ant.* 13.393–404).

5. It became an ancient Jewish custom to name sons after Alexander the Great. See Flusser 1978, 56–57. The grandson of Jannaeus and a son of Herod the Great and Mariamme were named Alexander. See *War* 1.158; *Ant.* 16.401. The Herodian family also used this name. See *Ant.* 15.342; 18.131, 139, 140.

6. Ariel 1982, 284, 322; Regev 2013, 174–82; Shachar 2004.

first century B.C.E. up to its 67 C.E. destruction.[7] They have also been uncovered with Roman coins from the fourth century C.E. at Khirbet Shema.[8] The discovery of Jannaeus coins from such a late period attests to their large production and widespread circulation. They may also indicate that some Jews during the Roman period preferred to use Hasmonean currency.[9]

Jannaeus, like his father, minted perutot with an inscription and a depiction of a cornucopia. He also issued coins with a lily on one side and an anchor on the other. These coins are an imitation of those his father minted in 130–129 B.C.E. in the name of Antiochus VII Sidetes.[10] They contain the Hebrew inscription יהונתן המלד along with the Greek equivalent ΑΛΕΞΑΝΔΡΟΥ ΒΑΣΙΛΕΙΟΣ. The choice of the lily and anchor on this particular coin was intentional: the lily was a symbol of Jerusalem and the temple while the anchor represented his family's ambition to conquer the coastal territories.[11] These coins incorporate both Seleucid and Jewish images and appear to have been manufactured at his father's mint in Jerusalem. What makes them unique is that we can use them to trace changes in the reign of Jannaeus over time, and his subjects' perceptions of him.

Jannaeus gradually introduced some innovations in his currency. Another series of coins he minted contains the same inscription found on his earlier currency, but in paleo-Hebrew letters. It also includes a depiction of an anchor on one side and a star surrounded by a diadem on the other. Meshorer suggests this star is a symbol of royalty and was based

---

7. Syon 1992/93, 35–36; 2004, 27, 38–41. Gamla's Western quarter contains 75% (2,370) Hasmonean coins of which 79% (1,885) are those of Jannaeus. This number is higher since many of the 213 otherwise worn and unidentifiable coins with an inscription and/or cornucopia are likely Jannaeus coins.

8. Hanson and Bates 1976, 151, 169.

9. Jannaeus also minted lead tokens. Because lead is a soft metal, these coins could not have been intended for extended circulation. They were typically issued to be redeemed for food or other commodities. Such types of currency are usually indicative of some crisis, such as civil war, when a government was forced to supply the needs of its population on a short term basis. See Hendin 1994/99. Hoover (2008, 83) suggests that the lead tokens minted by Jannaeus and Demetrius III were used as a special military currency during their conflict. Hirschfeld and Ariel (2005) suggest that a heap of 1,735 coins found along the Dead Sea, nearly all of which were minted by Jannaeus, was used to pay mercenaries.

10. Hoover 2003; 1994, 44–46.

11. Hoover 1994; Hendin 2007/2008, 79–84; Meshorer 2011, 37; Regev 2013, 208–9, 212–14. The lily also appeared on the Persian Yehud coins, which suggests that it was used as a symbol of Jerusalem prior to the Seleucid period.

on Num 24:17.[12] However, it is plausible that Jannaeus chose this symbol because of its royal and messianic associations. But there could be another reason: it may allude to his father's prophetic abilities to indicate that that Hyrcanus was the expected "true prophet" mentioned in 1 Macc 14:41 and to show that God had chosen the Hasmoneans to be the permanent kings and high priests.

Some of Jannaeus's coins only refer to his office of high priest (יהונתן הכהן הגדל וחבר היהודים).[13] Jannaeus also issued coins with both Greek (ΒΑΣΙΛΕΙΟΣ ΑΛΕΞΑΝΔΡΟΥ/ΛΚΕ) and Aramaic (אלכסנדרון שנה כה) inscriptions.[14] These coins are unique because they all date to the twenty-fifth year of his reign. Because they are the only dated coins he issued, they were presumably minted to commemorate the 25th anniversary of his rule. Jannaeus later overstruck many of these coins to remove the title king and replace it with high priest. This may suggest that he experienced some opposition to his use of a royal title.[15] Although Jannaeus is the only Hasmonean ruler to have erased titles from his coins, he is unique in another way: there has been some uncertainty concerning his name.

Josephus generally prefers to use Greek names for the Hasmoneans in his *War.* Consequently, he consistently refers to Jannaeus as Alexander. Only twice in the *War* does he provide Hebrew names. Josephus mentions four Hebrew names in the *Antiquities*: John for Hyrcanus, Judah for Aristobulus, Jannaeus for Alexander, and Salina for Alexandra.[16] Although he apparently copied these names from his sources, it cannot be ruled out that he occasionally inserted Hebrew names in his books.

In *Ant.* 13.320 Josephus departs from his custom of using Greek names for the Hasmoneans to give their Hebrew name and mentions that the Greeks called the wife of Salina by the name "Alexandra," while Jannaeus

---

12. Meshorer 2011, 37–38. For the messianic implications of this biblical passage, see further Collins 2010, 62, 68, 73–77, 85, 87–88. Regev (2013, 211–12) suggests that Jannaeus adopted the Hellenistic symbols of the star and diadem to represent his royal status and as a substitution for his self-portrait.

13. Meshorer 2011, 38–39; Schürer et al. 1973–87, 1:227; VanderKam 2004, 234. This inscription is placed between the rays of a star. Some of these coins contain the defective spelling (ינתן) of his name.

14. Mine 1981.

15. It has been suggested that hostility by the Pharisees compelled him to make this change. See Meshorer 2011, 40–41; VanderKam 2004, 334.

16. (Ἰωάννην) *Ant.* 13.228; (Ἰούδᾳ) *Ant.* 20.240; (Ἰανναῖον) *Ant.* 13.320; (Σαλίνα) *Ant.* 13.320. With the exception of Judah, all these names appear at the beginning of the narratives of each ruler. The name "Judah" also occurs twice in Josephus's list of high priests (*Ant.* 20.240–41).

was also known as "Alexander" ('Ιανναῖον τὸν καὶ 'Αλεξάνδρου). This passage is important because it reveals that Alexander's Semitic name was "Jannaeus." It is a Greek transliteration of the Hebrew name יהונתן that appears on his coins. This same spelling is found in 4Q448 (*Paean for King Jonathan Apocryphal Psalms*). The abbreviated form ינתן is inscribed on a bulla attributed to him and is also used on some of his coins.[17] The Talmud, however, refers to him as אלכסנדר ינאי.[18] Josephus uses the Greek spelling 'Ιανναῖον for יהונתן to refer to Jannaeus rather than 'Ιωνάθην that he uses elsewhere for Jonathan the high priest.[19] The Qumran texts use יונתן for Jonathan the High Priest (4Q245 i 10 [*4Qpseudo-Daniel*ᶜ *ar*]), John Hyrcanus (*4QpapHistorical Text C* [4Q331 1 i 7]), as well as for Jannaeus (*4QApocryphal Psalm and Prayer* [4Q448 ii 2 and iii 8] and perhaps 4Q523).[20] The transliteration of the Semitic name of Jannaeus in the writings of Josephus is closer to the form used in the Talmud rather than the spelling found on his coins and bulla. The different spellings of his name may lend some support to Ilan's suggestion that Jannaeus is an Aramaic hypocoristic of the Hebrew name Jonathan.[21] Although the extant evidence suggests that his official throne name was "Alexander Jonathan," the spelling of his name in Josephus and the Talmud suggest that he was also called "Yannai." It was perhaps his nickname. But there is an even more pressing issue that must be resolved before studying Jannaeus: the conventional dating for the start of his reign is incorrect.

The Beginning of His Reign

There is a chronological problem concerning the exact year when Jannaeus took power. This overlooked issue is important since it also changes the dates for the reigns of both his father and his brother.[22] Josephus lists the

17. Hendin and Shachar 2008, 89–91; Avigad 1975a; 1975b; Meshorer 1982, 76–81; Schürer et al. 1973–87, 1:602–4.

18. For the rabbinic literature, see Schürer et al. 1973–87, 1:219.

19. This Greek spelling is also found in his list of high priests in *Ant.* 20.238 and throughout his accounts of Jonathan (*War* 1.48–49; *Ant.* 13.1–212). It is also found in 1 Macc 2:5, where he is referred to as "Jonathan called Apphus" ('Ιωανθης ὁ καλούμενος 'Απφοῦς).

20. The name in 4Q245 is based on the reconstruction יונ[תן]. See Collins and Flint 1996, 157–60.

21. Ilan 1987, 7 n. 27.

22. A brief note of Dąbrowa (2010a, 84) is the only study of the Hasmonean state to acknowledge that our standard chronology for the reigns of Hyrcanus, Aristobulus, and Jannaeus are in error.

regnal years for the reigns of Hyrcanus, Aristobulus, and Jannaeus. The lengths he provides for each of them, along with their conventional dates, are as follows:

John Hyrcanus	31 years[23]	135/4–105/4 B.C.E. (*War* 1.68; *Ant.* 13.299)
Judah Aristobulus	1 year	104–103 B.C.E. (*War* 1.84; *Ant.* 13.318)
Alexander Jannaeus	27 years	103–76 B.C.E. (*War* 1.106; *Ant.* 13.430)[24]

The only fixed date we possess to determine the beginning of the reign of Hyrcanus is the statement in 1 Macc 16:14 that Simon died in the month of Shebat of the Seleucid year 177. This year is usually dated to February 135 or 134 B.C.E.[25] As we have previously discussed in relation to the beginning of the reigns of Simon and Hyrcanus, we are often uncertain which Seleucid calendar is used in the ancient sources to date the Hasmoneans from Hyrcanus to Jannaeus. There are actually two Seleucid calendars: the so-called Babylonian and the Macedonian calendars. According to the former dating system, the reign of Seleucus I as king of Babylon began in April 311 B.C.E.; the Macedonian dating system places it in autumn 312 B.C.E. The Macedonian calendar dates the second year of the Seleucid era in autumn 311 B.C.E.; the Babylonian calendar places the beginning of the second year of the Seleucid era in April 310 B.C.E. Both systems coincide during the summer months, from April to October, but in the winter months the Macedonian era is always greater than the Babylonian era by one year.[26]

A close look at the dates recorded throughout 1 Maccabees and Josephus suggests they used both dating systems.[27] Although the conventional interpretation is that the author of 1 Maccabees followed the

23. Josephus states in *War* 1.68 that Hyrcanus reigned for 33 years. This must be a copyist's mistake since Hegesippus reads *trigesimo et primo anno*. See Niese 1894, 16. Hegesippus copied the number from Josephus in *Ant.* 20.241, where he states that Hyrcanus ruled for 31 years. This number is certainly the correct figure. See further, Niese 1893, 217.

24. This information is adapted from the widely cited work of Schürer et al. 1973–87, 1:200.

25. See Goldstein 1976, 524; 541; Schürer et al. 1973–87, 1:200–201, 607–8.

26. For example, this means that February 310 B.C.E. is year 2 of the Macedonian era, but still year 1 of the Babylonian era. For this information, see further Van 'T Dack et al. 1989, 118–21.

27. See further, Bar-Kochva 1989, 572–75; Bickerman 1968, 25, 38, 66, 71; Goldstein 1976, 21–26; Schürer et al. 1973–87, 1:126–28. Schürer et al. (1973–87, 1:43) suggest that Josephus may have taken his figures from a chronological handbook such as the work of Castor of Rhodes, whose writings survive in quotations

Babylonian calendar to date the death of Simon, if we assume that the author used the Macedonian era to date the death of Simon to 135 B.C.E. the chronology of Josephus must be emended as follows:

Simon	d. 135 B.C.E.
John Hyrcanus	135–105 B.C.E.
Judah Aristobulus	105–104 B.C.E.
Alexander Jannaeus	104–76 B.C.E.[28]

The papyrological evidence from Egypt must be given prominence in any study of Jannaeus because these letters were written during his reign. An Egyptian demotic letter dated September 27, 103 B.C.E. shows that the first year of the reign of Jannaeus should be moved back from the traditional date of 103 B.C.E. to 104 B.C.E. It was discovered at Pathyris, south of Thebes, but was dispatched from Ptolemais. It was written during the conflict known as the "War of Scepters" (103–101 B.C.E.), which was a war between Cleopatra III and her son Ptolemy IX (Lathyrus) Soter II for the Ptolemaic throne.[29] This conflict began after Jannaeus became king: Josephus implies he caused it!

The Pathyrus letter shows that the army of Cleopatra III had not captured Ptolemais when it was written. Because her siege occurred after Jannaeus took power, the War of Scepters began before the date of this letter. Another Egyptian document found in the vicinity of Pathyris, dated June 29, 103 B.C.E., shows that Cleopatra III had mobilized troops in Egypt, and moved them from their normal garrisons to prepare them to go to Ptolemais.[30] The siege of Ptolemais by Jannaeus, and his previous encounters with Zoilus and Soter, all took place before this letter was written. Josephus provides no dates for this war or the arrival of Cleopatra III at Ptolemais. Yet if the traditional chronology is followed, and Aristobulus survived into 103 B.C.E., then all these events described in *Ant.* 13.320–51 took place within a period of, at most, eight months.[31] When we consider that Soter marched from Ptolemais to the Jordan River, then to Judea, fought several recorded battles throughout the Galilee, and

preserved in Eusebius and Syncellus. Josephus mentions him once (*Apion* 2.83–84), which shows that he had access to his chronicle.

28. Table adapted from G. Cohen 1989, 12.

29. *Ant.* 13.320–57. The *War* (1.86) merely alludes in passing to this event. The name of this conflict is taken from line 12 of the Cairo INV. 9205 (Van 'T Dack et al. 1989, 83–84), which reads "when a war of scepters came to Syria."

30. P. gr. 39 + Brit. Libr., P. gr. 626 (Van 'T Dack et al. 1989, 39–49).

31. G. Cohen 1989, 119.

certainly many undocumented engagements as well, before Cleopatra III arrived and besieged Ptolemais, there is insufficient time for all the events Josephus describes to have taken place in less than eight months.

The Seleucid coins of Soter minted in Cyprus that were found in the Golan date to this conflict and show that Soter reached this area during his invasion. His campaign was much longer and covered more territory than Josephus has indicated.[32] Because it is improbable that all the military actions recorded by Josephus in *Ant.* 13.320–51 could have occurred in the short time required by the traditional dating of the beginning of the reign of Jannaeus, the revised chronology is preferred. This modification in the traditional chronology also matches the date for Simon's death found in 1 Maccabees, once it is recognized that the author dated it according to the Macedonian era. The evidence suggests that Jannaeus began his reign in 104 B.C.E. Like his brother and predecessor, Aristobulus, his first act was the murder of a family member.

The Succession of Jannaeus

Josephus reports that after Salina Alexandra crowned Jannaeus king and high priest he set out to consolidate his power by eliminating all the royal heirs. He writes that he had two surviving brothers. One sibling, Absalom, eschewed politics. Although Jannaeus supposedly held him "in honor," he mysteriously disappears from Josephus's narrative; it is probable that he was assassinated. The other brother, whose name is unknown, staged an unsuccessful coup. Jannaeus murdered him.[33] Josephus places the story of the divine dream of Hyrcanus before his description of these events. According to his account, God warned Hyrcanus that Jannaeus would be "heir of all his possessions."[34] This apocryphal tale also may have been created to justify Jannaeus's murder of his brothers since it implies that he merely acted in accordance with God's plan that he was destined to assume sole power.

Josephus prefers not to dwell on Jannaeus's violence against his family. Rather, his account of Jannaeus's reign emphasizes his similarities with his father, Hyrcanus, and his great-grandfather, Mattathias. Jannaeus more than any other member of his family changed the Hasmonean state through military conquests to make it among the most powerful nations of the Middle East despite its small size. But what Josephus does not relate

---

32. Gitler and Kushnir-Stein 1999; Syon 2004, 31.

33. (Unnamed brother) *Ant.* 13.323; *War* 1.85. (Absalom) *Ant.* 14.71.

34. *Ant.* 13.322.

is the extent to which events to the north made Jannaeus's conquests possible. His reign happened to coincide with the disintegration of the Seleucid Empire, which henceforth was never ruled by a single monarch.[35] It was events there that initially got Jannaeus into trouble when he thought he could easily take the strategic port city of Ptolemais.

The Siege of Ptolemais

Josephus does not mention Jannaeus's siege of Ptolemais in the *War*. Rather, in this book, he merely provides a brief summary of a few events from the War of Scepters.[36] Consequently, historians must rely on the detailed account in *Ant.* 13.324–55 and Egyptian papyri to reconstruct this conflict. According to Josephus, Jannaeus's siege of Ptolemais started this war. He attacked the city, defeated its forces in battle, and then blockaded it. Zoilus, the ruler of Dor, feared Hasmonean encroachment on the coast and decided to intervene. Josephus writes that he held Straton's Tower at this time, where he maintained a company of mercenaries.[37] He sent this force to relieve the siege; these soldiers were unable to defeat the Hasmonean army. With no help forthcoming from any of the region's rulers, the citizens of Ptolemais asked Soter in nearby Cyprus for military assistance. The envoys from Ptolemais persuaded him that Zoilus, the Sidonians, and many others, would assist him.

Soter had a good reason to respond to the appeal from Ptolemais. Hyrcanus earlier had defeated him and Cyzicenus at Samaria. The invitation from Ptolemais to fight Jannaeus gave Soter the opportunity to seek revenge against the Hasmoneans. It also had the potential to help him overthrow his mother, Cleopatra III. Once in control of Ptolemais, he could potentially annex the Hasmonean state. This would provide him with secure bases on land and sea to invade Egypt.

---

35. See further Hoover 2007b, 284–300.

36. *War* 1.86.

37. *Ant.* 13.326. Josephus uses the word σύνταγμα, which can refer to a select body of troops, such as a battalion, as well as the constitution of a state. See LSJ, sv. Σύνταγμα. Josephus uses this same word with the latter meaning in a citation from Strabo in *Ant.* 14.116. In this instance, it is clear that Josephus refers to a specially trained band of soldiers that Zoilus kept at Straton's Tower. The exact location of Straton's Tower is unknown. It has been suggested, based on the findings of Hellenistic pottery and coins dating to the mid-second century B.C.E., that it was located in the northern portion of the city of Caesarea. The extant city wall in this spot may preserve a portion of it. See further G. Cohen 2006, 299–302.

According to Josephus, the political situation in Ptolemais changed before Soter arrived. A citizen by the name of Demaenetus had convinced the people of the city not to become involved in the dispute over the succession in Egypt.[38] He warned them that Cleopatra III would never allow Soter to gain a foothold in the region. Demaenetus also stated that if things went poorly then Soter would abandon them and return to Cyprus. This would leave Ptolemais vulnerable not only to the army of Jannaeus, but to the forces of Cleopatra III. Although Soter was told the people of Ptolemais no longer wanted his aide, he still sailed for Syria.

Soter landed at Sycamina, just south of the Carmel promontory, approximately twelve miles south of Ptolemais.[39] He disembarked with a force of over 30,000 infantry and cavalry and marched to the city. The people of Ptolemais refused to admit him or listen to the proposals of his envoys. Zoilus and an army from Gaza arrived while Soter was outside. Zoilus wanted to assist Soter because Jannaeus had just sent part of his force to attack Dor.[40] Faced with two hostile armies, Jannaeus had to make a treaty with Soter merely to survive. He offered him 400 talents and a pact of non-aggression if he promised to eliminate Zoilus and assign his territory to the Jews. Soter agreed and made an alliance with Jannaeus. It is unclear from Josephus's Greek whether Soter subsequently killed Zoilus or merely imprisoned him. According to later Jewish tradition, Jannaeus took advantage of the removal of Zoilus from the region to conquer the port cities of Straton's Tower and Dor.[41]

It is doubtful that Jannaeus could have successfully attacked the costal municipalities of Straton's Tower and Dor without the approval of Soter. It is highly implausible that Soter would have allowed him to take the strategic city of Dor unless he was certain of Hasmonean support. Josephus states that Jannaeus quickly betrayed his new ally by secretly contacting Cleopatra III. Once Soter realized that Jannaeus was in communication with his mother he invaded Hasmonean territory to remove Jannaeus from power.

38. *Ant.* 13.330.

39. The site is identified with Tel el-Samekh, which is situated on the lower, western slope, of the northern end of the Carmel Ridge. Because this spot does not overlook the modern Haifa Bay or the ancient city of Ptolemais, Soter clearly chose it for its strategic military advantages. It allowed him to gather and move his forces unobserved in either of two directions: northward to Ptolemais or southward to the coastal cities of Dor, Straton's Tower, and Gaza. See further Kasher 1990, 141.

40. *Ant.* 13.333–34.

41. *Megillat Ta'anit* (and Scholium) for 14th Sivan; *b. Meg.* 6a. See further, Lichtenstein 1931–32, 257–58.

Coins from Ascalon and Tyre suggest the *Antiquities* does not accurately describe the complicated political situation of the Jews at this time. Josephus portrays Jannaeus as a powerful regional monarch who sought to capture the major coastal cities at the beginning of his reign. He writes that Jannaeus planned to seize "Ptolemais, Gaza, Straton's Tower, and Dor."[42] Ascalon is notably absent from this list. During the Persian period it belonged to territory of Tyre.[43] In the third century B.C.E. the Ptolemies had jurisdiction over it, as well as all of Palestine and Phoenicia. Since the time of Antiochus III the Seleucids occupied the major coastal cities.[44] The Hasmoneans never controlled Ascalon. Judas and Jonathan had marched against it. On each occasion they were received favorably and did not attack it. The town's inhabitants paid them to leave.[45]

A series of tetradrachms minted at Ascalon suggests that Jannaeus faced more foes at the beginning of his reign than Josephus indicates. Coins have been found there bearing portraits of the following Ptolemaic rulers: one for Soter (84 B.C.E.), five for Ptolemy XIII Philopator (70, 66, 64, 63, and 54 B.C.E.), and at least two for Cleopatra VII (49 and 38 B.C.E.). All these coins are dated from the year of the city's independence, which the *Chronicon Paschale* places in the 169th Olympiad (650 A.U.C.).[46] This date correlates to between June 22, 104 B.C.E. to June 11, 103 B.C.E.[47] In her study of these coins, Brett notes that it is unusual for a supposedly independent city like Ascalon to render homage to Egyptian rulers.[48] It is also unexpected that Ascalon would mint expensive and less widely circulated silver pieces rather than more modest, and common, bronze coins with portraits of Egyptian monarchs. She notes that the date of Ascalon's independence coincides with the arrival of Soter in Ptolemais to oppose Jannaeus. Soter's defeat of Jannaeus at Ptolemais appears to have freed Ascalon from Seleucid domination; its inhabitants apparently remained on friendly terms with the Ptolemaic rulers for decades.

Ascalon declared its independence at this time. This would explain why it minted coins honoring the Egyptians, as well as its later friendly relationship with the Ptolemies.[49] This evidence not only suggests that

---

42. *Ant.* 13.324.

43. *Periplus of Pseudo-Scylax* 1.79. See further, Schürer et al. 1973–87, 2:105–6.

44. For the history of Ascalon, see Schürer et al. 1973–87, 2:104–8.

45. 1 Macc 10:86; 11:60.

46. *Chron. Pasch.* 1.346.

47. See Bickerman 1968, 150.

48. Brett 1937, 455–56.

49. Brett (1937, 456–58) also notes that Ascalon later issued portraits of Ptolemy Auletes, who sent cavalry to help Pompey in his 63 B.C.E. subjugation of Judea.

other coastal towns opposed Jannaeus, but it may indicate that Soter made alliances with them. Despite his supposed treaty with Jannaeus, it is plausible that Soter intended to invade the Hasmonean state and use its territory as a base to launch an attack against Egypt. Because the Hasmoneans had long tried to annex the major coastal cities, Soter had a good reason to support their leaders and try to weaken Jannaeus. With the coastal rulers and Soter allied against him, Jannaeus believed he had no option but to contact Cleopatra III for help.

A gold coin minted in Tyre may provide additional information to support this historical reconstruction. It celebrates the city's autonomy and depicts a bust of a veiled and turreted Tyche on its reverse with the inscription "Tyre sacred and inviolable." Dated to 103 B.C.E., this goddess, depicted for the first time on Tyrian currency, celebrates the independence that the city's residents managed to achieve with the assistance of Soter.[50] The Tyrians would have viewed the siege of Ptolemais by Jannaeus as a direct threat to their sovereignty. This is because the actual territory controlled by Ptolemais extended along a coastal strip approximately 28.5 miles long and from eight to 14 miles wide. Its northern border extended to the districts of Tyre and Sepphoris.[51] The citizens of Tyre had an interest in thwarting the plans of Jannaeus to annex coastal territory since it would have deprived them of lands they considered part of their city-state. Because the numismatic evidence suggests the major coastal cities were allied with Soter, it is doubtful that he agreed to eliminate Zoilus to win the support of Jannaeus. There is no evidence that Jannaeus controlled any coastal territories at this time.

Brett suggests that Soter chose to land at Sycamina not only to take advantage of its seclusion, but because the city of Tyre had joined his campaign against Jannaeus.[52] It would have been the perfect location for troops from Tyre and other cities to gather unobserved before setting out for Ptolemais to confront Jannaeus. The possible participation of Tyre may explain a later puzzling incident that Josephus omits from his books, but which is preserved in the *Chronicle* of George Syncellus. According to a source used by Syncellus, Jannaeus besieged Tyre just before his death.[53] No explanation is offered for this campaign. At this time, Jannaeus was free of both Ptolemaic and Seleucid domination; neither power was a

50. Hill 1910, cxxv, plate xliv no. 4; Brett 1937, 456.
51. Kindler 1978, 51–52; Kashtan 1988. Tyre became an autonomous city in 125 B.C.E. See Syon 2008.
52. Brett 1937, 456.
53. Syn. *Chron.* 1.559.

threat to the Hasmonean state. It appears that Jannaeus later attacked Tyre as retaliation for the earlier assistance it had given to Soter during the War of Scepters.

Soter expected Cyzicenus to supply him with troops and logistical support during his invasion of the Hasmonean state. Cyzicenus remained idle and chose not to become involved in this war. Despite this setback, Soter had enough time and forces to besiege Ptolemais, traverse the Galilee, and ravage many towns there before Cleopatra III sailed for Syria. The Hasmonean army was unable to stop his invasion. Jannaeus had no choice but to abandon much of the Galilee and to try to amass additional troops from the south to confront Soter. It took him some time to gather a sufficient military force since he had no option but to let Soter ravage his northern territories.

Soter invaded the Galilee unopposed. He captured the town of Asochis on the Sabbath and took 10,000 of its inhabitants prisoners.[54] His next major assault against the nearby metropolis of Sepphoris failed. Undeterred at this loss, he crossed the Jordan River to receive additional support from the Hellenistic cities in the region. He also may have planned to unite with the Nabatean Arabs before he continued southward towards Jerusalem.[55]

Jannaeus and Soter met east of the Jordan River at a place called Asophon.[56] Judea's army consisted of 50,000 to 80,000 men. It included a contingent known as the "hundred-fighters," all of whom carried long shields covered with bronze. Soter also had a special military unit equipped with identical weapons that was led by the tactician (τακτικὸς) Philostephanus. Both armies lined up on opposite sides of a river. Jannaeus decided to wait, hoping to lure Soter's forces across the river to impede their retreat. Philostephanus ordered his men to attack. When the two armies met the battle proved to be a stalemate until Philostephanus employed a classic stratagem. He kept one contingent of his men in reserve

---

54. Based on Josephus's descriptions in *Life* (207, 233, 384), the town was close to Sepphoris. It is possibly the pottery center known as Kefar-Shikhin, famous in rabbinic literature (*b. Šabb.* 120b), that is located on one of two small hills northwest of Sepphoris. See further, Mason 2001, 104 n. 926, 182; Grootkerk 2000, 196–97 no. 41.

55. See further, Kasher 1988, 86.

56. *Ant.* 13.337. Some manuscripts read Ἀσώχει. See Niese 1892, 214. Asophon's location is unknown. See Boettger 1879, 4. Kasher (1988, 86) suggests it should be identified with the biblical city of Saphon located on the border of Peraea and Gilead. See also Grootkerk 2000, 186–87 no. 28, 196–97 no. 41.

to join the fighting later. The unexpected appearance of seemingly new forces arriving on the battlefield created a panic: the Hasmonean army thought it was being outflanked by a new detachment. Under the false impression they were vastly outnumbered, self-preservation prevailed over military discipline. The soldiers in the army of Jannaeus fled. According to Josephus, Soter's troops pursued them "until their swords were blunt from murder."[57] They killed approximately 30,000 to 50,000 of Jannaeus's men.[58]

An inscription from Cyprus may provide some additional information about the battle of Asophon. It contains an invocation to Zeus Soter on behalf of Soter. It cannot date before 106 B.C.E. since Soter's brother, Ptolemy Alexandra, ruled Cyprus at that time.[59] The mention of Ἀθηνᾶ Νικηφόρος in the inscription suggests that it belonged to a monument that was erected to commemorate some military triumph. Mitford believes the only occasion that would justify such a dedication is either Soter's move to Cyprus or his victory over Jannaeus in 103 B.C.E. at Asophon. He believes the second option is more plausible. This suggestion is probable since his only success on the battlefield was his defeat of Jannaeus. This inscription also provides some additional insight into the composition of Soter's forces. It juxtaposes courtiers with aulic rank alongside men of overtly military ranks.[60] Soter promoted these administrative officials to senior military positions as an emergency measure to fill vacant offices in his army. This inscription also indicates that Kition was his base in

57. *Ant.* 13.342.

58. Josephus comments that the accounts he consulted provide conflicting figures for the number of men killed. He states that a few sources claim it was "30,000" while Timagenes places it at "50,000." See *Ant.* 13.344. M. Stern (1974–80, 1:226) suggests that Josephus quotes Timagenes through Strabo since he mentions this historian earlier in *Ant.* 13.347. Because Josephus also cites Nicolaus in this passage, it is equally possible that his lower figure derives from his lost history. Kasher (1988, 86) suggests these numbers are exaggerated since Josephus used sources hostile to the Hasmoneans. However, the Roman historian Livy (*History* 44.41) describes a similar incident that took place in 168 B.C.E. that may help us to understand the strategy of Philostephanus as well as show that Jannaeus could have lost a large number of men in this battle. The Romans, according to Livy, defeated the Hellenistic army of the Macedonians when they disrupted the discipline of their phalanx by bringing out men kept in hiding to attack their rear during the battle. The Macedonian soldiers became entangled in their weapons when they tried to rotate their spears: a phalanx is only designed to move forward.

59. For this inscription, see Mitford 1939; Clarysse, van der Veken, with Vlemming, 1983, 36, 99.

60. See Bagnall 1976.

Cyprus. Because it is a commemorative inscription, it further suggests that Soter's victory over Jannaeus was as decisive as Josephus claims.[61] If the variant reading of *Ant.* 13.345 is correct, and Soter "seized" Hasmonean lands, then Jannaeus lost some of his territory.[62]

According to Josephus, Soter took part of his army and launched a campaign that was designed to terrorize the Galilee. He writes that Soter commanded his soldiers to strangle Jews, cut them in pieces, and throw their body parts into boiling caldrons to fool people into thinking that his men were cannibals.[63] While striking fear in the Galilee through this action, Soter's other force captured Ptolemais.[64]

There is some archaeological evidence to support the account of Josephus concerning the campaign of Soter in the Galilee. Lead coins discovered in Coele-Syria minted by Cleopatra III and Ptolemy IX Alexander were struck as a form of emergency currency during the War of Scepters to finance military operations in the region.[65] A large number of bronze coins bearing the head of Zeus-Ammon on the obverse, and two eagles and the legend ΠΤΟΛΕΜΑΙΟΥ ΒΑΣΙΛΕΩΣ on the reverse, also have been uncovered at several sites in northern Israel. Most were found in the north-western shore of the Sea of Galilee (near ancient Taricheae). They also were also discovered at Ptolemais, Dor, Jotapata, and Gamla in the Golan. Because Ptolemaic coinage was not normally used for local circulation in Coele-Syria after the Seleucid conquest of the region in 202–195 B.C.E., these coins are connected with the War of Scepters.[66] Archaeological excavations at Paphos has confirmed the Cypriot origin of these coins, which indicates that they were brought to Palestine by a large group of people from Cyprus. Because the campaign of Soter is the only military expedition in these areas that involved solders from Cyprus, these coins should be attributed to his invasion of the Galilee and the Golan.[67]

61. If Soter decimated the Hasmonean army, this would account for the statement of Josephus that Jannaeus was powerless to stop him from taking additional Judean territory. Josephus also states that Soter committed numerous atrocities against Jews, which he mentions were recorded by both Strabo and Nicolaus (*Ant.* 13.346).

62. Niese's (1892, 215) text states that Soter "overran" (προσκαταδραμών) the territory of Jannaeus, but he comments that a variant reads "seized" (προσκαταλαβών).

63. *Ant.* 13.345–46.

64. Josephus (*Ant.* 13.347) mentions that he has elsewhere described the capture of Ptolemais by Soter. Because no such passage exists in the *Antiquities*, this may indicate that he copied this section from his source.

65. Hoover 2008.

66. Gitler and Kushnir-Stein 1999, esp. plate 5; Houghton, Lorber, and Hoover 2008, 57–58.

67. See further Gitler and Kushnir-Stein 1999; Syon 2004, 31.

This may provide some evidence that Soter reached the Golan, which would indicate that his campaign against Jannaeus was more extensive than Josephus has recorded.[68] When Cleopatra III arrived, matters only worsened for Jannaeus as he now had two Egyptian armies marching through his country: each undoubtedly leaving a trail of devastation in its wake.

The War of Scepters Reaches Judea

Josephus provides little information about the War of Scepters. His narrative mainly focuses on how Jannaeus retained power after the conclusion of this conflict. His account indicates that the fighting between the forces of Cleopatra III and Soter caused much damage to Judea. According to Josephus, Cleopatra III sailed for Syria after Soter invaded the Hasmonean state. He summarizes the events of this conflict, known as the War of Scepters, in a single paragraph in *Ant.* 13.348–51. Salvage excavations at Ptolemais uncovered widespread damage dating to this time. Among the most notable of these finds is a small shrine to Zeus Soter that appears to have been destroyed by the forces of Cleopatra III.[69] This archaeological evidence supports the statement of Josephus that she occupied the city.[70] She and her son, Ptolemy Alexander, chased Soter from Judea. Soter's departure from Gaza marked the end of the War of Scepters.[71]

Josephus suggests Cleopatra III planned to annex the Hasmonean state. Jannaeus apparently had no option but to approach her with gifts and plead that she not seize his kingdom. Her Jewish general, Ananias,

---

68. A coin minted by Jannaeus found in a Hellenistic tomb in the Royal Cemetery at Salamis may have been brought back to Cyprus by a member of Soter's invasion force. For this suggestion, see further G. Barkay 1977.

69. Applebaum 1975, 64–65.

70. *Ant.* 13.353. The autobiographical inscription of the Egyptian general Petimuthes mentions that Cleopatra III captured Ptolemais, which confirms Josephus's account (*Ant.* 13.348–51) that she took the city. See Turin, Museo Egizio cat. 3062 + Karnak, Karakol n° 258 (in Van 'T Dack et al. 1989, 88–108).

71. Josephus mistakenly writes that Soter fled to Egypt; it is clear from a later passage (*Ant.* 13.358) that he returned to Cyprus. Strabo (*Geogr.* 17.8) mentions that after Ptolemy Alexander left Syria he came to Egypt, where he violated the tomb of Alexander the Great. He implies this incident occurred after the conclusion of the War of Scepters. His account clearly conflates events from different times. A passage in Diod. Sic. (34/45 39a) sometimes associated with this conflict has been misplaced here by the excerptor. For these passages, and the extant references to the War of Scepters, see further Van 'T Dack 1981; Van 'T Dack et al. 1989, 33, 142–43.

supposedly threatened that if she took Hasmonean territory all the Jews (Ἰουδαίους) would turn against her.[72] Persuaded by Ananias, Cleopatra III made a treaty with Jannaeus at Scythopolis in Coele-Syria and allowed him to remain as king.[73] However, Egyptian records make it clear that Cleopatra III, Ptolemy Alexander, and native Egyptians—not the Jewish general Chelkias—commanded the Egyptian armies. The autobiographical inscription of the Egyptian general Petimuthes states that he was with Cleopatra III when she captured Ptolemais. This evidence shows that her expedition was a major undertaking in which Ptolemy Alexander and her highest-ranking Egyptian officers participated. Because the Egyptian records do not provide evidence of Jews in significant command positions among the units Cleopatra III sent to fight in the War of Scepters, we must conclude that Egyptian Jews played a minor role in this conflict.

No major political changes took place as a result of the War of Scepters in either the Seleucid Empire or the Hasmonean state. Soter still occupied Cyprus and threatened Egypt's maritime trade as well as the political stability of Syria and the Hasmonean state. Cleopatra III controlled Ptolemais, and had a garrison in Damascus. However, she already had relationships with Ptolemais and Damascus so she gained nothing from the War of Scepters. Her situation with Soter was now worse: he was still Cyprus and posed a continuing threat to her. Although Josephus attributes the survival of the Hasmonean state to the Jewish commander Ananias, Cleopatra III certainly realized that she was in no position to annex it because the Hasmonean family had been allies of the Roman Republic since 161 B.C.E.[74] Her takeover of the Hasmonean state would have threatened Rome's plans to dominate the Mediterranean trade routes. For this reason, Cleopatra III left Judea with no significant territorial gains and no change in her country's security.

The relationship between Cleopatra III and Ptolemy Alexander became strained after the War of Scepters.[75] He murdered her in October 101 B.C.E.[76] He ruled as Pharaoh with his wife, Berenice III.[77] In 88 B.C.E., Soter expelled his brother from Egypt and once again reigned in Alexandria. Ptolemy Alexander borrowed money from the Romans to recruit

72. *Ant.* 13.354.

73. Grainger (2010, 399) suggests Jannaeus's bestowal of gifts to Cleopatra III meant that he offered her the submission of Judea.

74. For this point, see further Van 'T Dack et al. 1989, 123.

75. Just. *Epit.* 39.4.3. For these events, see Hölbl 2000, 207–10; Huß 2001, 654–70; Whitehorne 1994, 142–48.

76. Justin, *History* 39.4; Paus. 1.9.3; Pestman 1967, 72–75, 156.

77. She was also his niece; she was the daughter of his brother, Ptolemy IX Soter.

an army to conquer Cyprus. He also willed his kingdom to the Roman Republic to obtain additional funds.[78] He died while trying to invade Cyprus in 88/87 B.C.E.[79] Soter passed away on December, 81 B.C.E. He left his kingdom to his daughter Cleopatra Berenice III.[80]

The political instability in Egypt following the death of Soter helped Jannaeus consolidate his hold over his territory, and recover militarily and economically after the War of Scepters. Egypt was too weak to attack the Hasmonean state. The Roman Republic was preoccupied with its war against Mithridates VI and unable to become involved in Hasmonean affairs. The subsequent Seleucid Empire's civil wars also made it doubtful that any of its monarchs would seek to annex Hasmonean lands. According to Josephus, Jannaeus took advantage of the weakened Ptolemaic and Seleucid Empires to begin a series of campaigns east of the Jordan River, and then along Egypt's border, without fear of any outside interference or military threat. But there is a problem with Josephus's accounts of this military activity: events in the Seleucid Empire actually delayed Jannaeus's conquests.

Jannaeus's Wars of Expansion: Chronological Problems

Josephus writes that immediately after the War of Scepters Jannaeus began his campaign in the Transjordan. He attacked and besieged Amathus for ten months.[81] Then he marched his army to the coast and captured Raphia and Anthedon.[82] He next went south and began a lengthy siege of Gaza that lasted approximately one year. But there is a chronological difficulty with Josephus's account of this siege. In *Ant.* 13.365 he writes that it coincided with the 96 B.C.E. murder of the Seleucid monarch Grypus. This would place the siege of Gaza by Jannaeus nearly five years after the War of Scepters. Yet, in *Ant.* 13.358, Josephus implies that it took place immediately after the cessation of the War of Scepters, which would place

78. Cicero, *Agr.* 1.1; 2.41. Badian (1967) believes the Romans remained content to take the money that Ptolemy Alexander had deposited in Tyre in lieu of actual possession of Egypt.

79. Porph. *FHG* 3.721–22; Paus. 1.9.3; Just. *Epit.* 39.5.1.

80. For this period, see further Hölbl 2000, 210–13; Huß 2001, 626–70; White-horne 1994, 174–75.

81. *War* 1.86; 13.356.

82. The toponym Anthedon is also found in Boeotia, which may suggest that it was established by Greek settlers. Josephus is the earliest writer to mention the town. Its exact location is unknown, although the ruins discovered at Khirbet Teda located three kilometers north of Gaza is a plausible site. See further G. Cohen 2006, 225–26.

it in approximately 101 B.C.E. Numismatic evidence allows us to refine the chronology in the *Antiquities* and provide a *terminus a quo* of 95/4 B.C.E. for the conquest of Gaza by Jannaeus.

In the second century B.C.E Gaza inaugurated its own era to celebrate its autonomy. Coins bearing this dating system exist up to "year 14" when it was no longer an independent city-state and under Hasmonean control.[83] We can calculate the exact year the latest known Gaza coin was minted by determining when the city began to use its own dating formula on its currency to celebrate its independence. Since Gaza stopped minting coins with Seleucid dates in 108/7 B.C.E., the city became an autonomous city-state in that year. Gaza produced the last of its autonomous coins in "year 14," which correlates to 95/4 B.C.E. This year is the *terminus a quo* for the conquest of Gaza by Jannaeus since he could not have captured it earlier when it was an independent city and still minting its own dated currency to celebrate its autonomy.[84]

The numismatic evidence from Gaza has some important ramifications for understanding the expansion of the Hasmonean state under Jannaeus. The coins of Gaza demonstrate that his expedition against the coastal region dates to the mid-90s B.C.E. at the earliest. It is, therefore, a separate military campaign that is unconnected with the termination of the War of Scepters. Josephus also provides another important chronological reference when he mentions that the citizens of Gaza expected the Nabatean monarch "Aretas, the king of the Arabs" (Ἀρέτας ὁ Ἀράβων βασιλεύς) to come to their aide. This king is Aretas II, who was alive in 95/4 B.C.E.[85] The claim in *Ant.* 13.365 that the siege of Gaza by Jannaeus took place about the same time as the 96 B.C.E. murder of the Seleucid monarch Grypus is correct.[86] Although this provides us with a firm date, it is still uncertain how to reconcile it with Jannaeus's other campaigns.

83. See Hoover 2007a, pls. 8–10; Kushnir-Stein 1995, pl. 2.

84. The coins of Gaza replace the Seleucid dating with this new autonomous dating. Although these coins do not contain the actual word ΑΥΤΟΝΟΜΟΣ, this is not an issue since other autonomous cities never placed this title on their currency. See Kushnir-Stein 2000.

85. Kushnir-Stein (2000, 24) suggests that if the account of Josephus is to be trusted, then he was clearly alive in 95/4 B.C.E. Aretas II is to be identified with the Arab king named Herotimus mentioned by Justin (*Epit.* 39.5). See Bowersock 1983, 22–23. Aretas II was soon afterwards replaced by Obodas I (ca. 95/94–85).

86. Although the coin evidence provides a *terminus a quo* of 95/4 B.C.E. for the conquest of Gaza by Jannaeus, it is close to the date of the death of Grypus and therefore shows that the chronology of *Ant.* 13.365 is accurate.

Kasher comments that the chronological order of the accounts of the conquests of Jannaeus in the works of Josephus are "quite confused and inconsistent, to the point where it is at times extremely difficult to extract any kind of historical truth."[87] Bar-Kochva, following a suggestion of Hölscher, proposes that Josephus has combined two sources. These scholars suggest that the expedition to the Transjordan (*Ant.* 13.352, 356–57) is from Nicolaus while the Gaza campaign (*Ant.* 13.358–64) is from Strabo.[88] The two also observe that Josephus connects the Gaza campaign and the War of Scepters in *Ant.* 13.358 when he recounts the city's fall to the army of Jannaeus. They believe Josephus copied this material from his source and did not fully integrate it into his narrative. This would explain some of the repetitions in his account of this period.[89]

The historical and numismatic evidence clearly shows that Jannaeus did not campaign outside Judea again until nearly five years after Egyptian troops had left the region. The date of his siege of Gaza suggests that both the Nabateans and the Hasmoneans had begun to take advantage of the absence of Egyptian forces in the region, and the rapid decay of the Seleucid Empire, to expand their territorial holdings along the southern coast. When Jannaeus attacked Gaza in 95/4 B.C.E, both Grypus and Cyzicenus were dead. For the next twelve years the Seleucid Empire experienced almost continual civil war between the five sons of Grypus (Seleucus VI Epiphanes Nicator, Antiochus XI Epiphanes Philadelphus, Demetrius III Eucaerus, Philip I Philadelphus, and Antiochus XII Dionysus) and the son of Cyzicenus (Antiochus X Eusebes Philopator).[90] If not for this political instability, it is doubtful that Jannaeus would have undertaken any foreign wars at this time. Josephus chose to highlight his siege of Gaza because Jannaeus's capture of this strategic port gave him control over many vital trade routes. The conquest of this city by Jannaeus also benefitted Cleopatra III.

The Siege of Gaza

Located near the Egyptian border, the strongly fortified city of Gaza was a major outlet for the Nabatean Arabs. They used its harbor to move their goods from Arabia to Europe. Its loss to the Hasmoneans threatened the

87. Kasher 1990, 154.

88. Bar-Kochva 1996, 293–94; Hölscher 1904, 15–16.

89. Josephus, for example, repeats himself in *Ant.* 13.348 and 352 when he describes the response of Cleopatra III to the invasion of Soter.

90. *Ant.* 13.365–71, 384–91; Porph. in *FHG* 3.715–16; App. *Syr.* 69.365–66; Bellinger 1949, 73–80; Ehling 2008, 231–56; Hoover 2007b, 288–301.

stability of the Nabatean economy, and Egypt's as well. Justin comments that the infighting between Cleopatra III and her sons led to a resurgence of Nabatean nationalism.[91] The Nabateans began to expand into Syria, made forays into Egypt, and attacked and captured Egyptian ships at sea.[92] Soter may have supported some of this Nabatean activity, which would explain why the citizens of Gaza welcomed him into their city. Because Gaza was a Nabatean ally at this time, the Ptolemaic maritime economy was in danger if its citizens cut off the Ptolemies from its port.[93] Because the Ptolemaic Empire feared this possibility, they began to reduce their dependence on the Arab tribes by making direct contact with the Far East to bypass Arabia.[94] Since the residents of Gaza had given Soter shelter, Cleopatra III considered the city a potential threat to the stability of her reign following the War of Scepters. She had no reason to disrupt the campaign of Jannaeus against Gaza since she had made a treaty with him and because there was no possibility the Hasmoneans would invade Egypt.

Gaza had the potential to bring great wealth to the Hasmonean state. For this reason, the claim in *Ant.* 13.364 that Jannaeus destroyed Gaza is unfounded. Josephus does not mention its devastation in his *War.* It is probable that he added this detail to his *Antiquities* to exaggerate the military conquests of Jannaeus: he attributed the complete destruction of one of the region's most fortified cities to him.[95] The historical evidence

91. Just. *Epit.* 39.5.6.

92. See also, Diod. Sic. 3.43.4–5; Strabo, *Geogr.* 16.4.18. Strabo's report is based on Artemidorus, whose *floruit* was approximately 100 B.C.E. It is commonly believed that Diodorus Siculus used Agatharchides of Cnidus, who wrote after 130 B.C.E.

93. During the time the Ptolemies controlled southern Syria and Phoenicia, aromatic goods passed through Gaza overland from Arabia to Egypt. The presence of an official in charge of incense in the mid-third century B.C.E. shows the importance of the city as a center for trade. See G. Cohen 2006, 33.

94. Ptolemy VIII Physcon, in 130 B.C.E., assigned a special official to investigate navigation in the Red Sea. The voyages of Eudoxus (Strabo, *Geogr.* 2.3.4) to India around 116 B.C.E., and the apparent appointment of an *epistrategos* for the Red Sea and Indian Ocean in 110/9 B.C.E., show that the Ptolemies from the time of Physcon sought to bypass the Nabateans and establish their own trade networks in the East. The Nabateans and the Egyptians also came into conflict over trade near Gaza. The Seleucid rulers appear to have supported the Nabateans to undermine Egyptian trade. See further Hamshary 1995, 26–28.

95. The claim that Jannaeus destroyed Gaza is also found in Strabo, *Geogr.* 16.2.30. Pastor (1997, 75) believes Jannaeus would not have demolished Gaza since he needed it as a port, and that the city's rapid recovery shows that it was not devastated.

suggests that Gaza suffered no adverse damage, and continued to function as a major center of trade. It was soon annexed to Idumaea. Jannaeus placed it under the authority of Antipas, the father of Antipater and grandfather of Herod the Great. Antipas established friendly relations with Gaza, the Nabateans, and the city of Ascalon.[96] This created a stable political situation in the region that made it possible for Jannaeus to take advantage of the rapidly disintegrating situation to the north, and expand his kingdom by annexing Seleucid territory. There are, however, major problems with this section of Josephus's accounts.

Chronological Problems with the Transjordan Campaign of Jannaeus

In his *Antiquities* Josephus claims that after the conclusion of the War of Scepters, Jannaeus campaigned beyond the Jordan River in Coele-Syria (*Ant.* 13.356–57). This expedition included a costly attack against the stronghold of Theodotus, the son of Zenon (*Ant.* 13.356). Jannaeus then besieged and destroyed Gaza before he returned to Jerusalem (*Ant.* 13.358–64). Josephus next includes a section about the Seleucid Empire's fratricidal wars (*Ant.* 13.365–72). By following this section with an account of how Jannaeus subdued his Jewish adversaries (*Ant.* 13.372–74), Josephus implies that the Hasmonean state was much more stable than the former great Seleucid Empire. Unlike Syria's monarchs, Jannaeus kept his kingdom intact. He then inserts a narrative about the campaign of Jannaeus beyond the Jordan River to portray him as a great military conqueror. His reputation preceded his arrival in the region, for a local ruler named Theodorus (*Ant.* 13.375) refused to fight him. However, Josephus mentions that Jannaeus fell into an ambush in rough terrain that forced him to return to Jerusalem (*Ant.* 13.374–76). His enemies took advantage of his weakened state to summon the Seleucid monarch Demetrius III (*Ant.* 13.377) to attack Jannaeus.

The chronology of these events in the *War* is similar to the *Antiquities*, but much shorter. In *War* 1.86 Josephus places the Transjordan campaign of Jannaeus, and his defeat by Theodorus, before the siege of Gaza (*War* 1.87). He then describes the subsequent Jewish revolt against Jannaeus (*War* 1.88), and a second Transjordan campaign. During this second expedition to the Transjordan, Jannaeus attacked the Arabs and found the fortress of Theodorus empty (*War* 1.89). The Arabs then defeated Jannaeus (*War* 1.90), which caused his subjects to revolt against him and summon Demetrius III (*War* 1.90–93).

96. *Ant.* 14.10.

It is rather doubtful that Jannaeus made two separate expeditions east of the Jordan River. Josephus connects his first Transjordan campaign with his conquest of the coast. The stories about the Transjordan expedition of Jannaeus in *Ant.* 13.356–57 and *War* 1.86–87 are reminiscent of his later accounts in *Ant.* 13.393–94 and *War* 1.103–105.[97] He twice recounts the capture of Amathus. In both instances he associates it with Theodorus. It is probable that Josephus has duplicated the details of one expedition to the Transjordan, during which Jannaeus was only partly successful and suffered considerable military losses. This defeat apparently encouraged Demetrius III to attack Judea.

It is difficult to reconstruct the relationship between Jannaeus and the Nabateans at this time. Josephus places his encounters with them in conjunction with the Transjordan expedition against Theodorus. However, he states in *Ant.* 13.374–75 that Jannaeus, after he had subdued the "Arabs of Moab and Galaaditis, whom he forced to pay tribute," he avoided Theodorus to fight the Nabatean king Obedas I. It appears either that Josephus has combined accounts of multiple battles, or the Nabateans regrouped their forces and engaged Jannaeus a second time. The location of the fighting is difficult to ascertain since the best manuscripts of *Ant.* 13.375 state that it took place in φάραγγα κατὰ Γάραδα κώμην τῆς Γαυλανίδος ("a deep ravine near Garda, a village of Gaulanis").[98] Josephus, or his source(s), apparently tried to identify the location of this battle with a known place. It occurred, as suggested by *Ant.* 13.375, in one of the

---

97. *War.* 1.104 states that Jannaeus attacked Theodorus whereas *Ant.* 13.393 reads "Zenon," which is presumably the name of his father. Cf. *War.* 1.87; *Ant.* 13.356. It cannot be ruled out that these stories refer to the same man.

98. The reading Γαυλανίδος is a conjecture of Niese for the manuscripts that read ᾽Ιουδάνιδος. For the Greek text and variants, see Niese 1892, 220. Because there were a number of towns named Gadara in southern Syria, it is often difficult to determine which location is referred to in the ancient sources. See further G. Cohen 2006, 284 n. 1. An inscription from Gadara (Umm Qēs) of the Decapolis shows that a tyrant named Philotas ruled the city in 85/4 B.C.E., which is during the period from 102/1 B.C.E. to 80 B.C.E. when Josephus claims Jannaeus supposedly had captured and remained in control of it. See Mittmann 2006. Earlier, in both *War* 1.86 and *Ant.* 13.356 Josephus states that Jannaeus conquered Gadara near Amathus. This suggests that this conquest cannot be associated with the site of Umm Qēs in the Decapolis. It is more probable that Jannaeus actually conquered Gadara in Peraea early in his reign and captured Gadara in the northern Golan later. Josephus appears to have merged different materials together from his source(s). This would account for the repetition of the account of Coele-Syria in *Ant.* 13.355–56, which erroneously implies that the Gadara in question was part of Syria. For this evidence, see further Piotrkowski 2011.

remote ravines in the Golan region. This rugged terrain gave the locals a decisive military advantage. The relatively inaccessible location of this defeat would account for the considerable loss of life in the Hasmonean army. It made him vulnerable to Demetrius III, who tried to conquer the Hasmonean state.

Internal Opposition to Jannaeus

Josephus does not describe in detail the factors that led to the invasion . of Demetrius III in his *War* 1.91–92. He merely states that Jannaeus had been at war for six years, which cost the lives of over 50,000 Jews. He also mentions that this tragedy compelled his enemies to appeal for aid to Demetrius III (*War* 1.92). However, Josephus inserts a rather lengthy account in his *Antiquities* (13.372–73) that is without any parallel in his *War.* This more detailed version nevertheless shows some dependence on the *War.* Both mention the six-year period of fighting between Jannaeus and his own people (*War* 1.1.91; *Ant.* 13.376). The two accounts also state that Pisidian and Cilician mercenaries were in the Hasmonean army (*War* 1.88; *Ant.* 13.374). In addition, his two books record a disturbance during a festival (*War* 1.88; *Ant.* 13.37). But only in the *War* does Josephus report that the mercenaries in the army of Jannaeus killed some of his opponents. In the *Antiquities* (13.374–76) Josephus also inserts a story about the second Transjordan campaign of Jannaeus. This disastrous expedition, according to this version, compelled his enemies to appeal to Demetrius III for military assistance.

Despite the differences in the *War* and the *Antiquities*, both books claim that a revolt against Jannaeus occurred during the Festival of Tabernacles. According to the *Antiquities*, the Jews attending this holiday pelted him with citrons and wands made of palm branches.[99] Some in the crowd yelled that he was a bastard and therefore unqualified to serve as high priest.[100] The similarity of this remark with *Ant.* 13.292 could indicate that Josephus did not know which Hasmonean was the object of this accusation, or that it was merely slander that was not based on fact and used against several members of this family. Even if untrue, this charge had the potential to undermine the religious authority of Jannaeus because it called into his question his legitimacy to serve as high priest. Jannaeus was so angry that he unleashed his soldiers against his opponents; they

99. *Ant.* 13.372. This is the earliest attestation of the use of the citron during this festival as mandated in Lev 23:40. See Rubenstein 1995, 82; Milgrom 2001, 236–42.

100. McLaren (1991, 57–58) suggests if there were any truth to this accusation, it would have been vocalized much earlier in his reign.

killed 6,000 in the temple precincts. He then placed a wooden barrier around the temple and the altar through which only the priests could pass to view the sacrifices.[101]

The Mishnah may preserve an account of this incident that is independent of Josephus. It describes a water ritual that took place at the altar during the Festival of Tabernacles. On one occasion, the high priest in an apparent ace of defiance poured the customary libation over his feet. The crowd responded by pelting him with their citrons.[102] The Talmud contains a similar story and states that the high priest who committed this sacrilege was a Sadducee.[103] Because there is only one recorded incident of such an event taking place, these rabbinic stories clearly refer to Jannaeus. If factual, they suggest that he inflamed an already tense situation when he publically mocked the Pharisees during a religious ceremony.[104] He also erected a high wooden partition wall around the temple and the altar. The major difference between the accounts of this incident in Josephus and the Talmud is that the rabbis were more concerned with the ritual performance of Jannaeus as high priest. Josephus merely uses this episode to introduce the Transjordan campaign and its great loss of Jewish life. By placing the story prior to this catastrophe, it serves to explain the Jewish opposition to his reign.

The harsh response of Jannaeus suggests that he considered this revolt a threat to his kingship. Josephus states that he would never have stopped this insurrection if his Pisidian and Cilician mercenaries had not come to his aide (*War* 1.88). In keeping with his theme in the *War* (1.10) that domestic strife (στάσις) was largely responsible for the First Jewish Revolt of 66 C.E., he writes (*War* 1.87) that festivals were times when στάσις was most apt to break out. He also states that Jannaeus attempted to conciliate the masses through changes of policy, which further angered his enemies (*War* 1.92).

---

101. *Ant.* 13.373.

102. *m. Sukkah* 4.9.

103. *b. Yoma* 26b; *b. Sukkah* 48b. Rubenstein (1995, 417–44) raises the possibility that the rabbis adapted the story from Josephus. Regev (2013, 155–60) proposes that the Pharisees opposed Jannaeus primarily because he was a Sadducee; therefore, they rejected his halakhic practices. Noam (2014) believes that the Talmudic stories regarding the opposition of the Pharisees to Jannaeus serving as high priest because his mother had been a captive, which parallel the *Ant.* 13.288–98, preserve an ancient Pharisaic polemical work.

104. See further Rubenstein 1995, 123–31.

Although it is possible there was a considerable period of time between the Transjordan campaign and the invasion of Demetrius III, it is probable that the Tabernacles incident occurred immediately after his disastrous Transjordan expedition. It was apparently the invasion of Seleucid territory by Jannaeus, and his defeat in the Transjordan, that caused widespread revolt against his reign and precipitated the 90/89 B.C.E. invasion of Demetrius III. If the claim of Josephus that the revolt against Jannaeus lasted for six years is factual, then it began beginning approximately at the time of his 95/4 B.C.E. siege of Gaza. It is likely that the local opposition to Jannaeus began shortly after this siege.[105] Josephus focuses on Jewish insurrectionists to highlight the instability they brought to their nation when they invited Demetrius III to invade their homeland to remove a Hasmonean king from power. The invasion of Demetrius III did not occur merely because of Jewish opposition to the Hasmoneans, but, as previously discussed, because of civil wars in the Seleucid Empire and possibly the interference of Jannaeus there.

The Invasion of Demetrius III

Demetrius III (97/6–88/87 B.C.E.), a son of Grypus, was the first Seleucid ruler to pose a threat to Jannaeus after the War of Scepters.[106] Coins of Damascus show that his reign in Damascus began in S.E. 216 (= 97/6 B.C.E.) and lasted until S.E. 225 (= 88/7 B.C.E.), with the exception of a short interruption in S.E. 220 (= 93/2 B.C.E.).[107] The first date conflicts with the claim of Josephus (*Ant.* 13.370) that Soter installed him there upon the death of Antiochus XI Epiphanes (ca. 93 BC). In this instance, the numismatic evidence is to be preferred over any literary accounts for reconstructing the reign of Demetrius III. This is because the Damascus coins are sequentially dated, bear his name, and record the years he ruled this city. They show that the chronology of Josephus, or a source he used, is mistaken for this period.[108]

---

105. Although Josephus does not mention conscription, Jannaeus would have needed to replenish his forces after so many battles. The large loss of life in his campaigns undoubtedly contributed to the opposition against him.

106. For sources, and the complicated history of this infighting between Demetrius III and his Seleucid rivals that ultimately affected Judea, see Atkinson 2014a, 9–13; Bellinger 1949, 73–86; Schürer et al. 1973–87, 1:134–35; Bevan 1902, 253–63; Ehling 2008, 231–46; Grainger 1997, 32, 34, 44, 52.

107. N. Wright 2010, 254–55.

108. For this evidence, see further Hoover, Houghton, and Vesely 2008, 306–8, 315–16.

Josephus calls Demetrius III "Akairos" ("Untimely) to highlight the failure of his invasion of the Hasmonean state.[109] He travelled with his army to Shechem. As the two forces lined up their armies for battle, the Greek soldiers in the army of Demetrius III urged the Greek mercenaries in Jannaeus's force to abandon him. The Jews in the Hasmonean legion likewise urged their fellow citizens in the Seleucid Empire's army to do likewise. Josephus stresses that Jannaeus lost the bulk of his mercenary force in this encounter. Jannaeus and the survivors fled to the mountains. According to Josephus, an unexpected event occurred during the battle that may have caused him, or his source, to give Demetrius III the unflattering moniker "Akairos." According to Josephus, Demetrius III supposedly feared he was now no match for Jannaeus. He abruptly abandoned his campaign and fled home after 6,000 Jewish soldiers in his army defected.[110]

The coins of Demetrius III from Damascus may help us to understand why he attacked Jannaeus at this time. Placing his invasion sometime in 90/89 B.C.E., most likely in 89 B.C.E. rather than 88 B.C.E., means that it took place approximately three to four years after Demetrius III temporarily lost and then regained Damascus. Currency minted in his name there stops in 93/2 B.C.E. Mint production rapidly rises in S.E. 222 (= 91/90 B.C.E.), the year he regained control of Damascus.[111] Coins were produced at a high rate there until S.E. 223 (= 90/89 B.C.E.). This increased output of currency represents his funding for his conflict with Jannaeus.[112] This rise in mint production for nearly two years preceding the invasion of Demetrius III suggests that he began to plan for an assault against Jannaeus once he recovered Damascus. If we place a Transjordan campaign of Jannaeus prior to the invasion of Demetrius III, perhaps around 93/2 B.C.E., it offers a possible explanation why this

---

109. *Ant.* 13.369; *War* 1.92. These passages refer to Demetrius III as Akairos (Δημήτριον τὸμ Ἄκαιρον). The table of contents to the writings of Josephus, as well as the Latin manuscripts of *Antiquities*, contain Eukairos (Εὔκαιρον). The nickname Akairos appears to presuppose the positive moniker Eukairos. For the view that the table of contents to the works of Josephus, which contain summaries of each book, were part of the original "published version," see Sievers 2007. Josephus is the only writer to provide an unofficial nickname for Demetrius III. However, the name Eukairos in the Table of Contents to Josephus's writings, the Greek editions, and the Latin translation of his works all appear to be a secondary reading. Because there is no ancient testimony or numismatic evidence that Demetrius III was known as Eukairos, it is best to abandon the use of this name. See further the extensive evidence compiled by Levenson and Martin (2009).

110. *War* 1.95; *Ant.* 13.379.

111. See further Hoover 2007b, 289–96.

112. For these data, see Hoover, Houghton, and Vesely 2008, 306–7.

Seleucid monarch invaded the Hasmonean state. Jannaeus may have taken advantage of the instability in the Seleucid Empire to campaign in the region of Damascus. Based on the numismatic evidence, it is plausible that earlier unrecorded Hasmonean activity in the areas surrounding Damascus weakened Demetrius III, and potentially made him vulnerable to attacks by Antiochus X Eusebes. Jannaeus may have contributed to Demetrius III losing the city for a year. Demetrius III quickly regained control of it and, as suggested by his increased production of currency, began to plan for an invasion of the Hasmonean state.[113]

Jannaeus barely survived the incursion of Demetrius III. Although Josephus claims the mass defection of Jews fighting alongside the Seleucid forces saved the Hasmonean state, Jannaeus refused to forgive them for their betrayal. He attacked and besieged many of them at Bethoma.[114] He captured the city and took many of its captives to Jerusalem. Jannaeus crucified 800 of these rebels and executed their wives and children while he feasted with his concubines. According to Josephus, the Jews gave Jannaeus the nickname "Thrakidas" (θρακίδαν) because of his excessive cruelty.[115] Then, in this weakened political state, Jannaeus faced another incursion by a Seleucid monarch.

The Invasion of Antiochus XII Dionysus

The invasion of Judea by Antiochus XII Dionysus is perhaps the most perplexing section of the account of the reign of Jannaeus in the writings of Josephus.[116] However, we should not blame Josephus for this difficult portion of his book. Antiochus XII Dionysus was apparently excluded from

113. Demetrius III ruled Damascus S.E. 216 (= 97/6 B.C.E.). He ruled the city until S.E. 225 (= 88/7 B.C.E.), with the exception of a brief interruption in S.E. 220 (= 93/2 B.C.E.). See Hoover, Houghton, and Vessely 2008, 307.

114. *Ant.* 13.380. The *War* 1.97 reads Bemeselis. The exact location of this conflict is uncertain, but it may be located somewhere north-east of Samaria at Misilye. See further, H. Eshel 2008, 119; Schürer et al. 1973–87, 1:224 n. 21.

115. *Ant.* 13.381. This name, apparently meaning Thracian, may have been intended to denote him as barbarous. It may also refer to the presence of Thracians among his mercenaries. See further Allegro 1959. Marcus (1966, 419) translates it as "the Cossack." The mass crucifixion is also mentioned in the *Nahum Pesher* (4Q169 3–4 I, 1–7). See further Atkinson 2013c, 16–19; Berrin 2004, 165–92; Charlesworth 2002, 112–17; Doudna 2001, 117–19.

116. Shatzman (1991, 120) writes of the encounters between Jannaeus, Antiochus XII Dionysus, and Aretas III: "Josephus' report is clearly incomplete and unsatisfactory; the motives and aims of the antagonists in this triple combat are anybody's guess." Dionysus was the brother of Seleucus VI, Antiochus XI, Philip I, and

the Seleucid sources, most of which were written from the perspective of the dynasty at Antioch. Josephus did not realize that Dionysus fought Jannaeus on multiple occasions. Once again, the fighting in the Seleucid Empire over Antioch and Damascus provides the necessary background for understanding why Dionysus, like his predecessor Demetrius III, invaded the Hasmonean state.

The kingdom of Dionysus was largely confined to Damascus. His rule there, mentioned by Josephus, is dated by the city's coins, which begin in S.E. 226 (= 87/6 B.C.E.) and end in S.E. 230 (83/2 B.C.E.).[117] The numismatic record provides some indirect evidence that Aretas III took Damascus from him in 83/2 B.C.E.[118] This date also appears to be the same year Aretas III killed him in battle. Jannaeus unwittingly found himself in the middle of the war between these two rulers: it nearly cost him his kingdom. Josephus's account is confusing because he only recounts the end of this conflict and not its beginning.

Dionysus actually conducted two campaigns against the Nabatean Arabs, who were at this time were extending their power northwards through the Transjordan region.[119] During his first expedition, his brother Philip I took advantage of his absence to march against Damascus.[120] A man named Milesius, the commander of the garrison, betrayed the city to him. Philip I was subsequently driven from Damascus for failing to reward Milesius for his support. There is, however, no currency to be attributed to Philip I at Damascus. Because the sequence of coins minted by Dionysus is unbroken, the occupation of the city by Philip I was quite brief. Josephus supports this numismatic evidence, which indicates that Philip held Damascus for a limited period of time.[121] The unsuccessful effort of Philip I to wrest Damascus from his brother Dionysus appears

---

Demetrius III. See further Grainger 1997, 34. For the campaign of Dionysus against Jannaeus as reflected in the Qumran literature, see further Atkinson 2013c, 19–23.

117. See *Ant.* 13.387–91; *War* 1.99–102. Newel 1939, nos. 132–34; Houghton and Spaer 1990, 4; Hoover 2007b, 298–99; Hoover, Houghton, and Vesely 2008, 314, 316.

118. Although the Nabatean coins of Aretas III (87–62 B.C.E.) lack dating marks, and their years of issue are uncertain, the Seleucid coins of Antiochus XII Dionysus and Tigranes minted at Damascus from 72–69 B.C.E. suggest that Aretas III occupied the city from 83/2 B.C. until 72 B.C.E. See further Hoover and Barkay 2010.

119. Roschinski 1980.

120. Only Josephus (*Ant.* 13.387) names him as the immediate successor of Demetrius III at Damascus.

121. He writes in *Ant.* 13.387–89 that the guard in Damascus kept the city safe for Dionysus.

to have taken place in late 88/7 B.C.E.[122] Given that his sibling was trying to invade his kingdom, it is doubtful Dionysus actually engaged the Nabateans in battle, or made it far into their territory. Rather, he had to abandon his campaign against the Nabateans and return to Damascus. Philip I presumably went back to Antioch.[123]

The account of the invasion of Dionysus in the writings of Josephus is confusing because he only chronicles his second attempt to attack the Nabateans. The numismatic evidence shows that several years intervened between the aborted effort of Philip I to take Damascus and the second Nabatean campaign of Dionysus, during which he attacked Judea.[124] According to Josephus's *War*, Dionysus attempted to transit Judea to invade the territory of the Nabatean Arabs. Jannaeus erected a fortified wooden wall and dug a trench for nearly seventeen miles, from Antipatris to Joppa, to halt his advance.[125] Dionysus set fire to these fortifications and marched through Judea to Arabia where he won a battle against an unidentified "Arab king."[126] This monarch, to be identified with Aretas III, feigned a retreat. He surprised the Seleucid army with a reserve force of 10,000 horses. Dionysus died in the ensuing battle. Josephus reports that the remnants of the Seleucid force fled to the "village of Cana." The region's inhabitants refused to supply them. Most of the Dionysus's army died of starvation while attempting to cross Judea to return home.[127] But what is most puzzling about these events is why Dionysus turned west to attack Jannaeus when he was en route to Nabatea in the opposite direction. The delay proved costly: Aretas III used the extra time to amass additional forces that he used to defeat Dionysus and kill him.

122. Bowersock (1983, 24) accepts this date and correctly notes that Dionysus conducted two campaigns against the Nabateans.

123. For these events, see *Ant.* 13.387–89; Hoover, Houghton, Vesely 2008, 316; Bellinger 1949, 77–78.

124. Josephus appears to portray Dionysus as the last of the Seleucid line. See *Ant.* 13.387–91. He, or his source, confuses this ruler with the similarly named Antiochus XIII Asiaticus. The latter monarch reigned in Syria for one year before the arrival of Pompey in 64 B.C.E. See App. *Syr.* 70; Dobias 1924, 224–27.

125. This distance of "150 stades," which Marcus (1966, 423 n. e) calculates as 17 miles. The distance is listed as "60 stades" in one manuscript. See Niese 1892, 390.

126. *War* 1.101; *Ant.* 13.391.

127. For this battle, see *Ant.* 13.390–91; *War* 1.99–102. Dionysus perished at the unknown location of Cana, which was presumably south or south-west of the Dead Sea. See Shatzman 1991, 119. This would indicate that he travelled from Joppa and Capharsaba through Judea to engage the Nabateans near the southern portion of the Dead Sea.

Archaeology provides some insight into Josephus's story. A series of rectangular and hexagonal-shaped stone foundations uncovered from the vicinity of Aphek (Herodian Antipatris) to Tel Aviv along with coins of Jannaeus support the identification of this structure as the barrier that Jannaeus constructed to stop Dionysus. Excavations at Horvat Mesad and Horvat 'Eqed have also uncovered Hellenistic coins along with other late Hellenistic remains, which suggest that this fortification barrier extended along the Jerusalem corridor as well.[128] This complex, immense, and lengthy barrier would have taken considerable time to construct. The placement of this line suggests that it was defensive in nature, and that it was built to impede Dionysus from entering southern Judea. Dionysus apparently destroyed this fortification both to avenge Jannaeus's earlier attack on his kingdom, and to prevent the Hasmoneans from taking advantage of his war with the Nabateans to invade Syria. This delay proved costly and undoubtedly contributed to Dionysus's death. Jannaeus then had some unexplained encounter with the Nabateans at Adida, during which he army was defeated.[129] Jannaeus made a treaty with Aretas III and then began an extensive series of conquests in the Transjordan.

Further Victories in the Transjordan

Jan Retsö comments that it is difficult to understand how Jannaeus could have made a treaty with Aretas III following the Hasmonean defeat at Adida, and then campaign in the Transjordan without any Nabatean objections. A close reading of the Josephus's account of the three-year campaign of Jannaeus in the Transjordan raises some further chronological difficulties. The appearance of Theodorus is suspect, as are the locations where he is said to have fought Jannaeus. Retsö observes numerous similarities and repetitions in Josephus's accounts of Jannaeus.[130] Theodorus and the battles of Amathus and Gadara are mentioned twice; it is unexplained why Jannaeus attacked the latter city again (*Ant.* 13.356;

---

128. Fisher 1987; Kaplan 1971. For a more skeptical view that this fortification does not date to the time of Jannaeus, which fails to take into consideration the revised chronology of this period based on the numismatic evidence, see Fantalkin and Tal 2003. The description of this fortification in the *Antiquities* states that it was large and had both wooden towers and firing-platforms. Pottery discovered in foundation trenches in the terrace walls of the City of David area of Jerusalem dates to the time of Jannaeus and suggests that he also fortified this city. For this evidence, see Berlin 2012. See also, *War* 1.99; *Ant.* 13.390.

129. *Ant.* 13.392; *War* 1.103.

130. Retsö 2003, 342–81.

War 1.86/*Ant.* 13.374; *War* 1.89). Jannaeus faces revolts on two occasions (*Ant.* 13.372–74; *War* 1.88–89/*Ant.* 13.375–76; *War* 1.92–95). Retsö proposes that Jannaeus also made an agreement with the Arabs against Dionysus. Aretas III took advantage of this Seleucid king's death on the battlefield to annex Damascus. Aretas III then broke his agreement and engaged Jannaeus in battle. Jannaeus was forced to make a treaty with him. Although this is a probable reconstruction, the exact sequence of events is impossible to determine because Josephus has combined several episodes and placed them in a single paragraph at the end of Jannaeus's life to make him look stronger.[131]

George Syncellus complicates matters by recording an otherwise unattested siege of Tyre by Jannaeus, and a counterattack by the Nabateans and Itureans. According to Syncellus, when Jannaeus sent his general Diagos to fight the Nabateans, he died while making preparations to fight the Itureans.[132] Jannaeus had apparently tried to take advantage of the collapse of the Seleucid Empire to attempt to annex Tyre. He apparently attacked the city because its residents had sided against him during the War of Scepters. The Nabateans and Itureans formed a military alliance, surprised Jannaeus there, and forced him to abandon his siege and sign a peace treaty. Josephus omits this embarrassing episode from his books; however, he mentions that Jannaeus, for unspecified reasons, surrendered many cities, including the valuable lands of Moab and Galaaditis beyond the Jordan River, to a Nabatean monarch named Aretas.[133] Only the threatened destruction of his army could have forced him to make such humiliating concessions. Jannaeus had to give up his Transjordan conquests and abandon his plan to annex the coastal territories.

Josephus in his *Antiquities* (13.395–97) includes a list of cities that formerly belonged to Syria, Idumaea, and Phoenicia that he claims were under Jewish domination approximately three years before the death of Jannaeus. Shatzman notes this catalog is not accurate because it includes territories (Marisa, Adora, Samaria, and Scythopolis) that had been conquered earlier while some regions Jannaeus controlled (Galilee and Judea) are absent. He suggests this is a partial list of former Gentile cities under the rule of Jannaeus around 79 B.C.E. Only a few of these sites were settled extensively or militarily occupied at this time. However, Seth Schwartz comments that the record of cities under the control of Jannaeus preserved by Syncellus is independent of Josephus's *Antiquities*. It appears ancient since it mentions Philoteria, which ceased to exist by the

131. *Ant.* 13.393–94.
132. *Chron.* 559.5–12.
133. *Ant.* 13.382. See further Shatzman 1991, 89–92; Kasher 1990, 153–60.

late first century B.C.E. and is never otherwise mentioned by Josephus.[134] Syncellus's statement that Basan is now called Scythopolis also dates the list a few centuries earlier than Josephus since by this time Scythopolis had reassumed its Semitic name. Josephus, in his inventory of cities under the control of Jannaeus at the time of his death states that he demolished Pella because its inhabitants refused to Judaize. Daniel R. Schwartz notes some textual difficulties in this passage and suggests that the claim that Jannaeus destroyed Pella, which is refuted by the archaeological evidence, comes from Strabo.[135] For these reasons, the list of Syncellus is preferable to that of Josephus, especially since it is much shorter. It suggests that the extent of the territory under the control of Jannaeus was much more limited than Josephus claims.

The Final Years of Alexander Jannaeus

In *Ant.* 13.398–407 Josephus includes a unique and rather strange story of the death of Jannaeus that conflicts with the accounts in his earlier *War* as well as the details provided by Syncellus. In this book, Josephus claims Jannaeus became fatally ill while on the battlefield at Ragaba. His wife, Shelamzion Alexandra, was there grieving and uncertain what to do. Jannaeus urged her to conceal his death from the soldiers until she had captured Ragaba and then, upon her return to Jerusalem, to yield some power to the Pharisees. He claims they were favorably disposed towards her and would let her rule.

134. Shatzman 1991, 76; S. Schwartz 1990a, 5–6. This list is found in *Ant.* 13.395–97. Josephus records the following towns under the control of Jannaeus at the time of his death: Straton's Tower, Apollonia, Joppa, Jamnia, Azotus, Gaza, Anthedon, Raphia, Rhinocorura, Adora, Marisa, all of Idumea and Samaria as well as Mt. Carmel and Mt. Tabor, Scythopolis, Gadara, Seleucia, Gamla, Essebon, Medaba, Lemba, Oronim, Agalain, Thona, Zoara, the Valley of the Cilicians, and Pella. Some of the towns in this list are unknown and a few are contested due to the corrupt text of Josephus. See further Shatzman 1991, 37, 90–91. The list of Syncellus (*Chron.* 558–59) adds Philoteria, Abilia, Hippus, and Lian (a mistake for Dian [= Dium] based on *Ant.* 13.393).

135. D. Schwartz (2011b) suggests that Josephus or an assistant put in the passage from Strabo, in addition to material from Nicolaus, and failed to notice the difficulties it created. This theory is plausible since Josephus acknowledges that he used Strabo (*Ant.* 13.284–87; 14.35, 68, 104, 112, 114–18), whose work mentions the forced conversion of the Idumaeans and Itureans. Josephus in his description of Pella in *War* 3.46–47 copies the boustrophedon structure of Strabo's geographical list. See further Shahar 2004, 236–37, 250–56.

Josephus states that Jannaeus made a last wish before he died: he asked Alexandra to allow the Pharisees to abuse his corpse and leave it unburied. Although this is a clear violation of the scriptural prohibition in Deut 21:22–23 against the mutilation or abuse of a dead body, Jannaeus had no fear they would accept his overture. He claimed that if Alexandra followed his request the Pharisees would give him a splendid burial. This puzzling story makes sense only if Jannaeus had violated this biblical commandment and abused the bodies of the 800 Jews he crucified, many of whom were Pharisees. The language and verbal parallels between this story and the brief account of his last campaign in the *War* suggest that both stories are the product of Josephus. Josephus likely wanted to conceal the undignified manner of his passing: Jannaeus appears to have never made it to Ragaba and presumably died in Jerusalem.

Josephus's accounts suggest that Jannaeus was the most widely hated Hasmonean king. But his reign ended with a political bombshell: he named his wife as his successor with the right to select the next high priest. Her nine-year reign is the most unique period of the Hasmonean monarchy; she affected both Middle Eastern and European history. We now turn to the remarkable Shelamzion Alexandra—the only Hasmonean queen regnant—and the final glorious period of the Hasmonean state.

Chapter 6

SHELAMZION ALEXANDRA: A HASMONEAN GOLDEN AGE

Her Name and Family Background

Josephus never tells us the Semitic name of the ruler commonly known as Shelamzion (Salome) Alexandra.[1] He only refers to her by her Greek name, "Alexandra" (Ἀλεξάνδρα). It is the only known Greek Hasmonean female name. Her two granddaughters by her sons, Hyrcanus II and Aristobulus II, were also named Alexandra.[2] The rabbinic literature never calls her Alexandra, but refers to her by a variety of Semitic names.[3] The Dead Sea Scrolls now provide the definitive answer concerning her actual Semitic name.

Alexandra is called "Shelamzion" (שלמציון) in *4QpapHistorical Text C* (4Q331 1 ii 7) and *4QHistorical Text D* (4Q332 2 4). She appears in 4Q331 after a line that Joseph Fitzmyer proposes read "Yohanan to bring to" (יוחנן להבי אל; 4Q331 1 I 7). He believes this passage refers to John Hyrcanus.[4] Because this Qumran text lists historical events in chronological order, and since Shelamzion is mentioned in the next column, Fitzmyer's proposal is the most plausible identification of the name Yohanan in this document.[5] Alexandra is certainly mentioned in line four 4Q332 which reads, "with secret counsel Shelamzion came" (ביסוד באה שלמציון). This identification is supported by the next two lines that

---

1. For the major historical sources for the life of Shelamzion Alexandra, see *War* 1.107–19; *Ant.* 13.407–32; Sync. *Chron.* 555.8–17; Moses of Kohren, *History of Armenia* 2.14; Atkinson 2012c; 2014b.

2. *Ant.* 14.126, 15.23. It was also the name of the daughter of Phasael. See *Ant.* 18.131.

3. For Alexandra's different names, see Ilan 1993; 2006, 53–54; Schürer et al. 1973–87, 1:229–30.

4. Fitzmyer 2000a; 2000b. Fitzmyer's identification was most recently accepted by VanderKam (2004, 308–9). Wise (2003, 68) is uncertain whether this text refers to John Hyrcanus or Hyrcanus II.

5. Atkinson 2007, 132–33; Vermes 2007, 137.

describe some confrontation (להקביל, "to confront," 4Q332 2 7) and a rebellion involving "Hyrcanus" (הרקנוס מרד, 4Q332 2 6).[6] Both Fitzmyer and Wise restore the name "Aristobulus" in the missing section of this line and reconstruct it to read: "Hyrcanus rebelled [against Aristobulus] ([ב הרקנוס מרד [בארסטבולוס).[7] Because the name Hyrcanus follows the reference to Shelamzion, Fitzmyer and Wise are certainly correct that it refers to Hyrcanus II rather than John Hyrcanus. This means that the earlier line with the name Shelamzion refers to Alexandra.[8]

Although the Dead Sea Scrolls now settle the longstanding scholarly debate over Alexandra's Semitic name, they do not dispel the mystery surrounding her background. Despite being the only female ruler of the Hasmonean state, Josephus records nothing about her parents. Because he identifies Alexandra as a lawful Hasmonean monarch, and does not state that she married into this family, it is plausible that she was a Hasmonean by birth.[9]

Alexandra and the Rise of the Pharisees

Josephus reluctantly admires Alexandra in his *War*. He portrays her as a forceful, dynamic, and powerful ruler. But he changed his mind about her when he wrote his *Antiquities*. In this book he stresses her lack of leadership and her gullibility; he highlights how easily the Pharisees tricked her into yielding power to them. He describes her as pathetic, submissive, and inconsolable when she learns her husband is dying. She does not think of her nation, but, Josephus writes, "when she realized that he was at the point of death with no possibility of recovering, she wept and beat her breast, fearful of what was about to befall her and her children."[10] It is Jannaeus who summons up the fortitude and courage

6. Fitzmyer 2000b, 284.

7. Fitzmyer (2000b, 284) accepts Wise's (1994, 208–10) proposal that the word ending in *bet* is the end of the name of a priestly course during which this action occurred. It could be either יהויריב or אלישיב, but apparently, as Wise suggests, the former ("in Jehoiarib Hyrcanus rebelled against Aristobulus").

8. There are no known coins of Alexandra. She presumably used those minted by her husband. If any were produced during her reign, they do not contain her name and therefore no Hasmonean coins can be attributed to her. See further Meshorer 2011, 42; Schürer et al. 1973–87, 1:228 n. 1. Although Regev (2013, 217) believes Jannaeus coins were minted after his death, there is no clear numismatic evidence for this thesis.

9. Ilan (1987, 3) assumes, without any evidence, that she was related to the Hasmoneans by marriage.

10. *Ant.* 13.398.

to save Judea. He accomplishes this by concocting an ingenious plan to trick the Pharisees into naming her as his successor. Jannaeus orders her to conceal his death from the army until she has captured the fortress, and then upon her return to Jerusalem to "yield a certain amount of power to the Pharisees."[11]

The different portrayals of the Pharisees in the *War* and the *Antiquities* may account for the conflicting accounts of Alexandra's reign.[12] In his *War*, Josephus depicts the Pharisees as a religious party that played a minimal role in politics. He states they were not closely associated with the anti-Roman rebels. In his *Antiquities*, however, he emphasizes that the Pharisees had been actively involved in politics. He blames them for the failure of her reign and claims they actually held the reins of power and determined her domestic and foreign policy.[13] According to Josephus, Alexandra favored the Pharisees and allowed them to seek revenge against those who persuaded her husband to crucify 800 of his enemies.[14]

Josephus did not intend to write a comprehensive account of the relationships between the various forms of Jewish sectarianism and the Hasmonean monarchy. Nevertheless, he provides a significant amount of information about the Hasmoneans and their religious beliefs that allows us to reconstruct their sectarian affiliations. His accounts agree that Alexandra's reign witnessed remarkable halakhic changes.[15] According to Josephus, Alexandra allied herself with the Pharisees and allowed them to restore all the regulations that had been abolished since the time of John Hyrcanus.[16] This suggests that Jannaeus allowed the Sadducees to dominate the temple cult throughout his entire reign. The Pharisees achieved unprecedented political power in her administration.[17] Her son Hyrcanus II, whom she appointed as high priest, must have also been a Pharisee since Josephus wrote that during her reign this sect dominated all matters that involved religion.[18] His brother, Aristobulus II, apparently remained a Sadducee like his father since, according to Josephus, he opposed the Pharisees.[19] Aristobulus II also stayed close to his father's

11. *Ant.* 13.400.

12. Rasp (1924) attributed the different portrayals of the Pharisees in the works of Josephus to the political changes that took place in Rome that altered his social circumstances and his attitude towards the Romans.

13. *Ant.* 13.409–11.

14. *Ant.* 13.410; *War* 1.110–12. See further Atkinson 2001b.

15. Atkinson 2012c, 161–73.

16. *Ant.* 13.408.

17. *Ant.* 13.408–18; *War* 1.107–14.

18. *Ant.* 13.408–10.

19. *Ant.* 13.423.

supporters and challenged Alexandra when she allowed the Pharisees to execute some partisans of Jannaeus.[20] Because the Pharisees were among the major enemies of Jannaeus, they were presumably among the most ardent opponents of Aristobulus II. The support Alexandra gave to the Pharisees during her reign worsened longstanding tensions between this religious sect and the Sadducees that largely began during her husband's period in office.

The account of the deathbed advice Jannaeus gave to Alexandra in the *Antiquities* shows that he had mistreated the Pharisees during his time in power, and that they had threatened to undermine the Hasmonean dynasty. Steve Mason suggests that the plan of Jannaeus for his wife to favor the Pharisees is both anti-Pharisaic and pro-Hasmonean, and therefore comes from Josephus and not Nicolaus of Damascus.[21] Jacob Neusner, however, proposes that this story has been revised to favor the Pharisees.[22] Daniel Schwartz observes that the language in *Ant.* 13.400–402 is similar to the editorial remarks in *Ant.* 13.288 and therefore comes from the same source, which he believes is Nicolaus of Damascus.[23] Although Josephus certainly consulted earlier works to write his account of Alexandra, we cannot determine the extent to which he revised them. Yet the common vocabulary in many of Josephus's presumed excerpts from his sources, particularly passages he possibly obtained from Nicolaus of Damascus, indicate that he did not copy them verbatim. Rather, he not only rewrote them, but he also determined what materials to insert, omit, and ignore. For these reasons, Josephus must be considered the author of these materials since they reflect his interests. This means that it is difficult, and highly conjectural, to attempt to determine the extent to which Nicolaus or the other writers Josephus consulted portrayed Alexandra and other women negatively.[24]

The deathbed speech of Jannaeus in the *Antiquities* is, as Mason suggests, almost certainly "formulated (or freely invented)" by Josephus since it displays many of the hallmarks of his rhetorical style.[25] It was written to show that Jannaeus's cynical view of the Pharisees was correct: they would accept the monarchy—even a female ruler—if they were given power. Unlike the *War*, in which Alexandra gave the Pharisees

20. *Ant.* 13.108–15; *War* 113–14.
21. Mason 1991, 248–54.
22. Neusner 1973, 60.
23. D. Schwartz 1983, 159.
24. For portrayals of women at this time, see also Atkinson 2001b; 2003b, 37–53; 2012c, 103–73.
25. Mason 1991, 250–52.

positions of influence because of her religious devotion to them, in the *Antiquities* she does so in order to maintain political sovereignty over the nation. Josephus often tends to give them the credit for her successes, and often blames them for her purported misdeeds.

Alexandra's Preparation for the Monarchy

Josephus implies in his *Antiquities* that Alexandra assumed a position of political authority before her husband bequeathed his kingdom to her. The evidence is found in his account of the Herodian dynasty that he likely copied from an earlier source. In a later section of the *Antiquities*, he states that Antipas, the grandfather of Herod the Great, came to political power when "King Alexander and his wife (= Alexandra) made him general of all Idumaea."[26] This passage may suggest that she exercised some royal powers at the time of this appointment.[27] Josephus does not mention that she held any political authority prior to her reign. If she did hold any executive powers, it was likely during her husband's final three years when he was fatally ill (ca. 79–76 B.C.E.). A plausible date for the promotion of Antipas would be sometime before 79 B.C.E. when Jannaeus was still physically active and able to campaign. Appointing his wife as his co-ruler, and Antipas as governor of Idumaea to reduce the danger of revolts to the south, would have helped to stabilize his kingdom during his infirmity.[28] This may explain why Alexandra became ruler instead of her two sons: Jannaeus likely appointed her as his successor several years before his death to ensure the survival of the Hasmonean monarchy. He also may have decided to restore the ancient separation of sacerdotal and secular powers and name his wife as his political successor to keep his family on the throne. It is plausible that he believed Alexandra—although a woman—alone in the family possessed the religious zeal and military might of Mattathias necessary to hold her nation together. If so, events proved him correct: Alexandra began her reign with a great victory at Ragaba and was a zealous follower of Jewish law. Even Josephus praised her piety: something he does not do for any other Hasmonean ruler. She greatly enlarged the Hasmonean state: after her death it rapidly diminished in size.[29]

---

26. *Ant.* 14.10.
27. Atkinson 2012c, 146.
28. *Ant.* 13.395–96; Kokkinos 1998, 94–95; Schürer et al. 1973–87, 1:226. Cf. Gruen 2016, 230.
29. *War* 1.111.

Political and Religious Strife during the Reign of Alexandra

Josephus praises Alexandra for her piety and her administrative abilities in his *War*. In this book he emphasizes that "she was indeed most precise" (ἠκρίβου γὰρ δὴ μάλιστα) in observance of Jewish law and expelled religious offenders from office (*War* 1.108). In the *War*, he makes a clear separation between the devout Alexandra and her impious husband. He portrays her as naive: she became easy prey for the Pharisees. They took advantage of her piety to dominate her administration. In the *Antiquities*, Josephus removes his earlier passage in his *War* that praises her "precise" observance of Jewish law. In the opening section of her reign in this book he describes her as carefully plotting, in conjunction with her husband, to placate the Pharisees so her family could continue to rule. Her solution is to court them. In the words of Steve Mason, in the *Antiquities* "Alexandra thus appears as a calculating politician."[30]

Josephus portrays the Pharisees as the major supporters of Alexandra. But he invented many of his disparaging remarks about them. This is clear from Josephus's Greek text. His account of the deathbed speech of Jannaeus in the *Antiquities* is similar to his story of the defection of John Hyrcanus from the Pharisees. According to Josephus, he left this sect when a man named Eleazar—it is implied he was a Pharisee—challenged the right of Jannaeus to serve as high priest. He claimed the mother of Jannaeus had been a captive during the reign of Antiochus IV Epiphanes and that his serving as high priest, in light of this unfortunate incident, violated the genealogical qualifications of Lev 21:14.[31]

In the story of the defection of John Hyrcanus from the Pharisees Josephus inserts an editorial remark in *Ant.* 13.288–98 to explain what the Pharisaic νόμιμα were. This section is widely regarded as Josephus's own contribution because it contains five words that he commonly uses in his books: τὰ νόμιμα, ἀναγράφω, οἱ πατέρες, παραδίδωμι/παράδοσίς and διαδοχή ("the ordinances," "to record or write down officially," "the people," "transmit/transmission," "succession").[32] Mason has emphasized that there are strong verbal parallels between this passage and the deathbed speech of Jannaeus in *Ant.* 13.400–402. These include the following words: φθονοῦντες/φθόνος, παρὰ τῷ πλήθει, πιστεύεσθαι, τι χαλεπὸν λέγωσιν/τι λέγοντες κατά, μάλιστα ("envy," "from the masses,"

30. See further, Mason 1991, 249.
31. Marcus 1966, 374 n. a.
32. For an extensive discussion of this list and additional evidence that Josephus composed this section on the Pharisaic laws, see Mason 1991, 227–45.

"confidence," "very badly treated, as he himself stated").[33] The presence of these same words, in addition to the common themes in these passages and other places in the writings of Josephus, show they are characteristically Josephan and that he invented the deathbed speech of Jannaeus.

The recognition that the accounts of Jewish sectarian conflicts in the *Antiquities* should be attributed to Josephus sheds some important light on his narratives of her reign. He clearly wanted to contrast her failure to acknowledge the corrupt nature of the Pharisees with the wise decision of John Hyrcanus to renounce them and become a Sadducee.[34] Her husband also recognized the potential danger they posed to her unless she appease them. For this reason he portrays the Pharisees as vicious partisan politicians to convince his readers they had deceived Alexandra.

The Damascus Campaign of Alexandra

Josephus summarizes the Damascus expedition of Alexandra, which was her first campaign, in two brief sentences in both of his books. He states it failed to accomplish anything noteworthy.[35] He writes that she sent her son Aristobulus II with her army there to oppose the Iturean leader Ptolemy, the son of Mennaeus, who was harassing the city. This campaign is puzzling because Damascus was too far from Jerusalem for her to control. This expedition also placed her forces in danger since none of the region's leaders would have tolerated her effort to seize this city. The monarch Aretas III—the most powerful ruler in the region—could have attacked and decimated her army to avenge previous incursions into his territory by Jannaeus, as well as her capture of Ragaba. The Seleucids, moreover, could have viewed this campaign as a potential threat to their country since the Hasmoneans in the past had captured several of their major cities and ports. A close look at the geopolitical situation at this time may offer a plausible explanation for her puzzling decision to send troops there.

The city of Damascus dominated Seleucia's eastern border. Many of the region's vital trade routes passed through it. Aretas III captured it in 83/2 B.C.E. after his forces killed Antiochus XII Dionysus in battle.[36] The

---

33. For this list, see Mason 1991, 248–52. In his discussion, Mason rejects the interpretation of D. Schwartz (1983, 159) that this common vocabulary shows this material emanated from Nicolaus of Damascus.

34. *Ant.* 13.293–300.

35. *War* 1.115–16; *Ant.* 13.418.

36. Because the coins of Antiochus XII Dionysus show that he occupied Damascus from 87/6 B.C.E. to 83/2 B.C.E., Aretas III could not have captured the city until 83/2 B.C.E. See further, Houghton and Spaer 1990, 4; Hoover 2007b, 298–99; Hoover, Houghton, and Vesely 2008, 314, 316.

political history of Damascus is obscure for the period from 84/3 B.C.E. to 72/1 B.C.E. Only Josephus reports the occupation of the city by Aretas III following the death of Dionysus.[37] Because the Seleucid monarch Cleopatra Selene minted three coins there between the death of Dionysus and the occupation of the city by Tigranes of Armenia in 72/1 B.C.E., Aretas III did not hold it for long. But the political situation in Damascus was more complicated than Josephus realized. Three coins minted in Damascus in 72/1 B.C.E. contain Cleopatra Selene's portrait. This supports the statement of Josephus that she was ruling over Syria in 72 B.C.E. when Alexandra sent Aristobulus II to Damascus.[38] She somehow lost the city in that year since coins minted in 72/1 B.C.E. show that the Armenian monarch Tigranes (II) was in possession of Damascus.[39] The numismatic evidence suggests that Cleopatra Selene, for reasons not stated in the extant sources, succeeded Aretas III at Damascus sometime prior to the conquest of the city by Tigranes in 72/1 B.C.E.[40] It is possible that Alexandra made an alliance with Aretas III and Selene, and possibly the Iturean ruler Ptolemy, to oppose Tigranes.[41]

Lucullus and Tigranes: The Impact of their Fighting for Understanding the Reign of Alexandra

The activity of the Armenian monarch Tigranes in the region may provide some additional background information that could explain why the Seleucids, the Nabateans, and the Itureans possibly made an alliance with Alexandra. Tigranes began construction of his new capital of Tigranocerta after his campaigns in Commagene and Syria. He forcibly transplanted Greeks from Cilicia, Cappadocia, and other regions there.[42] He also moved many citizens there from his strategic fortified river crossing at Jebel Khalid on the west bank of the Euphrates. He also settled Arabs in the Amanus region to guard one of the main roads between the Middle

---

37. *Ant.* 13.392.

38. *Ant.* 13.420; Bellinger 1949, 81–82; Bevan 1902, 263; Ehling 2008, 253–56; Hoover 2005; Macurdy 1932, 171; Grainger 1997, 45.

39. Nercessian 2000, esp. plates 26–27. The numismatic evidence shows that Tigranes produced coins in more than one mint in the city.

40. For this numismatic evidence, see Bellinger 1949, 81; Hoover 2005, 99; 2007b, 296; Newell 1939, 95; N. Wright 2010, 253.

41. For this thesis, see Atkinson 2007, 134–38; 2012c, 210–20.

42. Strabo, *Geogr.* 12.2.9; Plut. *Luc.* 21.4; N. Wright 2011b; cf. Strabo, *Geogr.* 11.14.15.

East and the Aegean.[43] The compulsory movement of these populations should be viewed as part of his effort to annex the entire region. But he did not travel south and threaten the Hasmonean kingdom of Alexandra or her neighbors until approximately 72 B.C.E. when tetradrachms minted in Damascus show that he had captured this city.[44] This placed him in a perfect position to annex the rest of Syria and invade the Hasmonean state. Then the Romans changed everything.

In 74 B.C.E., L. Licinius Lucullus became proconsul of Cilicia.[45] In the spring of 69 B.C.E., he invaded Armenia.[46] The Armenian historian Moses of Khoren suggests this campaign was unauthorized and undertaken without knowledge of the Senate. The classical sources support this claim. Sallust writes that he travelled to Cilicia to gather additional troops and gave the fortress of Tomisa to Ariobarzanes I, the king of Cappadocia, in exchange for provisions during his quick transit through his territory.[47] Lucullus then followed the caravan route from Melitene and secretly crossed the Euphrates.[48] He continued through Sophene to the Tigris River. The accounts of Appian and Plutarch suggest the inhabitants of the area were surprised at his unexpected arrival; they had no option but to surrender and supply his army.[49] Lucullus then travelled part of the "Royal Highway" of Achaemenid Persia through present-day Arghana towards Amid-Diarbekir. He crossed the Tigris River, which was considered the boundary of Armenia at this time, and marched the final 93 miles to Tigranes's new capital city of Tigranocerta.[50] The rapid march of Lucullus across much of present-day Turkey suggests he wanted to reach Armenia before his opponents in the Senate heard about his unauthorized campaign. Lucullus arrived in Tigranocerta in the spring of 69 B.C.E. while Tigranes was in the north. The Romans captured the city after a siege of several months.[51]

43. Cass. Dio 3362.5; Plut. *Luc.* 21.4; 25.5–6; 29.5–6; Plin. *HN* 6.142.

44. Hoover 2007b, 296–97.

45. In 75 B.C.E. he was elected to the consulship of 74 B.C.E. See further Broughton 1952b, 100, 107–8.

46. Plut. *Luc.* 19.1–7. For evidence in support of this date, see further Broughton 1952b, 107–8; Keaveney 2009, 142–47.

47. Strabo, *Geogr.* 5.12.2.1.

48. Sall. *Hist.* 4.60; Memnon, *Historiarum Heracleae Ponti* 56; Plut. *Luc.* 24.

49. App. *Mithr.* 84; Plut. *Luc.* 24.8.

50. For a detailed discussion of Lucullus's route through this region, see further K. Eckhardt 1910, 87–88.

51. The exact location of the city is uncertain. It is traditionally identified with the ruins southwest of Farkin in the valley located at the confluence of the Batman-Su and Farkin-Su Rivers. For this evidence, see K. Eckhardt 1910, 95–96, 102. The

A comparison of the accounts of the siege of Cleopatra Selene in Ptolemais by Tigranes in the works of Josephus and the classical sources may help us further refine the chronology of his invasion of Syria. These texts, which provide us with the route Lucullus took to reach Tigranocerta, allow us to determine his approximate rate of travel. Manandyan suggests that it would have taken Lucullus more than two weeks to march the nearly 186 miles from the Euphrates River to Tigranocerta in the spring of 69 B.C.E. He suggests Lucullus reached Tigranocerta in May of that year.[52] Because it took Lucullus at least two weeks to travel from the Euphrates to Tigranocerta, and a few more months to gather his forces and march from Ephesus to this river, Tigranes could not have departed from Ptolemais later than the first months of 69 B.C.E. We must also add to this estimate sufficient time for Tigranes's messengers to travel from Armenia to Ptolemais and back, and for him to gather his army, evacuate his capital, and prepare to defend his homeland. Because it would have taken considerable time for all these events to have occurred, it is improbable that Tigranes left Ptolemais before Lucullus reached Tigranocerta in May of 69 C.E. His siege of Cleopatra Selene in Ptolemais should also be placed in that year since it preceded the Roman siege of Tigranocerta.

In *War* 1.116 Josephus states that Tigranes was besieging Cleopatra Selene when he received news Lucullus had invaded Armenia. Josephus writes that Tigranes was forced to abandon his siege of Ptolemais and return home to expel Lucullus. However, in *Ant.* 13.421 Josephus writes Tigranes left for Armenia after he had captured Ptolemais. According to this account, Tigranes did not learn that Lucullus had invaded his homeland until after he had taken Ptolemais. There may be a connection between the sieges of Tigranocerta and Ptolemais. The siege of Ptolemais may have prompted Lucullus to attack Armenia. His abrupt and unexpected departure from Ephesus for Armenia suggests he never planned to invade the kingdom of Tigranes. Rather, it was apparently the news that Tigranes was in Syria besieging Cleopatra Selene in Ptolemais that made him realize that Armenia was unprotected. The speed of Lucullus's march across much

---

site of Arzan in the east half of the Tigris basin, along the east bank of the Garzan Su, has been put forth by Sinclair as the site of Tigranocerta. This proposal best accounts for the geographical details mentioned in the extant accounts of the siege and the evidence of the *Tabula Peutingeriana*, which is a fifteenth-century copy of a document that appears to contain descriptions of the region's roads and cities of the second and third centuries C.E. See Sinclair 1994–95; 1996–97. For the siege, see Plut. *Luc.* 26.6–7; 28.1–6; App. *Mithr.* 85; Memnon, *Historiarum Heracleae Ponti* 57; Frontin. *Str.* 2.1.14; 2.4.

52. Manandyan 2007, 80–81.

of present-day Turkey suggests he wanted to reach Tigranocerta while it was largely undefended. It is even probable that he received word on the way to Armenia that Alexandra had delayed Tigranes at Ptolemais.

Contrary to the assertion of Josephus that Tigranes captured Ptolemais, he certainly left the region with no territorial gains. According to Strabo, Tigranes later fought Cleopatra Selene in Syria.[53] This provides additional evidence that his siege of Ptolemais was unsuccessful: he neither captured Cleopatra Selene nor the city. Cleopatra Selene appears to have attacked him from the rear as he was returning home to confront Lucullus; Alexandra did not intervene to save her. Tigranes imprisoned Cleopatra Selene in the fortress of Seleucia, which was across from Zeugma. He ordered her execution in 69 B.C.E. before he returned to Armenia.[54]

Alexandra apparently forced Tigranes to abandon his plans to annex Syrian and Hasmonean territory and end his siege of Ptolemais. In exchange, she allowed him to leave in peace. His detour to deal with Alexandra likely slowed down his return home, and prevented him from saving his capital. This suggests that the action of Alexandra at Ptolemais inadvertently affected the future of the Roman Republic, and allowed it to gain a foothold in the Middle East that Pompey would later use to destroy the Hasmonean state.[55]

The Final Days of Alexandra

Alexandra ruled for nine years. She died in 67 B.C.E. at the age of seventy-three.[56] Josephus suggests she was ill for the two years preceding her death in 69 B.C.E. In his *War* he writes that she gave Hyrcanus II some royal

53. Strabo (*Geogr.* 24.4–8) also does not mention that Tigranes captured Ptolemais.

54. The majority of works on this period fail to recognize that Cleopatra Selene fought Tigranes twice. See, e.g., Bevan 1902, 266, 268; Kuhn 1891, 21, 42; Whitehorne 1994, 171; Schürer et al. 1973–87, 1:134. Manandyan (2007, 41–42, 105) and G. Cohen (2006, 191) recognize that Tigranes fought Cleopatra Selene on two occasions. Ehling (2008, 255–56) writes that Tigranes besieged Ptolemais in 70 C.E. He assumes, based on *Ant.* 13.421, that Tigranes captured and later murdered Cleopatra Selene in Mesopotamia.

55. Tigranes invaded Syria in 84/3 B.C.E. He expelled the Seleucid kings from northern Syria and lowland Cilicia. For fourteen years (83–69 B.C.E.) he ruled much of the Seleucid Empire until he was defeated by the Roman consul Lucullus in 68 B.C.E. During this time Tigranes controlled Antioch. For Tigranes, and the events of this period, see further Just. *Epit.* 40.1.1–3; Strabo, *Geogr.* 11.14.15; Atkinson 2012c, 202–17; Ehling 2008, 246–56; Sherwin-White 1994.

56. *Ant.* 13.430.

powers while she was alive. In the *Antiquities* Josephus correlates his reign with the tenures of the Roman consuls. According to the dates he provides, Hyrcanus II assumed power in early 69 B.C.E. This would mean that he served as her co-ruler for nearly two years.[57]

Josephus writes that Aristobulus organized a coup against his sibling at the end of her life. His assertion that Aristobulus II quickly took his mother's fortresses, and then acquired an army from Lebanon, Trachonitis, and the local princes, suggests that he had planned his revolt in advance.[58] Alexandra gave Hyrcanus II and her supporters the authority to do whatever necessary to stop Aristobulus II from taking power. It is uncertain whether she abdicated, or merely authorized Hyrcanus II to act on her behalf. She died shortly before her children began their civil war.

Josephus concludes his account of Alexandra with a short obituary that summarizes her reign. Although he praises her piety, he portrays her as a pawn of the Pharisees. He even blames her for the end of the Hasmonean dynasty: he claims she left her kingdom "filled with misfortunes and disturbances which arose from the public measures taken during her lifetime."[59] Yet, Josephus also states that she had kept the nation at peace during her time in power.

The death of Alexandra marks the true end of the Hasmonean state. The subsequent infighting between her sons caused the Romans to invade her homeland and terminate the Hasmonean monarchy. Their short reigns were tragic and full of misfortune. However, the Hasmonean family was so popular that the Romans had a difficult time maintaining control over the territories of the former Hasmonean state. The next chapter examines the 63 B.C.E. Roman conquest and the termination of the Hasmonean state by Pompey, and how Alexandra's son, Hyrcanus II, lost and regained his position as high priest.

---

57. *War* 1.120; *Ant.* 14.4. This period could also include part of the year 70 B.C.E.

58. *Ant.* 13.427. Aristobulus II received support from the Nabateans since Josephus mentions that he left Jerusalem and went to Ragaba. The text of this passage is corrupt, and states that he fled to the unknown city of "Agaba" (*Ant.* 13.425). Other Greek manuscripts read "Agabra" while the Latin translation of Josephus contains "Gabatha." The latter two spellings suggest that the original reading was "Ragaba," which is where Josephus later places Aristobulus's base of operation. See *Ant.* 14.4; *War* 1.120; Boettger 1879, 15, 209–10; Niese 1892, 231.

59. *Ant.* 13.432.

Chapter 7

POMPEY AND THE HASMONEANS:
HYRCANUS II, ARISTOBULUS II,
AND THE END OF THE HASMONEAN STATE

The Brief Reign of Hyrcanus II

According to Josephus, Aristobulus II believed the Pharisees would dominate the government if Hyrcanus II became king.[1] Before the death of Alexandra, Aristobulus II staged a coup from Nabatea to prevent his brother from assuming power. Josephus reports that the wife of Aristobulus II was the only person who knew of his plot.[2] She hid her husband's departure from her relatives. After Alexandra realized the magnitude of her daughter-in-law's deception, she confined her and the family of Aristobulus II in the Baris fortress.[3] Alexandra then urged Hyrcanus II and his supporters to do whatever necessary to stop Aristobulus II. Once she died, Hyrcanus II assumed sole power. Aristobulus II immediately declared war against him and assembled an army that included forces from Lebanon, Trachonitis, and the local princes of these regions.[4] The two brothers fought a battle

---

1. *Ant.* 13.423; Atkinson 2013a; 2013d. For the major historical sources for the reigns of Hyrcanus II and Aristobulus II, see *War* 1.120–58; *Ant.* 14.4–79; Flor. 1.40.29–31; Diod. Sic. 40.2.2.

2. *Ant.* 13.424.

3. *Ant.* 13.424; *War* 1.118.

4. Parts of Lebanon and Trachonitis were Iturean territories. Kasher (1990, 108) suggests that Aristobulus II recruited mercenaries from the Itureans and the neighboring tribes. A close reading of Josephus supports Kasher's conjecture. Alexandra sent Aristobulus II to Damascus in 72 B.C.E. because the Iturean ruler Ptolemy, the son of Mennaeus, was threatening the city (*Ant.* 13.418; *War* 1.115). Ptolemy's subsequent relations with Aristobulus II suggest the two made a peace treaty. Ptolemy later took in the orphaned children of Aristobulus II. Ptolemy even married Alexandra, a daughter of Aristobulus II. He also helped a son of Aristobulus II, Antigonus, return to Judea (*Ant.* 14.297). The actions of the Itureans at this time are best explained if Aristobulus II made a treaty with them sometime before his mother's death.

near Jericho. Hyrcanus II lost and fled to Jerusalem. He sought shelter in the Baris fortress where the wife and children of Aristobulus II were still held.[5] Hyrcanus then abruptly abdicated; he had reigned for three months.[6] Josephus writes that the two siblings made a public truce in the temple. According to the *War* (1.121), Aristobulus II gave Hyrcanus II special honors as the king's brother. But in the *Antiquities* (14.7) Josephus claims that Hyrcanus II became a private citizen and moved into his brother's house.

Josephus does not specify when the subsequent breach occurred between the two siblings. He attributes the renewal of hostilities to an Idumean noble named Antipater, father of the future king Herod the Great. Antipater convinced Hyrcanus II to make an alliance with the Aretas III to regain power. In exchange for his support, Hyrcanus II pledged to return to Aretas III lands east of the Jordan River that Jannaeus had annexed. Hyrcanus II and Antipater secretly left Judea for the city of Petra to gather an army to attack Jerusalem.

Josephus emphasizes that Antipater, whom he refers to as an "Idumaea," persuaded Hyrcanus II to remove his brother from power.[7] He also writes that Antipater largely supported Hyrcanus II because he hated Aristobulus II. According to Josephus, Antipater tried to persuade Hyrcanus II that the partisans of Aristobulus II were plotting his assassination and warned him to flee to Nabatea. Antipater eventually managed to convince Hyrcanus II to go with him to Nabatea to ask Aretas III to help them gather forces to overthrow Aristobulus II.

In his narrative of this period, Josephus emphasizes the "ineffectualness and weakness" (ἄπραγμον καὶ τὸ παρειμένον) of Hyrcanus II, which purportedly made him pliable to Antipater's deception. In his accounts he consistently portrays Hyrcanus II as lethargic and Aristobulus II as a hothead.[8] He also stresses that Hyrcanus II was inferior to his brother "in capacity and in intelligence was surpassed by Aristobulus" (δυνάμει

---

5. *War* 1.121.

6. Josephus does not explicitly state in his account of the cessation of hostilities (*War* 1.122; *Ant.* 14.5–6) that Hyrcanus II relinquished the high priesthood when he abdicated. Elsewhere (*Ant.* 14.97; 15.41; 20.243) he specifies that Hyrcanus II simultaneously gave up his positions as monarch and high priest. For the length of his reign, see *Ant.* 15.180. Josephus's accounts of Hyrcanus II and Aristobulus II contain numerous contradictions that are impossible to reconcile.

7. *War* 1.123–26; *Ant.* 14.8–13. For the Idumean ancestry Antipater and his family and the debate over their Jewishness, see S. Cohen 2001, esp. 18–20; Kokkinos 1998, 100–12; Richardson 1996, 40–43.

8. *Ant.* 14.12–13.

δὲ καὶ φρονήματι προεῖχεν ὁ Ἀριστόβουλος).[9] Josephus also implies that Hyrcanus II was a pawn of the Pharisees like his mother. Although the Pharisees were presumably powerful during his short reign, Josephus does not mention them in his accounts of Hyrcanus II. Nevertheless, his statement that they controlled Alexandra is clearly meant to imply that they also dominated Hyrcanus II since he had served as high priest during her nine-year reign. However, Josephus clearly presents a rather simplistic portrayal of the Alexandra's two sons that is designed to emphasize their hatred for one another.

A look at the career of Hyrcanus II suggests that he was an effective leader who was not hesitant to confront powerful individuals and groups. He served two lengthy reigns as high priest (76–67, 63–40 B.C.E.). If we add the time during which he was his mother's co-ruler, then he led his nation in various positions of political and religious leadership for over thirty years. During his second tenure as high priest several factions turned to him for support. Because a later decree of Julius Caesar to the people of Sidon praises Hyrcanus II for his contribution in the Alexandrian War, he certainly commanded troops there.[10] Despite his later disfigurement that rendered him ineligible to serve as high priest, Hyrcanus II was so popular that the public forced Herod the Great to allow him to return from his Parthian exile to Jerusalem. He even compelled Herod the Great to face charges made against him in the Sanhedrin.[11] Herod later felt that he was such a threat to his own reign that he ordered his murder.[12] Because Hyrcanus II managed to reign as high priest for a total of 33 years despite the conquest of his country by Pompey and opposition from Herod the Great, he clearly was a strong-willed person and a competent leader. There is no reason to doubt that Hyrcanus II played a major role in the plot to overthrow Aristobulus II.

The conflict between Hyrcanus II and Aristobulus II in the *War* and the *Antiquities* is shaped by the longstanding disagreements between the Pharisees and the Sadducees as described in these books. Josephus portrays the Pharisees in his *Antiquities* as vicious political partisans. They not only control the government, but they behaved violently against their enemies. Steve Mason writes of Josephus's depiction of them: "It is perfectly clear that Josephus sides with Aristobulus II and the leading citizens against

9. *War* 1.120.
10. *Ant.* 14.353. For evidence that Hyrcanus II fought in Alexandria, see VanderKam 2004, 353; Richardson 1996, 106–8.
11. *War* 1.210–15; *Ant.* 14.168–74.
12. *Ant.* 15.164.

Alexandra and her Pharisaic sponsors."[13] Because he believed the Pharisees played a major role in the termination of the Hasmonean dynasty, Josephus tends to denigrate Alexandra in the *Antiquities* because she brought them to power. As a consequence, his portrayal of Hyrcanus II often reflects his disdain for Alexandra: it is frequently inaccurate and overlooks his strengths. For Josephus, the infighting between Hyrcanus II and Aristobulus II not only led to the end of the Hasmonean state, but it was the direct result of their mother's reign. The historical evidence suggests that Hyrcanus II receives the worse treatment in Josephus's accounts. But there is an even greater reason why Josephus tends to portray him so negatively in his books: the effort of Hyrcanus II to regain power was the event that brought the Romans to Jerusalem and ended the Hasmonean state.

The Arrival of the Romans

In 65 B.C.E. Hyrcanus II, with the support of Aretas III, besieged the partisans of Aristobulus II in the temple in a bid to regain power. This assault occurred during Passover. Because the priests did not have sufficient animals for the festival they had to curtail the sacrifices. Josephus writes that only the priests remained loyal to Aristobulus II.[14] They agreed to pay one thousand drachma per animal; however, the supporters of Hyrcanus II kept the money. The priests then prayed for divine retribution. Josephus claims their petition was answered by a violent wind that destroyed crops throughout the Judean countryside and caused a famine.[15] This particular episode is significant because it places the priests among the partisans of Aristobulus II two years prior to the 63 B.C.E. siege of Jerusalem by Pompey. It suggests they provided much of Aristobulus II's support at this time, and during the later Roman conquest of the city.

---

13. Mason 1991, 54. Cf. Seeman 2013, 230–31.

14. *Ant.* 14.20.

15. Josephus (*Ant.* 14.22) also includes a story about how the supporters of Hyrcanus II murdered Onias (a.k.a. Honi), because he refused to curse the partisans of Aristobulus II. Onias instead prayed to God to prevent both factions from killing anyone. The Mishnah (*m. Ta'an* 3:8) also includes a story in which Onias successfully prayed for rain. See also *b. Ta'an* 23q; *y. Ta'an* 3:10; 66:4. The Talmud records a parallel, but greatly embellished, tradition about how Hyrcanus II prevented the priests from observing Passover during the siege and purportedly sent them a pig for the sacrifice. See *b. Menah.* 64b.

Pompey sent his envoy M. Aemilius Scaurus to Judea to investigate its political situation.[16] He arrived while Hyrcanus II was besieging Aristobulus II in Jerusalem. Both brothers sent delegations to meet him. Aristobulus II offered him 400 talents; Hyrcanus II promised him the same amount.[17] Josephus reports that Scaurus believed Aristobulus II was the stronger of the two siblings. He also implies that Scaurus considered Hyrcanus II untrustworthy. Josephus claims the Romans ultimately favored Aristobulus II because they believed he could fulfill his promises to them, and presumably serve as a loyal ally and help them stabilize the region. Scaurus returned to Damascus. In his absence Aristobulus II, with troops lent by Scaurus, attacked and killed 6,000 soldiers from the army of Aretas III. Antipater's brother Phallion was slain during the battle.[18]

The accounts of Josephus for this period are not in chronological order. He duplicates his story of Pompey's arrival in Syria. Paragraphs 34–36 of Book 14 of the *Antiquities*, which has no equivalent in the *War*, appears to describe events that took place in 63 B.C.E. The subsequent section, paragraphs 37–40, document the meeting of autumn of 64 B.C.E. when envoys from both brothers appeared before Pompey in Syria. At that time Antipater spoke on behalf of Hyrcanus II while a man named Nicodemus represented Aristobulus II.[19] Both Josephus and Diodorus state that three Jewish groups met Pompey in Damascus: the partisans of Hyrcanus II, the supporters of Aristobulus II, and a crowd that requested the abolition of the Hasmonean monarchy.[20] The faction seeking independence from the

16. Scaurus was Pompey's Questor in 66 B.C.E. and Promagistrate from 65 to 61 B.C.E. He subsequently held several high political positions until he was charged with corruption and exiled. See further Bucher 1995. For the details of Scaurus's career, see further Broughton 1952b, 159–80; Klebs 1929; Schürer et al. 1973–87, 1:244–45; D. Schwartz 2000.

17. The two accounts of Josephus often differ in their details. *War* (1.128) states that the "300 talents offered by Aristobulus outweighed considerations of justice."

18. For the suggestion that Scaurus helped Aristobulus II attack the Arabs, see Leach 1978, 91. For these events, and a discussion of Josephus's problematic and contradictory narratives of this time, see Greenhalgh 1981a, 138–46; Schürer et al. 1973–87, 1:233–42.

19. For the misplacement of these sections, see further Laqueur 1920, 153–54; Smallwood 1981, 22 n. 3, 153–54. For this meeting, see also Diod. Sic. 40.2.2. According to Cass. Dio (37.7.5) Pompey spent the winter of 65/4 B.C.E. in the unknown town of Aspis. Because he was still active in Asia Minor at this time, Gelzer (1959, 108) and Schürer et al. (1973–87, 1:237 n. 13) suggest that he spent the winter of 64/3 B.C.E. in Antioch. See also Seager 1979, 52–55.

20. *Ant.* 14.41; Diod. Sic. 40.2. For a discussion of variants in the text of Diodorus Siculus pertaining to this event, see further Fischer 1975.

Hasmoneans asked Pompey to establish a priestly form of government. It is difficult to determine when these delegations appeared before Pompey because Josephus's description of this contentious meeting in *Ant.* 14.41–45 likely belongs with the preceding paragraphs (*Ant.* 14.37–40), which describes the conference between Pompey and the Jewish parties in Syria. Benedikt Eckhardt suggests that the account of the third delegation, which asked for the restoration of a theocracy, is not historical since there is no evidence that it was contrary to Jewish tradition to be dominated by a king.[21] Because the high priests had led Judea during the post-exilic period, it is probable that some disaffected elements of the population wanted the restoration of the older theocratic form of government. There is no reason to doubt the existence of a faction that rejected the monarchy, especially since the Hasmoneans had no scriptural basis to reign as kings.

The account of the meeting between Pompey and the two Hasmonean brothers in the *Antiquities* is confusing. Josephus writes that Nicodemus, a partisan of Aristobulus II, told Pompey that the Roman officials Scaurus and Gabinius had accepted money from Aristobulus II. Pompey ordered both siblings to appear before him in Damascus the following spring. His decision to allow Aristobulus II to remain as king and high priest clearly shows that he still favored him over Hyrcanus II. In the meanwhile, Pompey conquered the rulers of several adjacent regions before he arrived in Damascus. He undertook this campaign to halt Nabatean territorial expansion in preparation for his planned campaign against Aretas III. The list of those Pompey fought includes a mysterious Jew named Silas who held a fortress at the unknown site of Lysias.[22] Josephus reports that Pompey also devastated the country of the Iturean monarch Ptolemy, the son of Mennaeus. Unlike the other rulers, Pompey allowed him to escape punishment and remain in control of his lands in exchange for a thousand talents.[23] It is probable that Aristobulus II may have convinced Pompey that Ptolemy was still a Hasmonean ally and that the Itureans would remain loyal to the Romans. This would account for the support the Itureans subsequently provided to Aristobulus II and his descendants.

The two Hasmonean brothers met Pompey in the spring of 63 B.C.E. Aristobulus II gave him a golden grapevine worth 500 talents that Strabo claims to have seen exhibited in the temple of Jupiter Capitolinius in

21. B. Eckhardt 2013.

22. *Ant.* 14.40. The *Tabula Peutingeriana* places a city called Lyca between Jerusalem and Elath (Aila). It is uncertain whether it is identical with the city of Lysias mentioned by Strabo (*Geogr.* 16.2.40). See G. Cohen 2006, 263–64. See also Boettger 1879, 164.

23. *Ant.* 14.39.

Rome.[24] Hyrcanus II claimed he was entitled to the throne because he was the eldest son of Jannaeus. He also accused Aristobulus II of piracy.[25] Aristobulus II told Pompey that he had been compelled to take power to prevent his nation from falling into worse hands. Josephus implies that he also accused Antipater, and the Nabateans, of taking advantage of the timid Hyrcanus II to control Judea.[26]

It is difficult to understand the two accounts of Josephus concerning the Jewish groups that met Pompey since they are not in chronological order. In his *Antiquities* he writes that Pompey condemned Aristobulus II for his violence. However, he also claims that Pompey treated him with deference because he feared he might incite an anti-Roman rebellion throughout Judea.[27] According to Josephus, Aristobulus II confirmed Pompey's suspicion when he travelled to Dium and then unexpectedly left for Judea to oppose the Romans.[28]

24. Strabo *apud* Josephus, *Ant.* 14.34–36. Some of the manuscript variants suggest that Jannaeus actually made this vine and that it bore his name. Aristobulus II may have given it to Pompey because of its value. See further, M. Stern 1974–80, 1:275.

25. *Ant.* 14.43. It appears that this section is a continuation of the narrative of the events described in paragraphs 34–36 since it describes the actual meeting between Pompey and the two Hasmonean brothers.

26. In *Ant.* 14.42–33, Josephus states that Hyrcanus II was ruling "a small part of the country" (μικρὸν ἔχοι μέρος τῆς χώρας ὑφ᾽ αὐτῷ, τὴν δὲ ἄλλην Βίᾳ λαβὼν Ἀριστόβουλος). This may refer to Idumaea, which is the one area over which Antipater had influence. Earlier (*Ant.* 14.6–7), however, Josephus wrote that Hyrcanus II had given up all his territory. It is possible that Hyrcanus II, due to the influence of Antipater, acquired a subordinate administrative post in Idumaea. For this possibility, see Smallwood 1981, 22 n. 4.

27. *Ant.* 14.47.

28. Dium is an emendation; it is sometimes spelled Dion. The manuscripts are corrupt and contain several variant spellings. Stephanus Byzantius (s.v. Δία) indicates that Dium was near Pella. See further, Boettger 1879, 104; Niese 1892, 247; 1894, 30; Schürer et al. 1973–87, 2:148. Josephus mentions it five times (*Ant.* 13.393; 14.47–49; 15.111; *War* 1.132, 366). Dium was among the most important cities in the region. It belonged to the Decapolis, which Pliny (*Nat.* 5.16.74) lists as Damascus, Philadelphia, Raphana, Scythopolis, Gadara, Hippos, Diun, Pella, Gerasa, and Canatha. The collective term "Decapolis" was linked to the submission of the region's rulers by Pompey in 64/3 B.C.E. For this evidence, see Lichtenberger 2003, 6–20. Josephus's accounts show that Dium was along the road from Damascus to Judea and in the possession of the Hasmoneans until Pompey's arrival. Because Dium is also the name of an important Macedonian town as well as several other cities in Northern Greece, it is possible that it was named after one of these places. The most probable location for Dium is Tel Ash'ari in the northern Transjordan where funerary stelae have been discovered that bear dates according to a new city era that begins in

Josephus does not explain why Aretas II went to Dium. He suggests that he did so at the request of Pompey.[29] Aristobulus II was expected to accomplish some unrecorded mission there to prepare for the Roman invasion of Nabatea. For reasons unexplained, Josephus reports that he subsequently left Dium and went to the Judean fortress of Alexandrium.[30] Because of his unexpected departure from Dium, Pompey no longer trusted Aristobulus II. Pompey immediately abandoned his planned invasion of Nabatea and set out with his army to pursue him.[31] But why did Pompey send Aristobulus II to Dium and what happened there?

If the identification of Dium as Tel Ash'ari is correct, this helps us understand its importance for Pompey. This city was located in the contested borderland between the Jews and the Nabateans. It was the location Pompey planned to use as his base from which to enter Nabatean territory. But there was a major problem with using Dium as a base of operations. Stephanus Byzantinus mentions that it was unhealthy because of its poisonous water. If this is Dium that Aristobulus II was sent to garrison, then he needed to supply it with potable water so Pompey's troops could use it as a base to invade Nabatea.[32] Aristobulus II—either willingly to undermine Pompey's campaign or through sheer ineptitude despite his best efforts to assist the Romans—clearly failed to make the necessary preparations. This forced Pompey to abandon his planned invasion of Nabatea.[33] It was a costly failure for him, both politically and monetarily. It caused him to turn against Aristobulus II and back Hyrcanus II.

64 B.C.E. Although two unused coins bearing the name "Dium" were found at Tel Ash'ari, because coins are highly portable objects they cannot be used to confirm the site's identification. Although Tel al-Husn, close to Aydoun near Irbid, is also identified as Dium, surveys make this improbable since no Roman road reached it. The Roman-era archaeological remains, its proximity to a major Roman road, and the historical sources appear to support the identification of Dium with Tel Ash'ari. See further Mittmann 1964, 134 n. 36; G. Cohen 2006, 245–47; Schürer et al. 1973–87, 2:148–49.

29. *War* 1.132.

30. *War* 1.122–34.

31. *War* 1.122–34.

32. Stephanus Byzantinus even quotes from an epigram warns against drinking Dium's water. For this text, see Athanassiadi 1999, 302–3, no. 135.

33. Pompey recognized the importance of the Nabateans in the region's trade and planned to annex their territory for its wealth. See further van Ooteghem 1954, 228, 237–38; Abel 1947; Bellmore 1999; 2000; Sarte 1979.

The Romans at this time considered the Seleucid Empire part of the spoils of war connected with their subjugation of Tigranes. Pompey believed this gave him the legal authority to annex the Seleucid Empire, which they apparently believed included Judea.[34] The Romans appear to have adopted previous Seleucid policy when it came to their administration of the Hasmonean state. The Heliodorus Stele shows that the Seleucid rulers earlier had tried to exercise the same control over the Jerusalem temple and the royal administration in Coele-Syria and Phoenicia they already had accomplished elsewhere by taking direct control of the shrines in their territories. This included the Jerusalem temple and its priests.[35] Pompey apparently considered the Seleucid dynasty terminated following the Roman defeat of Tigranes, and adopted a similar view of the Hasmoneans. He regarded the Hasmonean monarchs merely as local rulers of a region of the former Seleucid Empire that was now under the jurisdiction of Rome.[36] Therefore, he could do whatever he wanted with the Hasmonean state. Pompey merely treated Aristobulus II the same as he had Antiochus XIII: he annexed both their kingdoms because he regarded their lands as the rightful property of the Roman Republic.[37] Pompey's earlier meeting with Alexandra's sons may account for his decision to terminate the Hasmonean monarchy and take direct control of Judea.

Diodorus preserves a slightly expanded account of Pompey's relationship with the two Hasmonean siblings. He describes a meeting between Hyrcanus II, Aristobulus II, and Pompey that took place in Damascus. He claims that Pompey denounced Hyrcanus II at this gathering for the "lawless behavior of the Jews" (παρανομίας τῶν Ἰουδαίων) against Rome. Pompey, according to Diodorus, threatened to invade Judea to remove Hyrcanus II from power.[38] Josephus writes that Hyrcanus II accused Aristobulus II of raiding neighboring territories and committing acts of piracy at sea.[39] Laqueur suggests that Josephus took the reference to

34. See Sartre 2005, 38–39.

35. See further Atkinson 2013c, 8–16.

36. See further van Ooteghem 1954, 226–30; Baltrusch 2002, 125–32; Shatzman 1999, 79.

37. The Roman consul Lucullus defeated Tigranes and replaced him in Syria with Antiochus XIII Asiaticus in 69 B.C.E. Asiaticus ruled a small territory centered around Antioch until Pompey deposed him in 65/4 B.C.E. See further Assar 2006a, 60; Hoover 2009, 279, 299–300; Ehling 2008, 256–77.

38. Diod. Sic. 40.2.2. The parallel account preserved by Flor. (1.40.29–31) is unreliable. He suggests that the two brothers met Pompey after the defeat of Aristobulus II and states that the Arabs were ready to help Pompey attack Jerusalem.

39. *Ant.* 14.43.

pirates in *Ant.* 14.43 from Theophanes.[40] The allegation of piracy in the *Antiquities* replaces the theme in *War* (1.128) that Hyrcanus II had justice on his side: in *War* he did not resort to bribery to win Pompey's support.

The accusation that Aristobulus II had engaged in piracy, if factual, only could have taken place during his brother's reign. Hyrcanus II ruled in 67 B.C.E. Because this was also the year of Pompey's war against pirates, if there is any truth to the account of Josephus it is more probable that Hyrcanus II, and not his sibling, was accused of involvement in piracy. Hyrcanus II was in power at the time; he had been his mother's co-ruler for the preceding years.[41] It is probable that pirates operated from the Judean coast during his tenure, either with or without his consent. Nevertheless, the Romans would have held him responsible for any such activity regardless of whether or not he was involved.

Pompey's campaign to protect the Mediterranean trade routes was part of a larger Roman operation against banditry in the Mediterranean.[42] He

40. Theophanes wrote his works between 63 and 40 B.C.E. Despite his support for Pompey, Julius Caesar forgave him. Theophanes eventually returned to Italy. See further, Harvey 2013; Laqueur 1920; Yarrow 2006. Bellmore (1999, 107–18) suggests that Josephus used local Jewish works in his *War* and consulted Nicolaus of Damascus, Strabo, and Livy for the material about Pompey in the *Antiquities*. Josephus's incorporation of selected materials from these writers, she believes, accounts for his different portrayals of events. It is also possible that these writers used other unknown sources. Because Strabo and Diodorus Siculus consulted Theophanes, it is probable that Josephus obtained information from his work through quotations or summaries in these later writers.

41. For this view, see Laqueur 1920, 153–54. It is plausible that some Jews engaged in piracy along the coasts between Cilicia and Judea during the reign of Hyrcanus II. See, Zonar. 10.5. This is possible since Pompey gave many of the pirate's clemency. Some settled along the Mediterranean coast, where they may have returned to piracy on a smaller scale. It is also plausible that these pirates settled in Hasmonean territory, which at this time was not under direct Roman control. See further, Greenhalgh 1981b, 91–100. For piracy in Phoenicia, see Sarte 2005, 32–34, 37–38. Josephus provides some indirect support for Jewish piracy when he mentions that Pompey later cut the Jews off from the sea by removing their harbors from their control (*War* 1.156). This suggests that Pompey felt that the Jews, presumably because of some unrecorded past action by their rulers, could not be trusted with possession of these ports.

42. Shatzman (1999, 79–80) comments that Pompey's commission to eradicate pirates effectively acknowledged Roman supremacy over the world. Many Romans believed that it gave him the right to campaign where he wished because by this time the Roman Republic believed that its power should extended everywhere. Earlier, in 100 B.C.E., the Roman Republic passed a law (*lex de piratis persequendis*) that

and his legates pursued brigands on the coast from Lycia to Phoenicia, as well as the Amanus passes. It is probable that Pompey suspected Hyrcanus II of failing to eradicate pirates in the region, which may have been another factor that led the Romans to end the Hasmonean monarchy and take direct control over the country by besieging Jerusalem. Unlike their Hasmonean ancestors, the Roman Republic did not consider Alexandra's sons trustful allies.

The 63 B.C.E. Roman Siege of Jerusalem

The decision of Pompey to abandon his campaign against Aretas III and attack Jerusalem before he returned to Asia Minor shows the importance of the Hasmonean state. Pompey was clearly worried about a possible alliance between the Nabateans and the Jews. He feared this could threaten Rome's control over the region and the Mediterranean. Because he presumably could not spend much time in Judea since his presence was required to deal with Tigranes and the former kingdom of Mithridates VI, Pompey needed an ally to capture Jerusalem quickly. The surviving sources suggest that Hyrcanus II played a major role in the Roman victory.

According to Josephus and Cassius Dio, civil war quickly erupted in Jerusalem between the supporters of both brothers. The partisans of Aristobulus II took refuge in the Temple Mount. Hyrcanus II fulfilled Pompey's expectations for a client when he convinced his partisans to open Jerusalem's gates and surrendered its palaces to the Roman legions.[43] Pompey pitched his camp to the north of Jerusalem, which was the Temple Mount's only vulnerable side. Although he was in possession of the Upper City, and had the support of Hyrcanus II, his forces still faced considerable obstacles. The Temple Mount was protected by deep valleys on all but its northern wall. It was also surrounded by a high wall with defensive towers. A fosse 60 feet in depth and 250 feet in width protected its northern wall.[44] The Baris fortress was attached to the northwest corner of the Temple Mount and provided further defense to this vulnerable section

required the Seleucid and Ptolemaic rulers to stop pirates in the Mediterranean. See Pestman 1967, 72, 156. This law shows that the Roman Republic at this time expected the nations of the Middle East to comply with its edicts and that it was especially concerned with piracy there.

43. See *Ant.* 14.79; *War* 1.157–58; Cass. Dio 37.15.2–17.4; Plut. *Pomp.* 39.3.

44. *Ant.* 14.58; *War* 1.143. For Jerusalem's defenses and the location of Pompey's attack, see further Strabo, *Geogr.* 16.2.34–46. For archaeological evidence of this fosse, and the location of the Baris fortress at this time, see Bahat 1996, 44–45; van Ooteghem 1954, 232–33; Smallwood 1981, 24–25.

of the city's fortifications. The partisans of Aristobulus II destroyed the bridge that spanned the ravine that connected the Temple Mount with the Upper City, which was difficult for the Roman forces to approach.

Pompey ordered his men to cut down the trees around Jerusalem to construct earthworks and platforms for his siege engines that he had brought from Tyre.[45] His troops filled in the fosse and then battered the city's northern walls and towers. Nevertheless, despite the size and equipment of the Roman army, it took Pompey's forces three months to capture the Temple Mount. According to Josephus, the priests continued to perform their duties while his soldiers entered through a breach in the wall. The Romans and some partisans of Hyrcanus II killed many of them; others committed suicide. Josephus reports that 12,000 perished during the final assault; the Romans suffered minimal casualties.[46] Although Pompey did not plunder the sanctuary, he entered the Holy of Holies.[47] He also took Aristobulus II to Rome and later forced him to march in his triumph.[48] Hyrcanus II was allowed to remain as high priest to keep order, but was forbidden from taking the title "king." It looked like the Hasmonean state was over. But the Romans underestimated the resilience of the Hasmonean family and their supporters: many of them would continue to fight the Romans to regain their independence.

45. *Ant.* 13.62.

46. *Ant.* 14.69–70; *War* 1.149–51. The *War* says that 12,000 perished while manuscripts of the former read 22,000. See Niese 1892, 251.

47. *Ant.* 14.72; *War* 1.152. Cicero (*Flac.* 28.670) insists that Pompey did not lay his hands on any item in the Jerusalem Temple.

48. Pompey also took two sons, Alexander and Antigonus, and two daughters of Aristobulus II to Rome. Absalom, the uncle and father-in-law of Aristobulus II, was among the captives. *Ant.* 14.71, 79; *War* 1.154, 157–58; Plut. *Pomp.* 39.2; 45.4; App. *Mithr.* 116–17. For Pompey's triumph, which was held September 21, 61 B.C.E., see Vell. Pat. 240.3; Plin. *HN* 7.97–98; Broughton 1952b, 181; Girardet 1991. For Jewish responses to Pompey's termination of the Hasmonean monarchy, see Atkinson 2001a, 414–16; 2003a; 2004, 64–86; 2012a; 2015c.

Chapter 8

AFTER THE ROMAN CONQUEST

Judea after the Departure of Pompey

None of our extant sources acknowledge it, but something was clearly wrong in the former Hasmonean state after Pompey's 63 B.C.E. conquest of Jerusalem. The escape of Alexander, one of the two sons of Aristobulus II, from his Roman captivity provides proof that the Romans were not fully in control of the former Hasmonean kingdom. His return required a sophisticated level of organized support among the Jewish community of Europe and the Middle East. He managed to travel by land, and possibly sea, undetected and return to Judea. Unlike Hyrcanus II, Aristobulus II and his sons remained persistent enemies of Rome following the events of 63 B.C.E.[1] They personified the religious zeal and military might of Mattathias, and desired the removal of all foreigners from Jewish soil. Alexander quickly amassed 10,000 heavily-armed soldiers and 1,500 cavalry to fight the Romans. When Hyrcanus II realized Alexander was back, he panicked. He even began to repair Jerusalem's wall in defiance of Pompey's edict that it not be rebuilt.[2]

Alexander's support was considerable, for Josephus states that he captured the strongholds of Alexandrium and Machaerus.[3] Gabinius sent his second-in-command, Mark Antony, with some soldiers to Judea to prevent him from taking control of the country. Antony's troops included Jewish contingents commanded by Malichus and Peitholaus. Gabinius arrived shortly afterwards with infantry. Josephus suggests he was unable to contain the situation when he mentions that Antony armed some Romans already living there.[4] The identity of these men is unknown; they were

---

1. See further, Baumann 1983, 51, 58; Richardson 1996, 100; VanderKam 2004, 347.
2. *War* 1.160.
3. *War* 1.160–68; *Ant.* 14.82–89.
4. *Ant.* 13.84.

presumably soldiers or veterans left behind to help stabilize the region. The addition of these men to the army of Gabinius allowed the Romans to confront Alexander with an overwhelming force. Gabinius fought Alexander near Jerusalem. The Romans killed 3,000 men and captured almost the same number. Alexander fled to the fortress of Alexandrium.

Josephus's account of the conclusion of the siege of Alexandrium is rather confusing. He states that Alexander sent envoys to Gabinius to request a pardon. Alexander's mother convinced him to accept her son's offer of surrender. Gabinius then destroyed the fortresses formerly under the control of Alexander.[5] Despite his loss, Alexander still had a sizable military force. He was able to launch new attacks against the Romans from Alexandrium. Josephus writes that the Romans prevailed only because of Mark Antony's courage on the battlefield. Gabinius stationed a portion of his army outside the fortress to prevent Alexander's partisans from reoccupying it. Although Josephus's account of this period is rather terse, he mentions in passing that Gabinius travelled throughout the country to rebuild ruined cities.[6] This suggests that the revolt of Alexander was widespread, and caused considerable devastation that required Roman supervision, and money, to repair. The economic losses for the region are unknown, but must have been considerable.

Gabinius now had no confidence in the abilities of Hyrcanus II and Antipater to govern Judea. Gabinius confined Hyrcanus II in Jerusalem, but allowed him to administer the temple as high priest. The Romans realized the power this office held, but failed to consider that nationalism would cause many Jews to continue to take up arms against them. As an effort to weaken the rebels' hold over portions of the former Hasmonean state, Gabinius divided the country into five districts (συνόδους): Jerusalem, Gadara, Amathus, Jericho, and Sepphoris.[7]

The efforts of the Romans to fragment the former Hasmonean state into smaller administrative units proved unsuccessful at quelling dissent. Soon after Gabinius reorganized the country, Aristobulus II evaded his captors in Rome and returned to Judea. None of our extant sources describe how he managed to escape his confinement in Rome and return home. His ability to recruit large armies to fight the Romans upon his arrival not only indicates that many Jews, despite the recent victory of Gabinius over

---

5. *Ant.* 14.90. Josephus in *War* 1.168 adds that Gabinius destroyed Alexandrium, Hyrcania, and Machaerus, to prevent the Jews from using them as bases for future hostile actions against the Romans.

6. *Ant.* 14.87.

7. *Ant.* 14.90–91.

Alexander, were still committed to the restoration of the Hasmonean state and willing to fight to obtain it.

Josephus suggests that news of the arrival of Aristobulus II caused widespread insurrections throughout the country. The Jewish legate Peitholaus—apparently the Roman-appointed deputy-governor of Jerusalem—went over to Aristobulus II with 1,000 men. Josephus writes that Aristobulus II fled with his supporters, many of whom arrived unarmed to resist the approaching Roman forces, to the fortress of Machaerus.[8] Aristobulus II turned away a large number of potential warriors because they did not possess weapons. His decision to send home so many men willing to fight the Romans suggests that he believed he had sufficient armed soldiers to oppose the forces of Gabinius. According to Josephus, he had some 8,000 men.

The Romans besieged Aristobulus II in Machaerus. Josephus does not record what happened during the blockade, but he suggests that the Jews and the Romans fought a fierce battle during which Aristobulus II sustained many wounds. The Romans eventually captured him together with his son Antigonus. Gabinius sent Aristobulus II in chains to Rome for a second time. Josephus writes that Gabinius requested the Senate allow the children of Aristobulus II to return home because he had promised this favor to their mother in exchange for the surrender of Machaerus. Despite the threat they posed to the stability of the region, the Senate upheld Gabinius's promise.[9] She was allowed to remain free for her assistance to the Republic.[10] But her presence did not stop her family from fighting to regain their independence.

The Final Hasmonean Revolt against Roman Rule and the Roman Civil Wars

In 54 B.C.E. M. Licinius Crassus arrived in Syria to replace Gabinius as proconsul.[11] Unlike his predecessors, he oppressed Judea. He plundered the temple treasury to finance his planned Parthian campaign; he seized 2,000 talents of gold, and an additional 8,000 talents worth of precious objects. A priest and custodian of the temple's curtains named Eleazar offered Crassus a bar of solid gold from the treasury if he would agree

8. For these events, see *War* 1.171–74; *Ant.* 14.92–97. Josephus implies in *Ant.* 14.92 that he may also have fortified Alexandrium.

9. See further, Atkinson 2013a.

10. See *War* 1.185–86; *Ant.* 14.123–26.

11. Crassus governed Syria from 57–55 B.C.E. For his tenure, see further Broughton 1952b, 195–96, 203, 211, 218; Schürer et al. 1973–87, 1:246.

not to take anything else from the sanctuary.[12] Hyrcanus II plays no role in the accounts of this incident. Josephus indirectly criticizes him in a lengthy digression that describes the wealth of the diaspora Jews and their loyalty to the temple.[13] He implies that Hyrcanus II, unlike the heroic Eleazar, failed to protect the temple offerings that faithful diaspora Jews had entrusted to him.

Crassus crossed the Euphrates in 54 B.C.E. to invade Parthia. He had to return to Syria for the winter. The following spring he traversed the Euphrates at Zeugma. Josephus does not provide a complete account of the succeeding events.[14] The Parthians defeated him in battle and retreated to Carrhae. The Parthian general Surenas offered to make a treaty if the Romans would renounce their claim to all territories beyond the Euphrates. Crassus accepted these conditions and left Carrhae to meet Surenas. He rode into a Parthian ambush. It is uncertain whether enemy troops murdered him, or whether his soldiers killed him to prevent his capture.[15] The Parthians imprisoned many Romans. Nevertheless, some survivors of the campaign managed to reach Syria under the leadership of the quaestor C. Cassius Longinus. He subsequently assumed command of Syria.[16] He repulsed a Parthian invasion at Antioch in the autumn of 51 B.C.E.[17] It was during the tenure of Longinus that the Romans faced another revolt by the supporters of Aristobulus II.

Longinus travelled to Tyre after his Parthian victory. During his absence Peitholaus gathered the remaining partisans of Aristobulus II and led an insurrection to evict the Romans from the country.[18] Josephus describes this rebellion in a single sentence; he provides little detail as to what transpired. However, the location of Longinus's battle with the rebels in the Galilee suggests that Peitholaus led a widespread uprising that threatened Roman control over the former Hasmonean state. This

12. *War* 1.179; *Ant.* 14.105–9. Crassus also looted a temple in Hierapolis. Plut. *Crass.* 17.

13. *Ant.* 14.110–18.

14. Josephus comments that it is not appropriate to repeat the story (*War* 1.179) of Crassus's campaign since other historians have described it in detail (*Ant.* 14.119).

15. For the Parthian campaign of Crassus, see Cass. Dio 40.12–27; Ov. *Fast.* 6.465; Plut. *Crass.* 17–31; Livy, *Per.* 106; Just. *Epit.* 43.4; Debevoise 1938, 78–93; Schürer et al. 1973–87, 1:246.

16. Longinus governed Syria from 53 to 51 B.C.E. For his tenure, see Broughton 1952b, 229, 237, 242–45; Schürer et al. 1973–87, 1:247.

17. Cass. Dio 40.28–29; *Ant.* 14.119; Livy, *Per.* 108; Just. *Epit.* 42.4; Cic. *Att.* 5.20.1–7; *Fam.* 2.10; *Phil.* 11.14.35.

18. For this revolt, see *War* 1.180–81; *Ant.* 14.120.

may indicate that the partisans of Aristobulus II were prominent in the north. Longinus defeated the forces of Peitholaus somewhere in the Galilee; Josephus does not specify the location. He captured Peitholaus and enslaved 30,000 of his soldiers. According to Josephus, Longinus executed Peitholaus at the request of Antipater.[19] Then events in Rome unexpectedly changed Judea's political situation.

The decision of Julius Caesar in 49 B.C.E. to cross the Rubicon led to a civil war between him and Pompey that ultimately ended all hope for a restoration of the Hasmonean state.[20] Much of this conflict took place in the Middle East and directly affected Judea. Pompey and a large portion of the Senate fled Italy at the outbreak of the fighting. Caesar took advantage of their departure to seize Rome. He defeated Pompey at the Battle of Pharsalus on August 9, 48 B.C.E.[21] This event cut Pompey off from any of his supporters in Europe. Pompey decided to use his ally Hyrcanus II to acquire troops from the Middle East. This action forced Caesar to back Aristobulus II. Caesar released him from prison and gave him two legions to fight the supporters of Pompey in Syria.[22] The partisans of Pompey in Rome poisoned Aristobulus II before he could depart the city. His corpse was preserved in honey until Mark Antony could send it back to Judea to be interred in the royal sepulcher.[23] Pompey ordered the execution of Alexander, the son of Aristobulus II, to prevent him from helping the partisans of Caesar. Q. Metellus Scipio, Pompey's father-in-law, beheaded him at Antioch.[24]

Josephus does not include a detailed account of the civil war between Pompey and Caesar. He instead highlights the favors the Romans bestowed upon the Jews at this time for their loyalty to Caesar. He mentions that Caesar gave Antipater Roman citizenship and exemption from

---

19. *War* 1.180; *Ant.* 14.120.

20. For a summary of the events and the literature on the civil wars between Caesar and Pompey, see further Goldsworthy 2006, 358–79; Rawson 1994.

21. Caes. (*B. Civ.* 3.92–99) claims that Pompey lost 15,000 men, and that 24,000 were taken prisoner along with the eagles of nine legions and 180 standards. The sources provide different figures for the number killed in this battle. See App. *B. Civ.* 2.72–82; Plut. *Caes.* 42–47; Cass. Dio 41.58.1–63.6. For a detailed account of the Roman Civil War between Pompey and Caesar and the battle of Pharsalus, see further Goldsworthy 2006, 358–431; Greenhalgh 1981b, 197–255.

22. *War* 1.183; *Ant.* 14.123; Cass. Dio 41.18.1.

23. *War* 1.184; *Ant.* 14.124. For this practice, see Marcus 1966, 512–13 n. d.

24. *War* 1.185; *Ant.* 14.125–26. It is difficult from Josephus's accounts to trace the whereabouts of the sons of Aristobulus II for much of the period following Pompey's 63 B.C.E. siege of Jerusalem.

taxation everywhere. He also recognized Hyrcanus II as the lawful high priest and gave him permission to rebuild Jerusalem's walls.[25] Caesar ordered the consuls to record these grants in Rome.[26] Despite Caesar's public acknowledgement of Roman support for Antipater and Hyrcanus II, many Jews still maintained hope that a descendant of Aristobulus II would restore the Hasmonean state. This appeared to be feasible when, in 40 B.C.E., the Parthians placed Antigonus, the second and only surviving son of Aristobulus II, on the throne. Antipater's son, Herod, fled Judea to escape the invasion. Antigonus cut off the ears of Hyrcanus II to render him ineligible to serve as high priest.[27] From 40–37 B.C.E., Antigonus held the office of high priest: he was *de facto* ruler of a small quasi-Hasmonean state.[28]

The Roman Republic realized that it would never suppress the movement to restore Hasmonean rule in the absence of any viable alternative. Octavian and Antony viewed Antipater's son Herod as the only feasible candidate who could pacify the country. In 40 B.C.E. they convinced the Senate to proclaim Herod king of Judea. But the problem was that Herod was a man with no kingdom: Antigonus controlled the country. The Romans would have to fight a war to destroy the dream of a restored Hasmonean state by placing Herod on the throne.

In 37 B.C.E. Herod, with forces supplied by the Roman governor C. Gaius Sosius, fought a brutal war to crush the anti-Roman opposition and the remaining partisans of the Hasmoneans.[29] During their siege of the Temple Mount, the temple porticoes were burnt and Roman soldiers tried to enter the temple's inner sanctuary. Sosius argued with Herod that his men were entitled to pillage Jerusalem; Herod was forced to bribe him and his troops to prevent the utter ruin of the city. Sosius, nevertheless, defiled the temple by offering a crown of gold to God in it. Sosius also insulted the Hasmonean family by addressing Antigonus as "Antigone" when he captured him.[30]

---

25. The position of ethnarch is mentioned in Josephus's extensive passage documenting Caesar's favorable decrees to Hyrcanus II and the Jews found in *Ant.* 14.190–216.

26. *Ant.* 14.144.

27. *Ant.* 14.366.

28. For his tenure, see further VanderKam 2004, 385–93; Schürer et al. 1973–87, 1:281–86.

29. For these events, see *War* 1.342–57; *Ant.* 14.386–491. See further, Atkinson 1996, 320–22.

30. For these events, see *War* 1.346–57; *Ant.* 14.468–76. See further, Atkinson 1996, 320–22.

Antigonus was sent to Antony to confine for the triumphal celebration in Rome. Herod bribed Antony to execute him. Antony beheaded Antigonus in Antioch. According to Josephus, Antony consented to Herod's request because he believed this was the only way to prevent further Jewish revolts to restore the Hasmonean monarchy. Antony is the only Roman to have beheaded a reigning Hasmonean king.[31] It had taken the Romans three years to place Herod on the throne. Yet the trouble was not over for the new Jewish king: the Hasmonean state would arise again, although briefly and considerably smaller.

Josephus ends his account of the Hasmonean dynasty with the murder of Antigonus. He states that his death marked the end of the Hasmonean line, which had lasted for 126 years.[32] In his obituary of the dynasty, Josephus contrasts the lineage of Herod with that of the Hasmoneans. Writing that the Hasmonean dynasty came from a splendid pedigree and had held the high priesthood, he comments that this family had lost their royal power through internal strife. The throne, Josephus believed, rightly passed to Herod—a mere commoner and a former Hasmonean subject! Josephus concludes his account with a final statement that Herod's coronation marks the end of the Hasmonean line. But he is certainly wrong! There was one other Hasmonean state. A woman created it, led it, and fought to preserve it!

31. *Ant.* 14.489–90; Plut. *Ant.* 36.4. Strabo (apud *Ant.* 15.9–10) claims that Antigonus was beheaded because he had refused to accept Herod as king. In *War* 1.357 Josephus merely states that Antigonus fell beneath the axe. According to Cass. Dio (49.22.3–5), the Romans crucified and flogged him. The anthropologist Nicu Hass, in an unpublished study, identified the human remains found in an ossuary in the Abba Cave at Giv'at ha-Mivtar as Antigonus. He based his conclusion both on the Aramaic inscription on the wall of the chamber and the skeletal evidence that this person had been beheaded. This identification was challenged by P. Smith (1997), who published the bones from this cave after the death of Hass. However, a recent investigation of the findings from this cave has revealed that Smith was apparently given the wrong set of skeletal remains. This confusion was due to the accidental mixing of skeletons that were formerly in the possession of Hass. The jawbone of the male found in this tomb was cut from behind with a sharp instrument that is consistent with decapitation. In 1982 another subterranean niche was discovered in this cave with an ossuary that contained the bones of a male approximately 35 to 40 years of age and a child. This male skeleton may be the remains of Abba the priest who was responsible for the inscription and for placing the bones of Antigonus in the tomb. For this new evidence, see Elitzur 2013.

32. *Ant.* 14.490–91. VanderKam (2004, 392) notes that this figure places the beginning of the family to 163 B.C.E.

In his *War*, Josephus mentions in passing the last effort to revive the Hasmonean kingdom. And it was successful! According to his account, a sister of Antigonus, Alexandra, captured the fortress of Hyrcania.[33] Once again, this shows that Herod and his Roman supporters were unable to secure the country's fortresses. Josephus is reluctant to tell us anything about her or how long her desert kingdom lasted. She likely captured Hyrcania in 37 B.C.E.—the year the Romans executed her brother—and held it until Herod besieged it in 31 B.C.E. But what is most surprising about her is what Josephus claims in his single-sentence summary of her kingdom: "Now when the Battle of Actium began, Herod prepared to come to the assistance of Antony, since he was freed from his troubles in Judea, but he instead had to capture Hyrcania, which Antigonus's sister held."[34] This passage reveals that this desert queen had kept Herod from participating in the Battle of Actium.[35] What is unstated is whether she actually posed a military threat to Jerusalem, or whether Herod decided to eradicate her and her partisans at this time to avoid fighting at Actium. We will never know. But his absence at that epic battle changed the course of Western history: it is possible that with Herod's forces, funds, and the allies he could have summoned, Antony and Cleopatra VII could have defeated Octavian. But that is mere speculation and Josephus did not want us to know more about it: he literally erased this Alexandra from history by omitting her story in his *Antiquities*.

Josephus tells us nothing about Herod's siege of Hyrcania. Alexandra presumably died in battle or Herod captured and then executed her. Her passing ended any hope for the restoration of the Hasmonean dynasty: she was the last ruler of an independent Hasmonean state.

33. This woman, named Alexandra (III), is to be distinguished from the daughter of Hyrcanus, Alexandra (II). See further the genealogy of Hyrcanus II and Aristobulus II in Kokkinos 1998, 114–15.

34. *War* 1.364.

35. An observation tower, camp, and remains of a defensive wall at the site show that he undertook an extensive military operation there. See H. Eshel 1998.

Chapter 9

CONCLUSION:
JOSEPHUS, ROME,
AND THE HASMONEAN HISTORY

Stasis in Josephus's Books:
Their Impact on His Accounts of the Hasmonean State

Josephus was greatly influenced by the historian Polybius, who emphasized that historians should stress the relationship between cause and effect.[1] Josephus believed it was important to begin his *War* with an account of the Hasmoneans because this family had created a successful state that had been allied with Rome (*War* 1.38). This, to a great extent, accounts for its creation and continued survival. For this reason, Josephus expanded his account of the Hasmonean monarchy in his *Antiquities* to include Roman decrees that honored the Jews. Judea, he was convinced, had not fallen to the Romans during the First Jewish Revolt because of the military might of its vaunted legions. Rather, this war ended in disaster for the Jews because of the poor leadership of tyrants that provoked divine punishment.[2] Josephus emphasizes the theme of internal sedition (στάσις οἰκεία) in his account of this conflict. This topic would have resonated with his Flavian-period audience, all of whom had experienced civil war (*bellum civile*). Through allusions to Thucydides, Josephus portrays *stasis* as a disease that not only afflicted Judea, but Rome as well.[3] It had doomed the Hasmonean state.

---

1. Polyb. 3.1–4.

2. *War* 1.9–10. Josephus also stresses that internal factionalism destroyed Judea and the temple. See also, *War* 1.10–12. Sulpicius Severus (*Chron.* 2.30.3, 6, 7) also contrasts the moderation of the Romans with the undisciplined actions of the Jewish rebels, who had failed to respect their own sanctuary. Cf. *War* 3.501; 4.92, 96; 5.334, 450, 519; 6.324, 383; 7.112.

3. For Josephus's use of Thucydides to highlight the theme of stasis, see further Mader 2000, 55–103; D. Schwartz 2013, 79–82. Mason remarks that this theme is

Civil war is a prominent theme in Roman literature. The prestige of the Flavian dynasty was largely based on their successful victory over the Jews and their capture of Jerusalem. By linking the recent Roman civil war with the First Jewish Revolt, Josephus downplays the involvement of the priests in the fighting against the Romans in Judea. He writes that conflict within this institution existed from the beginning with Korah. Nevertheless, the priests preserved order: they represent stability. Josephus emphasizes that the Jewish rebels sought to overthrow the established priestly aristocracy with their appointment of Phanni. This move was illegitimate because it was an effort to replace the leaders of the egalitarian theocracy with an alternative tyrannical form of government that was loyal solely to the rebellion.[4]

Josephus struggled to explain the First Jewish Revolt to his Roman audience while praising Judaism. He could not completely absolve the Judean ruling class of complicity in the revolt. For this reason, he praises the Flavians to call attention to Rome's recent civil war and its own history of *stasis*. He demands respect for his people and their rightful aristocratic leaders who, despite their qualifications to govern, had given the Romans no choice but war. Josephus too praises the heroes of both sides of the First Jewish War to emphasize the manly virtues of the Jews and the Romans.[5] Personalities form the basis for much of his storytelling. He found many of his best subjects among the rulers of the Hasmonean state. He stresses that its best Hasmonean rulers had sought alliances with Rome.

Personalities and Roman Supremacy in Josephus's Books

Josephus, like Polybius, considered individual moral virtue and vice to constitute the main forces behind historical causation. Both writers believed Rome had evolved from a Republic into an Empire because of the self-discipline of its leaders. Like other ancient historians, Josephus focuses on personalities.[6] His historical narrative is largely a collection of character studies that revolve around individuals and communities. He tends to include summaries of each of his subjects, often in obituaries,

prominent in Roman writings and calls attention to *War* 1.4 where Josephus explicitly makes the connection between disease in Rome and trouble in Judea. Mason 2009, 80–92.

4. *War* 4.147–57. For this theme, see Mader 2000, 78–79.

5. For this understanding, and opposing views, see Mason 2009, 257.

6. As Varneda (1986, 1–4) observes, this type of history, with its focus on causes, substantially differs from annalistic history (ἐφημερίδες) and commentaries (ὑπομνήματα).

that not only highlight their intellectual and moral qualities, but which often include some words of praise.[7] Josephus is also the object of special treatment in the *War*. He highlights his own resistance as a general against Vespasian at Jotapata. Josephus also emphasizes the discipline and military training of the Roman army. He wants his readers to infer that the Romans had a difficult time capturing Jotapata because he had adopted many of the best aspects of Roman values and self-discipline. Josephus implies that his acceptance of Roman virtues eventually led to his favored position in Flavian Rome.[8]

The *War* is largely a book about violence. It reaches its climax with the fall of Jerusalem. In contrast, the *Antiquities* merely describes the historical evolution of the Jewish people. Wars in this book merely serve as political events and are therefore included within the lives of rulers and peoples. Because Josephus does not focus on his own achievements in the *Antiquities*, he devotes more time to describing the personalities of the Hasmonean leaders and their wars. These events largely serve to illustrate the character of each person. Like Polybius, Josephus in his *Antiquities* uses past events—particularly the history of the Hasmonean state—to understand the present. Both writers believed their accounts could serve as models to guide present and future political activity.[9] Polybius, whose book greatly influenced Josephus, believed that a correct reading of history could serve as a guide to predicting the future behavior of leaders. Josephus imitates Polybius through his inclusion of exemplary actions of influential persons.

Although the *Antiquities* may not appear to be as obsessed with Roman supremacy as the *War*, it too is a book that is intended to explain Rome's rise. In this work Josephus highlights the longstanding relationship between the various Hasmonean leaders and Rome. He emphasizes that this alliance led to stability and even helped the Hasmonean monarchs in times of trouble.[10] For this reason, he devotes much space to documenting treaties between the Hasmoneans and the Romans to highlight the theme

7. For this theme in other ancient authors, and the use of obituaries to recount history as the actions of individuals and communities, see further Kraus and Woodman 1997, 32–37.

8. See further Varneda 1986, 27–28.

9. Polyb. 3.31; 12.25b; 30.6.4. See further Marincola 1997, 98; Fornara 1983, 112–14.

10. The influence of Rome in ending the siege of Antiochus VII Sidetes is one example. For Josephus, this incident shows the advantages of cooperation with Rome, and also speaks well of the character of John Hyrcanus. He implies that Hyrcanus's reign was a success because he kept his family's treaty with the Roman Republic.

clearly expressed in the *War* that the Romans did not dominate the Jewish nation during the First Jewish Revolt because of chance, but because of their valor, their foresight, and their discipline. Josephus was convinced that God had allowed the Jewish people to be defeated during the First Jewish Revolt, and τύχη had gone over to the Romans.[11]

Rome is a central character throughout the *War* and the *Antiquities*. This is especially true of the former book, which recounts in great detail Rome's triumph over the Jews and their destruction of Jerusalem. The Flavians to a great extent based their legitimacy on their victory over the Jews. They transformed the city of Rome to commemorate this event. Just as Augustus in 29 B.C.E. had marked the end of the civil wars of the late Republic with the closing of the doors to the Temple of Janus, Vespasian likewise undertook the same public action in 71 C.E. to declare the end of the First Jewish Revolt.[12] Living in Flavian Rome, Josephus would have been reminded constantly of this event in which he had participated.[13]

Josephus occupied a unique position in Roman society. As the most famous citizen to have fought against Rome during the First Jewish Revolt, he was also the chief spokesperson for his people and their faith. Yet, as a Roman he socialized with those who still rejoiced at his nation's defeat. He observed the Flavian celebration of his country's loss to the Romans in the First Jewish War in which many of his fellow Jews were marched in chains to the jeers of onlookers. His apparent eyewitness account of the Flavian triumphal procession of June 71 C.E. is the fullest extant ancient description of any Roman victory parade.[14] Yet, despite the tragic consequences of the First Jewish Revolt for the Jewish people, Josephus's portrayal of the Flavian triumphal procession is quite positive.[15] It shows that he had become somewhat comfortable with the Romans, even though they were devoting so much of the monies they had acquired from their recent defeat of the Jewish rebels to turn the city of Rome into a massive memorial to celebrate their victory.

Living, speaking, and writing in Rome, Josephus would have seen and undoubtedly walked through the Forum frequently, which the Flavians completely redesigned with the construction of several structures to commemorate their successful suppression of the First Jewish Revolt. He undoubtedly watched the building of several of these monuments,

11. *War* 5.367. For these Roman values, see *War* 3.71, 98–100, 105–6.

12. See further Boyle 2003.

13. For the importance of his works as a foundation myth for the Flavian dynasty, and the popularity of his writings among Romans, see further Barnes 2005.

14. *War* 7.123–58.

15. Beard 2003, 556; Eberhardt 2005, esp. 258–59.

including the Colosseum. The 80 C.E. dedication inscription on this structure proclaimed that spoils that had been taken from Judea during the First Jewish Revolt paid for its construction.[16] The Flavians not only built the famed Arch of Titus, but also a second arch in 81 C.E. and a third arch of unknown date, to commemorate their victory over the Jews.[17] But there was an even greater monument dedicated to the destruction of Josephus's homeland and its temple. As a priest, it undoubtedly grieved him greatly every time he walked past it.

For Jews, the most important of the structures built to commemorate the First Jewish Revolt was Vespasian's Temple of Peace. Pliny the Elder claimed it was one of the world's most beautiful edifices.[18] It was both a temple and a museum: it contained paintings, sculptures, and the vessels of gold taken from the Jerusalem temple. This treasure included the table of shewbread and the temple menorah. Both were carried in Vespasian's triumphal parade and are depicted on the Arch of Titus.[19] Honora Howell Chapman suggests that Jewish visitors to Rome went to the Temple of Peace to pray before these objects that had once been in the Jerusalem temple.[20] Josephus devotes much space to Vespasian's parade and the placement of these sacred items from Jerusalem's temple in this pagan shrine to imply that the God of the Jews had abandoned Jerusalem and now favored the Romans.[21]

The First Jewish Revolt was a unique event for the Romans. Unlike other wars, which were waged against nations, the Flavian triumph, with its extraordinary quantity of booty and religious objects from Jerusalem on display, was different than previous celebrations to commemorate a successful campaign. The Romans typically fought nations, and not their

16. Alföldy 1995.

17. *CIL* 6.944. This second arch is no longer extant. It marked the spot where Vespasian and Titus passed during their triumph. The arch of Titus in today's Forum was erected by Domitian after his brother's death. See Pfanner 1983, 119–21. A third arch was also built to commemorate the First Jewish Revolt. It is represented on one of the Haterii reliefs near the Colosseum, close to the temple of Isis, and may have been constructed by Vespasian. It contained depictions on each side of a palm-tree with prisoners tied at the base of its trunk. For this evidence, see Kleiner 1990, 131–34. Archaeological remains from Jerusalem suggest that Flavius Silva erected an arch near, or on top of, the Temple Mount following the 70 C.E. Roman destruction of Jerusalem. See Grüll 2006.

18. Plin. *HN* 36.101–2. This building was dedicated in 75 C.E.

19. *War* 148–62. A Torah scroll was the final item carried in the procession. It was placed with the temple curtains in the royal palace.

20. Chapman 2009, esp. 113–17.

21. Magness 2008, 208–9.

deities. Victorious Roman generals customarily performed the ritual of *evocation* to invite the patron deity of an enemy to accept a better home and worship in the city of Rome.[22]

The display and commemoration of the objects from the Jerusalem temple was a clear demonstration that the Flavian triumph celebrated not just the conquest of Judea, but also Rome's triumph over the religion of Judaism.[23] Jodi Magness suggests this explains why the Romans departed from their custom of constructing a temple for a recently conquered god in the city of Rome after the First Jewish Revolt.[24] She proposes the Romans associated the Jewish God with Capitoline Jupiter and worshipped the former as the latter. From the Roman perspective, the Jewish God had been subjugated to Capitoline Jupiter and was now captive in Rome. Because of the association between these deities, there was no need to build a new temple to house the Jewish god. The irony for Josephus was that although he was free in the city of Rome and enjoyed all its benefits as a citizen, many of his pagan readers believed that the very God he worshipped was a captive in their capital. The Jewish God, moreover, was a prisoner close to Josephus's house![25]

Although the account of the Flavian triumph shows that Josephus is decidedly pro-Roman, he at times includes subversive elements in his writings. He emphasizes that fortune ($\tau\acute{\nu}\chi\eta$) has now passed over to the Romans. But Josephus stresses that their dominance would not last forever since God does not bestow his favor permanently upon any nation.[26] By the time Josephus wrote his *Antiquities*, he had become slightly more optimistic about Judaism's future. In this book, in his description of the restoration of the temple under Cyrus, he even imagines the conditions under which sacrifice could be restored in the Jerusalem temple.[27]

The belief of the Romans that the Jewish God had abandoned his people, for many pagans effectively severed the connection between the

22. Kloppenborg (2005, esp. 442–44) proposes that Titus may have performed this ritual in Jerusalem. The Flavian triumph and subsequent treatment of the items taken from the temple strongly suggests that Titus did not conduct it in Jerusalem.

23. For the Flavian Triumph as a victory celebration of over Judaism, and it effect upon the subsequent treatment of Jews, see further Goodman 2007, 428–44.

24. Magness 2008, 208–9.

25. *Life* 423. Josephus writes that Vespasian gave him the house he had lived in before he became emperor. It was located on the Quirinal hill on a street called "The Pomegranate." Suet. *Dom.* 1.5. See further, Mason 2001, 168.

26. *War* 5.367. This view also reflects the periodization of Daniel and such apocalypses as *4QApocryphon of Jeremiah C^e* (4Q390).

27. *Ant.* 11.1–18. See further Magness 2008, 216–17.

Jews and the land of Judea in the Flavian period. Roman writers now called the former homeland of Josephus either "Idumaea" or "Palestine," rather than "Judea." Jews in the first century C.E. are commonly referred to in pagan writings in connection with Jewish religious practices and not with the land of Judea.[28] According to Cassius Dio, Vespasian and Titus both received the title of "imperator," but not "Judaicus" (Ἰουδαϊκοῦ), for their victory during the First Jewish Revolt.[29] Jews were now forced to pay dues to the cult of Capitoline Jupiter. This punishment and the closing of the temple at Leontopolis represented an effort by Vespasian to assimilate the Jews throughout the Roman Empire by making them more like other national groups. Ultimately, this policy failed because the Jewish Scriptures and history allowed for the continued practice of Judaism, and the maintenance of Jewish identity, without a sacrificial cult.[30]

Josephus, living as a Flavian client in a city redesigned to commemorate the defeat of his people, was in a difficult position. It was important for him to distance himself from the fanatics he blamed for the revolt, while urging support for the Roman Empire. He tries to achieve this difficult balance by affirming the power of the Jewish God while emphasizing that the Jews had abandoned their deity. At the same time, he urges loyalty to Rome because it is the nation that the God of the Jews has now chosen to favor. Although Josephus urges accommodation with Rome, he was especially worried that many Romans did not trust the Jews. Among the most sensitive issues of his time was the longstanding accusation that the Jews continued to maintain relations with the Parthians. This charge had its origin in the Hasmonean period and led many of Josephus's pagan contemporaries to mistrust Jews: some certainly distrusted him.

Roman Doubts Concerning Jewish Loyalty: The Parthians and the Hasmoneans

Many pagans doubted the loyalty of the Jews to the Roman Empire in the aftermath of the First Jewish Revolt. Tensions between the Romans and the Jews did not diminish following this conflict, but only increased.

---

28. See further D. Schwartz 2005, 69. For references to Judea by other names in Flavian writers, see M. Stern 1974–80, 1:316; 2:403. As Stern notes, Cassius Dio is an exception and uses "Judea" instead of "Palestina."

29. Cass. Dio 66.4.60. M. Stern (1974–80, 2:377) comments that Cassius Dio was surprised the Flavians did not assume the title "Iudaicus" since it was customary for Roman emperors to adopt an epithet based on the name of a nation conquered during their reign.

30. Rives 2005; Magness 2008, 206–9.

This was due to the persistent belief that the Jews continued to have a longstanding relationship with Rome's enemy, the Parthians. Rome's fear of Parthia during the first century C.E. may explain Josephus's decision to add an account of the participation of John Hyrcanus in the campaign of Antiochus VII Sidetes to the *Antiquities*. His *War* was not without its detractors in Rome. Many challenged its accuracy before its publication.[31] It is probable that the other books about the First Jewish Revolt were known to some of his critics and may have caused them to question the historical reliability of his descriptions of the relationship between the Jews and Rome's enemies. Some may have asked him why he had omitted this story in his *War*.

Josephus likely avoided any discussion of the involvement of Hyrcanus in the Parthian campaign of Sidetes because of longstanding suspicions among some Romans that the Jews were not loyal to the Roman Empire. This accusation was not new, but extended back to the Roman Republic. In 54 B.C.E. the Parthians defeated Crassus and captured the Roman standards. This tragedy made it appear to many nations in the Mediterranean that the Parthians were equal to Rome. Augustus was successful in his efforts to remove this disgrace and enhance Rome's prestige when he regained the lost standards around 23 B.C.E. Josephus would have been reminded of this event daily since the Romans had redesigned the Forum of Rome to commemorate this victory. Augustus even took the title *Imperator* and issued coins to celebrate this event even though no actual battle had taken place.[32]

The Jews had a long relationship with the Parthians that extended back to the early period of Hasmonean rule. Some Romans may have considered this long history troubling following the 70 C.E. destruction of Jerusalem. The Roman Republic had sought to win the support of the Jews to counter Parthian expansion. A circular letter from Rome sent to various Middle Eastern nations, including the Parthians, mentioned Rome's friendship with the Jews.[33] Antiochus III had transported 2,000 Jewish families from Parthia and resettled them as military colonies in troubled

---

31. For critics of Josephus, see Mason 1991, 322–24; Bilde 1988, 107–13.

32. For these events and the importance of the Parthians, as depicted in Roman coins and monuments, in relationship to the writings of Josephus, see further Overman 2009, esp. 284–93.

33. This document is preserved in 1 Macc 15:16–24 as well as Josephus (*Ant.* 14.145–47) who, as previously noted, erroneously dated it to the time of Hyrcanus II. Goldstein (1976, 493–94) comments that this document is out of place in 1 Maccabees, which he attributes to the misplacement of the passage in the original Hebrew edition.

areas.[34] The Roman letter to the Eastern nations was written about the time the Arsacid court conquered Babylonia where many Jews resided.[35] During the campaign of Tigranes against Shelamzion Alexandra, a number of Jews had been exiled to Armenia.[36] Because the Romans had a long interest in controlling this region, they viewed these Jewish resettlements as a potential threat to their eastern border.

The existence of a large Jewish community in Parthia led many Romans to question the loyalty of the Jews during the periods of the Roman Republic and the Roman Empire. Several early conflicts that involved Jews further increased tensions between Jews and Romans. After the death of Crassus in Parthia, many Jews revolted against his general, Cassius, when he and the survivors reached the Galilee.[37] In 40 B.C.E. the Parthians made Antigonus king, which forced Mark Antony to seek support in the Senate to install Herod as Judea's monarch to halt their advance.[38] Pheroras, who was accused of plotting to poison Rome's ally, Herod the Great, was supposedly prepared to flee to Parthia to avoid capture.[39] In 54 C.E, at the beginning of Nero's reign, Tiridates, the brother of the king of Parthia, claimed the throne of Armenia. It was this Parthian expansion that caused the *legatus* of Syria and his forces to delay moving to Judea until the Passover of 66 C.E.[40] Vespasian worsened relations between Rome and Parthia when, in 75 C.E., he refused the request of the Parthian ruler Vologases for aid to help him fight the Alani. In 79 C.E. fears of the Parthians increased in Rome when a pseudo-Nero took refuge in the East with some pretenders to the Parthian throne. In 82/3 C.E. Domitian forced the Parthian monarch Pacorus II to surrender

34. *Ant.* 12.147–53. For Jews in the diaspora, including Parthia and Asia Minor, see Smallwood 1981, 120–28.

35. For the importance of this letter's timing, see Neusner 1965, 24.

36. Moses of Khoren, *History of Armenia* 2.14; Neusner 1965, 26.

37. This insurrection was inspired by Peitholaus, who attempted to rally the followers of Aristobulus II in the region to fight against Rome. *Ant.* 14.120; *War* 1.180; Cass. Dio 40.28.

38. See further, VanderKam 2004, 385–93; Schürer et al. 1973–87, 1:281–86. Several authors comment that many of the residents of Syria and the neighboring lands favored the Parthians. Cass. Dio 49.19; Hor. *Odes* 3.6; Tac. *Germ.* 37. Jewish sources record the visit of a Parthian delegation to the Hasmonean court during the reign of Jannaeus. This may confirm to the existence of an earlier treaty, made by Hyrcanus, between the Jews and the Parthians. For this and favorable relations between Jews and Parthians, see further, Debevoise 1938, 94–95, 111.

39. *War* 1.485.

40. See further, Millar 1993, 66–69.

another pseudo-Nero.[41] Toward the end of his reign, Domitian planned a campaign against Parthia because he believed it posed a threat to the Roman Empire. This did not occur until Trajan (113–117 C.E.) fought his Parthian war.[42]

Josephus not only had to deal with allegations that the Jews were in league with the Parthians, but also the fact that many Romans seem to have considered him a traitor. The accusations against him became problematic when Catullus, the procurator of Libya, captured a man named Jonathan. Catullus believed he was a fugitive *sicarius*. He appropriated Jonathan's goods and sent him in chains to Rome. When Jonathan arrived he alleged that Josephus had sent him weapons and supplies to foment a revolt among the Cyrenaican Jews. Josephus claimed he was innocent. Vespasian believed him and executed Jonathan; Josephus was given custody of his land in Judea.[43] This story may suggest that other Jews were not happy that Josephus enjoyed a privileged position in Rome while many of them continued to suffer as a result of the First Jewish Revolt.

Josephus began his literary career in Rome shortly after the Roman destruction of Jerusalem when Vespasian was concerned with Parthia. In late 71 or 72 C.E. Vespasian began his reorganization of the Empire's eastern frontier. He removed several rulers and fortified Syria's eastern border.[44] The Romans undertook this effort largely to monitor the Parthians. While troops were sent to the region to counter the Parthian threat, some in Rome were suspicious of the members of the royal house of Adiabene

41. For these incidents, see Debevoise 1938, 200–202, 214–15.

42. For this period, see Millar 1993, 80–89.

43. See *War* 7.437–51; *Life* 424–25.

44. Because M. Ulpius Trainus won the *ornamenta triumphalia* while governor of Syria in the 73/4–77/79 C.E., it is commonly assumed that some fighting took place beyond the border between Roman and Parthian forces. For this view, see further van Berchem 1983; Bowersock 1973; Millar 1993, 84–86; Pliny the Younger, *Pan.* 9.16. Because emperors achieved imperatorial acclamations through their own military successes or through the victories of their commanders, the awarding of this commendation to Trainus should have been accompanied by an award to Vespasian, or possibly also Titus as his *de facto* co-ruler. Because the number of Vespasian's imperatorial ovations remained unchanged, and since the belief that there was a conflict between the Romans and the Parthians is based on an interpretation of literary references that are difficult to date, there is no evidence for any serious clash at this time. It was the threat of a Parthian invasion that compelled Vespasian to appoint the experienced commanders A. Marius Celsus and M. Ulpaius Traianus to the border region. However, Traianus appears to have undertaken some non-military action that led to peaceful relations between Parthia and Rome. For this evidence and interpretation, see further Dąbrowa 1998, 60–61.

in the city who may have participated in the First Jewish Revolt.[45] This alliance made some distrustful of the Jews.

As the leading spokesperson in Rome for the Jewish community, Josephus was aware that some questioned his loyalty since he had fought in the war against Rome. It was Vespasian's concern for future trouble in Parthia that compelled him to commission Josephus to produce a propagandistic tract in Aramaic on the First Jewish Revolt for the Parthians, the Babylonians, the Arabs, the Adiabenians, and the trans-Euphratine Jews.[46] Nevertheless, despite his imperial patron, many Romans undoubtedly wondered why Josephus had omitted an account of the Parthian campaign of Sidetes in his *War*. This expedition made many speculate what had taken place since Hyrcanus and his Jewish forces alone survived, and the Parthians helped the Jews several times afterwards. This omission may have been among the criticisms of his book that prompted him to write his more detailed account of the campaign of Sidetes in his *Antiquities*.[47]

Josephus not only expanded his account of Hyrcanus in his *Antiquities* to answer his critics, but he did so to enhance his own reputation. He stresses that he and John Hyrcanus were priests and military leaders. Throughout his works Josephus emphasizes that he was not an ordinary priest, but a child prodigy of the Jewish Scriptures. By equating the Jewish priesthood with Jewish nobility, Josephus emphasizes the abilities of those Hasmoneans who, like himself, were natural leaders.[48] His emphasis on his priestly status and his Hasmonean ancestors who had supported Rome enhanced his own credentials. It allowed Josephus to portray himself to his Roman readers as the leading representative of his people. His

45. *War* 6.356–57. The spread of Jewish customs in Roman society in the first century C.E., and several conflicts that involved Jews throughout the Roman Empire, caused many Roman elites to become more hostile towards Jews. See further, Zeev 2010. In his *War* Josephus acknowledges the participation of Adiabeneans in the First Jewish Revolt and tries to shape his account of the Adiabene royal family to highlight their piety and to distinguish them from the Parthians. See further, Marciak 2011.

46. *War* 1.4–6. Cass. Dio (65.3; 66.19) suggests that participants from the trans-Euphratine region in the First Jewish War were more numerous than Josephus claims.

47. Varneda (1986, 271–72) includes an extensive list of anachronisms, discrepancies, and variants between the *War* and *Antiquities* that show Josephus not only enlarged the latter work, but that he changed his opinions of himself in his subsequent writings.

48. For the importance of Josephus's self-presentation as a priest and member of Jewish nobility to enhance his credibility with the Romans, see further Tuval 2011. Grojnowski (2015) believes that Josephus also incorporated traditions from the book of Nehemiah in *Life* to enhance his authority within the Jewish communities.

self-presentation also influenced his accounts of the Hasmonean rulers, which must be read in light of Josephus's social situation in Flavian Rome.

The Accuracy of Josephus's Accounts of the Hasmonean State

In the preface to the *War* (1.1–3), Josephus criticizes other historians of the First Jewish Revolt for producing accounts that exhibit "alternatively invective and encomium, but nowhere historical accuracy" (τὸ δ' ἀκριβὲς τῆς ἱστορίας οὐδαμοῦ). Josephus stresses historical accuracy as the goal of the historian in the *Antiquities*, where he interrupts his narrative following the death of Alexandra to state: "...historians should make their chief aim to be accurate (ἀκριβείας)" (*Ant.* 14.3). He stresses the reliability of his accounts to show that he is a faithful and meticulous researcher who has attempted to present the truth. Like Polybius, Josephus believes that history is of great benefit to the reader, especially that which is accurate, instructive, and pedagogic with a focus on events, especially political actions.[49] Nevertheless, the standards of Josephus's time are different than our own. He sought to produce entertaining, yet didactic, histories. What makes him unique is that he not only bridged two worlds as an elite Jew and a Roman citizen, but he participated in many of the most significant events of his day. These clearly affected his historical writings, and influenced his histories of the Hasmonean state.

Josephus was greatly shaped by models of writing history current in the city of Rome. Yet, he also was a product of Judea and a rich Jewish literary tradition. His works often convey history through the psychology of the Greek novelists. This is especially true of his description of the downfall of Judah Aristobulus, which focuses on his inner turmoil. Josephus combines his portrait of Aristobulus's physical and mental decline with dramatic elements to create a gripping story. In many places, particularly his accounts of Seleucid history, Josephus cannot be entirely faulted for his inaccuracies since he had few reliable sources. It is only as a result of recent archaeological and numismatic discoveries that we can now correct his works and present a chronologically accurate narrative of what transpired. This evidence also shows that the Seleucid Empire's civil wars played a greater role in the creation of the Hasmonean state than previously recognized because it brought about the necessary conditions for John Hyrcanus to annex considerable Seleucid territories. This was possible because his alliance with the Roman Republic allowed him

49. For the historical methods of Josephus and Polybius, see further Varneda 1986, 251–56.

to seize Seleucid territories. This relationship allowed his successors to maintain their state amid continued threats from the Seleucid Empire. The termination of this longstanding alliance with the Romans eventually doomed the Hasmonean state.

The Hasmonean State and the Seleucid Empire

The Hasmonean state appeared during a period of Seleucid decline—it is doubtful that Mattathias's revolt would have been successful without a destabilized Seleucid Empire. The Parthians from this time forward also took advantage of the declining Seleucid Empire to annex its eastern lands. Demetrius II and Antiochus VII Sidetes were forced to wage distant wars to regain this lost territory. The defeat of Sidetes in Parthia marked the end of the Seleucid Empire as a major power in the region: it only survived as a divided and weakened series of small kingdoms until Pompey's arrival.

The Jews were positioned to take advantage of the rapid decline of the Seleucid Empire following the death of Sidetes. As the Seleucid rulers fought constant civil wars and Parthian incursions, they increasingly had to make treaties with the Hasmonean rulers. From Hyrcanus onwards, the Hasmoneans proved quite skilled at playing one Seleucid monarch against the other. In times of great turmoil in Syria, Hasmonean rulers such as Hyrcanus and Jannaeus managed, like the Parthians, to annex significant portions of Seleucid lands. It was only in the latter days of the Seleucid Empire, largely during the reign of Alexandra, that the Hasmoneans truly ruled an independent nation free from the threat of Seleucid intervention. This period of was short-lived. The Roman Republic permanently changed the political structure of the region when it annexed the Seleucid Empire and neighboring kingdoms. In hindsight, the end of the Hasmonean monarchy was inevitable once the Romans conquered the Seleucid Empire: there was nothing the Hasmoneans could have done to prevent the end of their state.

Conclusion

The history of the nine decades of the Hasmonean rule of Judea (152–63 B.C.E.) is the remarkable tale of a family whose zeal for their ancestral faith helped them survive a turbulent period of Middle Eastern history and create an independent state surrounded by hostile powers. Like Mattathias, many Jews later took up arms to expel the Romans during the first century B.C.E. and well into the first century C.E.; Josephus is the most famous of them. For this reason, it is not surprising that he featured the Hasmoneans in both his major historical works, and chose to begin his account of the First Jewish Revolt with the history of the family that had successfully fought the Seleucid Empire for its political and religious freedom. He was proud and unapologetic of the role he had played in the First Jewish Revolt, as well as of his Hasmonean forebears who likewise fought against formidable opponents for their independence. For this reason, he undertook the task of recounting the history of the Hasmonean state to his former foes as part of his great epic of the First Jewish Revolt. When all the extant evidence is compared with his writings, Josephus emerges as a truly exemplary chronicler of one of history's most remarkable dynasties, the Hasmoneans who, alone of all Jewish families, still has its own holiday to celebrate its struggle for religious and political freedom.

BIBLIOGRAPHY

Abel, F. M. 1947. "Le siège de Jérusalem par Pompée." *Revue Biblique* 54: 243–55.

Allegro, J. M. 1959. *"Thrakidan*, the 'Lion of Wrath' and Alexander Jannaeus." *Palestine Exploration Quarterly* 91: 47–51.

Alföldy, G. 1995. "Eine bauinschrift aus dem Colosseum." *Zeitschrift für Papyrologie und Epigraphik* 109: 195–226.

Amit, D. 2002. "The Aqueduct of the Fortress of Dok (Dagon). Pages 330–35 in *The Aqueducts of Israel*. Edited by D. Amit, J. Patrich, and Y. Hirschfeld. Portsmouth, RI: Journal of Roman Archaeology.

Applebaum, S. 1975. "Hellenistic Cities of Judaea and Its Vicinity—Some New Aspects." Pages 59–73 in *The Ancient Historian and His Materials*. Edited by B. Levick. Farnborough: Gregg International.

Ariel, D. T. 1982. "A Survey of Coin Finds in Jerusalem (Until the End of the Byzantine Period)." *Liber Annus Studii biblici franciscani* 32: 273–326.

———1990. *Excavations at the City of David 1978–1985.* Jerusalem: Institute of Archaeology, Hebrew University of Jerusalem.

Assar, G. F. 2006a. "A Revised Parthian Chronology of the Period 91–55 BC." *Parthica* 8: 55–104.

———2006b. "A Revised Parthian Chronology of the Period 165–91 B.C." *Electrum* 11: 87–158.

Athanassiadi, P. N. 1999. *Damascius the Philosophical History*. Athens: Apamea.

Atkinson, K. 1996. "Herod the Great, Sosius, and the Siege of Jerusalem (37 B.C.E.) in Psalm of Solomon 17." *Novum Testamentum* 38: 313–22.

———2001a. *An Intertextual Study of the Psalms of Solomon*. Lewiston, NY: Edwin Mellen.

———2001b. "Queen Salome Alexandra and the Dead Sea Scrolls: A Period of Enlightenment for Women in Ancient Judea During the First Century B.C." Pages 15–29 in *Proceedings of the Central States Regional Meeting of the Society of Biblical Literature and the American Schools of Oriental Research*. Edited by S. S. Elliott. Kansas City, MO: Central States Society of Biblical Literature.

———2003a. "Theodicy in the Psalms of Solomon." Pages 546–75 in *Theodicy in the World of the Bible*. Edited by A. Laato and J. C. de Moor. Leiden: Brill.

———2003b. "Women in the Dead Sea Scrolls: Evidence for a Qumran Renaissance During the Reign of Queen Salome Alexandra." *The Qumran Chronicle* 11: 37–56.

———2004. *I Cried to the Lord: A Study of the Psalms of Solomon's Historical Background and Social Setting*. Leiden: Brill.

————2006. "Noble Deaths at Gamla and Masada? A Critical Assessment of Josephus's Accounts of Jewish Resistance in Light of Archaeological Discoveries." Pages 349–71 in *Making History: Josephus and Historical Method*. Edited by Z. Rodgers. Leiden: Brill, 2006.

————2007. "Representations of History in 4Q331 (4QpapHistorical Text C), 4Q332 (4QHistorical Text D), 4Q333 (4QHistorical Text E), and 4Q468e (4QHistorical Text F): An Annalistic Calendar Documenting Portentous Events?" *Dead Sea Discoveries* 14: 125–51.

————2008. "The Salome No One Knows: Long-Time Ruler of a Prosperous and Peaceful Judea Mentioned in Dead Sea Scrolls." *Biblical Archaeology Review* 34, no. 4: 60–65, 72–73.

————2010. "Masada." Pages 919–22 in *Eerdmans Dictionary of Early Judaism*. Edited by J. J. Collins and D. C. Harlow. Grand Rapids: Eerdmans.

————2011. "The Historical Chronology of the Hasmonean Period in the *War* and *Antiquities* of Flavius Josephus: Separating Fact from Fiction." Pages 7–27 in *Flavius Josephus: Interpretation and History*. Edited by M. Mohr, P. Stern, and J. Pastor. Leiden: Brill.

————2012a. "Enduring the Lord's Discipline: Soteriology in the *Psalms of Solomon*." Pages 145–63 in *This World and the World to Come: Soteriology in Early Judaism*. Edited by D. M. Gurtner. London: T&T Clark International.

————2012b. "Josephus the Essene at Qumran? An Example of the Intersection of the Dead Sea Scrolls and the Archaeological Evidence in Light of Josephus's Writings." *Scripta Judaica Cracoviensia* 10: 7–35.

————2012c. *Queen Salome: Jerusalem's Warrior Monarch of the First Century B.C.E.* Jefferson, NC: McFarland.

————2013a. "Aristobulus II." Pages 694–95 in *Encyclopedia of Ancient History*. Edited by R. Bagnall, K. Brodersen, C. Champion, A. Erskine, and S. Huebner. Oxford: Wiley Blackwell.

————2013b. "Eupolemus." Pages 2571–72 in *Encyclopedia of Ancient History*. Edited by R. Bagnall, K. Brodersen, C. Champion, A. Erskine, and S. Huebner. Oxford: Wiley Blackwell.

————2013c. "Historical References and Allusions to Foreigners in the Dead Sea Scrolls: Seleucids, Ptolemies, Nabateans, Itureans, and Romans in the Qumran Corpus." *Qumran Chronicle* 21: 1–32.

————2013d. "Hyrcanus II." Pages 3613–14 in *Encyclopedia of Ancient History*. Edited by R. Bagnall, K. Brodersen, C. Champion, A. Erskine, and S. Huebner. Oxford: Wiley Blackwell.

————2013e. "John Hyrcanus in the Dead Sea Scrolls: Hasmonean History, the Samaritans, and Messianism." *Qumran Chronicle* 21: 103–16.

————2014a. "Judah Aristobulus and Alexander Jannaeus in the Dead Sea Scrolls." *Qumran Chronicle* 22: 1–19.

————2014b. "Shelamzion Alexandra, Hyrcanus II and Aristobulus II in the Dead Sea Scrolls." *Qumran Chronicle* 22: 20–38.

————2015a. "Hanukkah: Second Temple and Hellenistic Judaism." Pages 253–55 in *Encyclopedia of the Bible and Its Reception*. Vol. 11, *Halah-Hiquni*. Edited by H. J. Klauck, Hans-Josef. Berlin: de Gruyter.

————2015b. "Hasmoneans: Second Temple and Hellenistic Judaism." Pages 373–77 in *Encyclopedia of the Bible and Its Reception*. Vol. 11, *Halah-Hiquni*. Edited by H. J. Klauck, Hans-Josef. Berlin: de Gruyter.

————2015c. "Perceptions of the Temple Priests in the Psalms of Solomon." Pages 79–96 in *The Psalms of Solomon: Language, History, Theology*. Edited by E. Bons and P. Pouchelle. Atlanta: Society of Biblical Literature.

————2016. "Understanding the Relationship Between the Apocalyptic Worldview and Jewish Sectarian Violence: The Case of the War Between Alexander Jannaeus and Demetrius III." Pages 45–57 in *The Seleucid and Hasmonean Periods and the Apocalyptic Worldview*. Edited by L. L. Grabbe. London: Bloomsbury T&T Clark.

Atkinson, K., and J. Magness. 2010. "Josephus's Essenes and the Qumran Community." *Journal of Biblical Literature* 129: 317–42.

Attridge, H. 1984. "Josephus and His Works." Pages 185–232 in *Jewish Writings of the Second Temple Period*. Edited by M. Stone. Philadelphia: Fortress.

Aucher, J. B., ed. 1818. *Eusebii Pamphili Caesariensis episcopi Chronicon bipartitum nunc primum ex Armeniaco textu in Latinum conversum, adnotationibus auctum, Graecis fragmentis exornatu*. Venice: Typis Coenobii PP. Armenorum in Insula S. Lazari.

Aviam, M. 1993. "Galilee: The Hellenistic to the Byzantine Periods." Pages 453–58 in vol. 2 of *New Encyclopedia of Archaeological Excavations in the Holy Land*. Edited by M. Stern. Jerusalem: Israel Exploration Society.

Avigad, N. 1975a. "A Bulla of Jonathan the High Priest." *Israel Exploration Journal* 25: 8–12.

————1975b. "A Bulla of King Jonathan." *Israel Exploration Journal* 25: 245–46.

Babota, V. 2014. *The Institution of the Hasmonean High Priesthood*. Leiden: Brill.

Badian, E. 1967. "The Testament of Ptolemy Alexander." *Rheinisches Museum für Philologie* 110: 178–92.

Bagnall, R. S. 1976. *The Administration of the Ptolemaic Possessions Outside Egypt*. Leiden: Brill.

Bahat, D. 1996. "Jerusalem Down Under: Tunneling Along Herod's Temple Mount Wall." *Biblical Archaeology Review* 21, no. 6: 30–47.

Baltrusch, E. 2002. *Die Juden und das Römische Reich*. Darmstadt: Wissenschaftliche Buchgesellschaft.

Bar-Kochva, B. 1989. *Judas Maccabaeus*. Cambridge: Cambridge University Press.

————1996. *Pseudo Hecataeus, "On the Jews"*. Berkeley: University of California Press.

Barag, D. 1982/83. "Tyrian Currency in Galilee." *Israel Numismatic Journal* 67: 7–13.

————1992/93. "New Evidence on the Foreign Policy of John Hyrcanus I." *Israel Numismatic Journal* 12: 1–12.

Barag, D., and S. Qedar. 1980. "The Beginning of Hasmonean Coinage." *Israel Numismatic Journal* 4: 8–21.

Barkay, G. 1977. "A Coin of Alexander Jannaeus from Cyprus." *Israel Exploration Journal* 27: 119–20.

Barkay, R. 1992/93. "The Marisa Hoard of Seleucid Tetradrachms Minted in Ascalon." *Israel Numismatic Journal* 12: 21–26.

Barnes, T. D. 2005. "The Sack of the Temple in Josephus and Tacitus." Pages 129–44 in *Flavius Josephus and Flavian Rome*. Edited by J. Edmondson, S. Mason, and J. Rivers. New York: Oxford University Press.

Baumann, U. 1983. *Rom und die Juden*. Frankfurt am Main: Lang.

Baumbach, G. 2005. *Josephus – Jesusbewegung – Judentum*. Berlin: Institute Kirche und Judentum.

Baumgarten, A. I. 1997. *The Flourishing of Jewish Sects in the Maccabean Era*. Leiden: Brill.

Bautch, K. C. 2003. *A Study of the Geography of 1 Enoch 17–19*. Leiden: Brill.

Beard, M. 2003. "The Triumph of Flavius Josephus." Pages 543–58 in *Flavian Rome*. Edited by A. J. Boyle and W. J. Dominik. Leiden: Brill.

Begg, C. 1996. "Athaliah's Coup and Overthrow According to Josephus." *Antonianum* 71: 189–210.

Bellinger, A. R. 1949. "The End of the Seleucids." *Transactions of the Connecticut Academy of Arts and Sciences* 38: 51–102.

Bellmore, J. 1999. "Josephus, Pompey and the Jews." *Zeitschrift für Geschichte* 48: 94–118.

———2000. "Pompey's Triumph Over the Arabs." Pages 91–123 in *Studies in Latin Literature and Roman History 10*. Edited by C. Deroux. Brussels: Latomus Revue d'études latines.

Ben-Dov, M. 1985. *In the Shadow of the Temple: The Discovery of Ancient Jerusalem*. New York: Harper & Row.

Berlin, A. M. 1977. "Between Large Forces: Palestine in the Hellenistic Period." *Biblical Archaeologist* 60: 2–57.

———2006. *Gamla I: The Pottery of the Second Temple Period*. Jerusalem: Israel Antiquities Authority.

———2011. "Identity Politics in Early Roman Galilee." Pages 69–106 in *The Jewish Revolt Against Rome*. Edited by M. Popović. Leiden: Brill.

———2012. "The Pottery of Strata 8–7 (The Hellenistic Period)." Pages 5–29 in *Excavations at the City of David 1978–1985 Directed by Yigael Shiloh Volume VIIB Area E: The Finds*. Edited by A. De Groot and H. B. Greenberg. Jerusalem: Hebrew University of Jerusalem.

Berrin, S. L. 2004. *The Pesher Nahum Scroll from Qumran*. Leiden: Brill.

Berthelot, K. 2003. *Philanthrôpia Judaica: le débat autour de la 'misanthropie' des lois juives dans l'Antiquité*. Leiden: Brill.

Bevan, E. R. 1902. *House of Seleucus*. London: E. Arnold.

———1927. *House of Ptolemy*. London: E. Arnold.

Bickerman, E. J. 1937. *Der Gott der Makkabäer*. Berlin: Schocken.

———1938. *Institutions des Séleucides*. Paris: P. Geuthner.

———1944. "Notes on Seleucid and Parthian Chronology." *Berytus* 8: 73–76.

———1968. *Chronology of the Ancient World*. London: Thames & Hudson.

———1988. *The Jews in the Greek Age*. Cambridge, MA: Harvard University Press.

Bilde, P. 1988. *Flavius Josephus Between Jerusalem and Rome*. Sheffield: Sheffield Academic.

Boettger, G. 1879. *Topographisch-historisches Lexicon zu den Schriften des Flavius Josephus*. Leipzig: L. Fernau.

Bohak, G. 2010. "Heliopolis." Pages 721–23 in *Eerdmans Dictionary of Early Judaism*. Edited by J. J. Collins and D. C. Harlow. Grand Rapids: Eerdmans.

Bond, H. 2000. "Josephus in Recent Research." *Currents in Research: Biblical Studies* 29: 162–90.

Borchardt, F. 2015. "Sabbath Observance, Sabbath Innovation: The Hasmoneans and Their Legacy as Interpreters of the Law." *Journal for the Study of Judaism* 46: 159–81.

Bowersock, G. W. 1973. "Syria under Vespasian." *Journal of Roman Studies* 63: 123–29.

———1983. *Roman Arabia*. Cambridge, MA: Harvard University Press.

Boyle, A. J. 2003. "Introduction: Reading Flavian Rome." Pages 1–69 in *Flavian Rome*. Edited by A. J. Boyle and W. J. Dominik. Leiden: Brill.

Brett, A. B. 1937. "A New Cleopatra Tetradrachm of Ascalon." *American Journal of Archaeology* 41: 452–63.

Brighton, M. A. 2009. *The Sicarii in Josephus's Judean War*. Atlanta: Society of Biblical Literature.

Bringmann, K. 1983. *Hellenistische Reform und Religionsverfolgung in Judäa*. Göttingen: Vandenhoeck & Ruprecht.

Broughton, R. S. 1952a. *The Magistrates of the Roman Republic*. Vol. 1, *509 B.C.–100 B.C*. New York: American Philological Association.

———1952b. *The Magistrates of the Roman Republic*. Vol. 2, *99 B.C.–31 B.C*. New York: American Philological Association.

Brutti, M. 2006. *The Development of the High Priesthood During the Pre-Hasmonean Period*. Leiden: Brill.

Bucher, G. S. 1995. "Appian BC 2.24 and the Trial *De Ambitu* of M. Aemilius Scaurus." *Zeitschrift für alte Geschichte* 44: 396–421.

Büchler, A. 1896. "Les sources de Flavius Josèphe dans ses *Antiquités* (XII,5–XIII,1)." *Revue des é juives* 32 (Janurary–March): 179–99.

Bull, R. J. 1967. "A Note on Theodotus' Description of Shechem." *Harvard Theological Review* 60: 221–28.

Bull, R. J. 2008. "Er-Fas, Tell." Pages 1015–22 in vol. 4 of *The New Encyclopedia of Archaeological Excavations in the Holy Land*. Edited by E. Stern, A. Leyinzon-Gilbo'a, and J. Aviram. Jerusalem: Israel Exploration Society.

Bull, R. J., and G. E. Wright. 1965. "Newly Discovered Temples on Mt. Gerizim in Jordan." *Harvard Theological Review* 58: 234–37.

Chapman, H. H. 2009. "What Josephus Sees: The Temple of Peace and the Jerusalem Temple as Spectacle in Text and Art." *Phoenix* 63: 107–30.

Chapman, H. H. 2012. "Reading the Judeans and the Judean War in Martial's *Liber spectaculorum*." *Journal for the Study of the Pseudepigrapha* 22: 91–113.

Chapman, H. H., and Z. Rodgers, eds. 2016. *A Companion to Josephus in His World*. Malden, MA: John Wiley & Sons.

Charlesworth, J. H. 2002. *The Pesharim and Qumran History: Chaos or Consensus?* With Appendixes by L. Novakovic. Grand Rapids: Eerdmans.

———2015. "הברכה על הר גריזים"—An Unknown Dead Sea Scroll and Speculations Focused on the Vorlage of Deuteronomy 27:4." Pages 393–415 in *Jesus, Paulus und die Texte von Qumran*. Edited by J. Frey and E. E. Popkes. Tübingen: Mohr Siebeck.

Clarysse, W., and G. van der Veken with S. P. Vlemming. 1983. *The Eponymous Priests of Ptolemaic Egypt (P. L. Bat. 24): Chronological Lists of the Priests of Alexandria and Ptolemais with a Study of the Demotic Transcriptions of their Names*. Leiden: Brill.

Cohen, G. 1989. "The Beginning of the Reign of Alexander Jannaeus." Pages 118–21 in *The Judean–Syrian–Egyptian Conflict of 103–101 B.C.: A Multilingual Dosier Concerning A "War of Sceptres"*. Edited by E. Van 'T Dack, W. Clarysse, G. Cohen, J. Quaegebeur, and J. K. Winnicki. Brussels: Publikatie van het Comité KlassiekeStudies, Subcomité Hellenisme Koninklijke Academie voor Wetenschappen, Letterèn en Schöne Kunsten van België.

———2006. *Hellenistic Settlements in Syria, the Red Sea Basin, and North Africa*. Berkeley: University of California Press.

Cohen, S. J. D. 1979. *Josephus in Galilee and Rome*. Leiden: Brill.

———2001. *The Beginnings of Jewishness*. Berkeley: University of California Press.

Collins, J. J. 1980. "The Epic of Theodotus and the Hellenism of the Hasmoneans." *Harvard Theological Review* 73: 91–104.

————1993. *Daniel*. Minneapolis: Fortress.

————1999. *Between Athens and Jerusalem*. 2nd ed. Grand Rapids: Eerdmans.

————2003. "The Zeal of Phinehas: The Bible and the Legitimation of Violence." *Journal of Biblical Literature* 122: 3–21.

————2010. *The Scepter and the Star*. 2nd ed. New York: Doubleday.

Collins, J. J., and P. W. Flint. 1996. "245.4Qpseudo-Danielᶜ ar." Pages 153–64 in *Qumran Cave 4.XXVII: Parabiblical Texts, Part 3*. Edited by G. Brooks et al. Oxford: Clarendon.

Cotton, H. M., and W. Eck. 2005. "Josephus's Roman Audience: Josephus and the Roman Elites." Pages 37–52 in *Flavius Josephus and Flavian Rome*. Edited by J. Edmondson, S. Mason, and J. Rivers. New York: Oxford University Press.

Cotton, H. M., and D. Gera. 2009. "Olympiodoros, Heliodoros and the Temples of Koile Syria and Phoinike." *Zeitschrift für Papyrologie und Epigraphik* 169: 125–55.

Cotton, H. M., and M. Wörrle. 2007. "Seleukos IV to Heliodoros: A New Dossier of Royal Correspondence from Israel." *Zeitschrift für Papyrologie und Epigraphik* 159: 192–205.

Cromhout, M. 2005. "The Reconstruction of Judean Ethnicity in Q." PhD diss., University of Pretoria, Pretoria.

Dąbrowa, E. 1992. "Könige Syriens in der Gefangenschaft der Parther: Zwei Episoden aus der Geschichte der Beziehungen der Seleukiden zu den Arsakiden." *Tyche* 7: 48–50.

————1998. *The Governors of Roman Syria from Augustus to Septimius Severus*. Bonn: Rudolf Habelt.

————2007. "Samarie entre Jean Hyrcan et Antiochos IX Cyzicène." *Mélanges de l'Université Saint Joseph* 60: 447–59.

————2010a. *The Hasmoneans and Their State*. Kraków: Jagiellonian University Press.

————2010b. "The Hasmoneans and the Religious Homogeneity of Their State." *Scripta Judaica Cracoviensia* 8: 7–14.

Dar, S. 1988. "The History of the Hermon Settlements." *Palestine Exploration Quarterly* 120: 26–44.

Dar, S. 1993. *Settlements and Cult Sites on Mount Hermon, Israel*. London: BAR International Series.

Dar, S., and N. Kokkinos. 1992. "Greek Inscriptions from Senaim on Mount Hermon." *Palestine Exploration Quarterly* 124: 9–25.

De Troyer, K. 2003. *Rewriting the Sacred Text*, Atlanta: Society of Biblical Literature.

de Vaux, R. 1961a. *Ancient Israel*. Vol. 1, *Social Institutions*. New York: McGraw-Hill.

de Vaux, R. 1961b. *Ancient Israel*. Vol. 2, *Religious Institutions*. New York: McGraw-Hill.

Debevoise, N. C. 1938. *A Political History of Parthia*. Chicago: University of Chicago Press.

dei Rossi, A. 2001. *The Light of the Eyes*. Trans. J. Weinberg. New Haven: Yale University Press.

Dentzer, J.-M. 1985. *Hauran I*. Paris: Librairie Orientaliste Paul Geuthner.

Dimant, D. 2001. *Qumran Cave 4.XXI: Parabiblical Texts, Part 4: Pseudo-Prophetic Texts*. Oxford: Clarendon.

Dobias, J. 1924. "Φίλιππος Βαρύπους: A Contribution to the History of the Last Seleukids." *Listy Filoggické* 51: 214–27 (in Czech).

Doudna, G. L. 2001. *4Q Pesher Nahum*. Sheffield: Sheffield Academic.

Downey, G. 1961. *A History of Antioch in Syria: From Seleucus to the Arab Conquest*. Princeton: Princeton University Press.

Eberhardt, B. 2005. "Wer Dient Wem? Die Darstellung des Flavischen Triumphzuges auf dem Titusbogen und bei Josephus." Pages 257–77 in *Josephus and Jewish History in Flavian Rome and Beyond*. Edited by J. Sievers and G. Lembi. Leiden: Brill.

Eckhardt, B. 2013. *Ethnos und herrschaft*. Berlin: de Gruyter.

Eckhardt, K. 1910. "Die armenischen Feldzüge des Lukullus: II. Das Kriegsjahr 69." *Klio: Beiträge zur alten Geschichte* 10: 72–115, 192–231.

Egger, R. 1986, *Josephus Flavius und die Samaritaner*. Göttingen: Vandenhoeck & Ruprecht.

Ehling, K. 2008. *Untersuchungen zur Geschichte der späten Seleukiden (164–63 v. Chr.)*. Stuttgart: Steiner.

Elitzur, Y. 2013. "The Abba Cave: Unpublished Findings and a New Proposal Regarding Abbas's Identity." *Israel Exploration Journal* 63: 83–102.

Eph'al, I. 1982. *The Ancient Arabs*. Jerusalem: Magnes.

Eshel, E., and H. Eshel. 2003. "Dating the Samaritan Pentateuch's Compilation in Light of the Qumran Biblical Scrolls." Pages 215–40 in *Emanuel*. Edited by S. M. Paul. Leiden: Brill.

Eshel, E., H. Eshel, C. Newsom, B. Nitzan, E. Schuller, and A. Yardeni. 1998. *Qumran Cave 4.VI: Poetical and Liturgical Texts, Part 1*. Oxford: Clarendon.

Eshel, H. 1999. "Josephus' View on Judaism Without the Temple in Light of the Discoveries at Masada and Murabba'at." Pages 229–38 in *Gemeinde ohne Tempel*. Edited by B. Ego, A. Lange, and P. Pilhofer. Tübingen: Mohr Siebeck.

———2008. *The Dead Sea Scrolls and the Hasmonean State*. Grand Rapids: Eerdmans.

———2012. "The Growth of Belief in the Sanctity of Mount Gerizim." Pages 509–35 in vol. 1 of *A Teacher for All Generations: Essays in Honor of James C. VanderKam*. Edited by E. F. Mason, et al. Leiden: Brill.

Fantalkin, A., and O. Tal. 2003. "The 'Yannai Line' (BJ I,99–100; AJ XIII, 390–391): Reality or Fiction?" *Palestine Exploration Quarterly* 135: 108–23.

Feldman, L. H. 1984. *Josephus and Modern Scholarship (1937–1980)*. Berlin: de Gruyter.

Finkielsztejn, G. 1998. "More Evidence on John Hyrcanus I's Conquests: Lead Weights and Rhodian Amphora Stamps." *Bulletin of the Anglo-Israel Archaeological Society* 16: 33–63.

Fisher, M. 1987. "Die Strassenstation von Hòrvat MəṢād (Ḥirbet el-Qaṣr) Ein Beitrag zur Geschichte des Weges von Jerusalem nach Emmaus." *Zeitschrift des deutschen Palälstina-Vereins* 103: 117–36.

Fischer, T. 1970. *Untersuchungen zum Partherkrieg Antiochos' VII*. Munich: privately published.

———1972. "Zu Tryphon." *Chrion* 2: 201–13.

———1975. "Zum jüdischen Verfassungsstreit vor Pompejus (Diodor 40,2)." *Zeitschrift des deutschen Palälstina-Vereins* 91: 45–49.

———1992. "Tryphons verfehlter Sieg von Dor?" *Zeitschrift für Papyrologie und Epigraphik* 9: 29–32.

Fitzmyer, J. A. 2000a. "4QpapHistorical Text C." Pages 275–80 in *Qumran Cave 4.XXVI: Cryptic Texts*. Edited by S. J. Pfann. Oxford: Clarendon.

———2000b. "4QHistorical Text D." Pages 281–86 in *Qumran Cave 4.XXVI: Cryptic Texts*. Edited by S. J. Pfann. Oxford: Clarendon.

Flusser, D., ed. 1978. *Josippon [Josephus Gorionides]*. Jerusalem: Bialik Institute (in Hebrew).

Fornara, C. W. 1983. *The Nature of History in Ancient Greece and Rome*. Berkeley: University of California Press.

Freyne, S. 1980. *Galilee from Alexander the Great to Hadrian 323 B.C.E. to 135 C.E.* Wilmington, DE: Michael Glazier.

————2001. "Galileans, Phoenicians and Itureans: A Study of Regional Contrasts in the Hellenistic Age." Pages 188–95 in *Hellenism in the Land of Israel.* Edited by J. J. Collins and G. E. Sterling. Notre Dame: University of Notre Dame Press.

Fuks, G. 1990. "Josephus and the Hasmoneans." *Journal of Jewish Studies* 41: 166–77.

Gal, Z. 1992. *The Lower Galilee During the Iron Age.* Winona Lake: Eisenbrauns.

Garbrecht, G., and Y. Peleg. 1994. "The Water Supply of the Desert Fortresses in the Jordan Valley." *Biblical Archaeologist* 57: 161–70.

Gelzer, M. 1959. *Pompeius.* Munich: F. Bruckmann.

Gera, D. 1985. "Tryphon's Sling from Dor." *Israel Exploration Journal* 35: 153–66.

Giovannini, A., and H. Müller. 1971. "Die Beziehungen zwischen Rom und den Juden im 2 Jh. V. Chr." *Museum Helveticum* 28: 156–71.

Girardet, K. M. 1991. "Der Triumph des Pompeius im Jahre 61 v.Chr.—ex Asia?" *Zeitschrift für Papyrologie und Epigraphik* 89: 201–15.

Gitler, H., and A. Kushnir-Stein. 1999. "The Chronology of a Late Ptolemaic Bronze Coin-Type from Cyprus." *Israel Numismatic Journal* 13: 46–53.

————2009. "A Late Hellenistic Anonymous (?) Coin from Southern Phoenicia." *Swiss Numismatic Revue* 88: 169–72.

Goldstein, J. A. 1976. *I Maccabees.* Garden City: Doubleday.

————1983. *II Maccabees.* New York: Doubleday.

————1989. "The Hasmonean Revolt and the Hasmonean Dynasty." Pages 292–351 in *The Cambridge History of Judaism.* Vol. 2, *The Hellenistic Age.* Edited by W. D. Davies and L. Finkelstein. Cambridge: Cambridge University Press.

Goldsworthy, A. 2006. *Caesar.* New Haven: Yale University Press.

Goodblatt, D., A. Pinnick, and D. R. Schwartz, eds. 2001. *Historical Perspectives.* Leiden: Brill.

Goodman, M. 2007. *Judaism in the Roman World.* Leiden: Brill.

Grabbe, L. L. 1991. "Maccabean Chronology: 167–164 or 168–165 BCE." *Journal of Biblical Literature* 110: 59–74.

————1992. *Judaism from Cyrus to Hadrian.* Vol. 1. Minneapolis: Fortress.

————1997. "The Seventy-Weeks Prophecy (Daniel 9:24–27) in Early Jewish Interpretation." Pages 595–611 in *The Quest for Context and Meaning.* Edited by C. A. Evans and S. Talmon. Leiden: Brill.

————2003. "Poets, Scribes, or Preachers? The Reality of Prophecy in the Second Temple Period." Pages 192–215 in *Knowing the End from the Beginning.* Edited by L. L. Grabbe and R. D. Haak. London: T&T Clark International.

Grainger, J. D. 1991. *Hellenistic Phoenicia.* Oxford: Oxford University Press.

————1997, *A Seleukid Prosopography and Gazetteer.* Leiden: Brill.

————2010. *The Syrian Wars.* Leiden: Brill.

Greenhalgh, P. 1981a. *Pompey: The Republican Prince.* Columbia: University of Missouri Press.

————1981b. *Pompey: The Roman Alexander.* Columbia: University of Missouri Press.

Grojnowski, D. 2015. "Flavius Josephus, Nehemiah, and a Study in Self-Presentation." *Journal for the Study of Judaism* 24: 345–65.

Grootkerk, S. E. 2000. *Ancient Sites in Galilee: A Toponymic Gazetteer.* Leiden: Brill.

Gruen, E. S. 1984. *The Hellenistic World and the Coming of Rome.* 2 vols. Berkeley: University of California Press.

————2016. "The Hasmoneans in Josephus." Pages 222–34 in *A Companion to Josephus in His World*. Edited by H. H. Chapman and Z. Rodgers. Malden: John Wiley & Sons.

Grüll, T. 2006. "A Fragment of a Monumental Roman Inscription in the Islamic Museum of the Haram ash-Sharif, Jerusalem." *Israel Exploration Journal* 56: 183–200.

————2010. "The Date and Circumstances of the Heliodoros Affair: Consideratinos on the Seleucus IV Dossier from Maresha." *Acta classica Universitatis Scientiarum Debreceniensis* 46: 9–20.

Habicht, C. 1989. "The Seleucids and their Rivals." Pages 324–87 in *Cambridge Ancient History*. Vol. 8, *Rome and the Mediterranean to 133 B.C.* Edited by A. E. Astin, F. W. Walbank, M. W. Frederiksen, and R. M. Ogilvie. Cambridge: Cambridge University Press.

Hamshary, M. A. 1995. "Nabateans Reactions Towards Alexandrians Trade Activity in the Ptolemaic Period." Pages 26–35 in *Alessandria e il mondo ellenistico romano*. Edited by N. Bonacasa. Rome: L'Erma di Bretschneider.

Hanson, R. S. 1980. *Tyrian Influence in the Upper Galilee*. Cambridge: American Schools of Oriental Research.

Hanson, R. S., and M. L. Bates. 1976. "Numismatic Report." Pages 146–69 in *Ancient Synagogue Excavations at Khirbet Shema, Upper Galilee, Israel 1970–1972*. Edited by E. M. Meyers, A. T. Kraabel, and J. F. Strange. Durham: American Schools of Oriental Research/Duke University Press.

Harington, D. J. 1988. *The Maccabean Revolt*. Wilmington, DE: Glazier.

Hartel, M. 1987. "Khirbet Zemel 1985–6." *Israel Exploration Journal* 37: 270–72.

Harvey, P., Jr. 2013. "Theophanes of Mytilene." Pages 6688–89 in *Encyclopedia of Ancient History*. Edited by R. Bagnall, K. Brodersen, C. Champion, A. Erskine, and S. Huebner. Oxford: Wiley Blackwell.

Hendin, D. 1994/99. "Four New Jewish Lead Coins or Tokens." *Israel Numismatic Journal* 13: 63–65.

————2007/2008. "Numismatic Expressions of Hasmonean Sovereignty." *Israel Numismatic Journal* 16: 76–91.

————2009/2010a. "Another Style of Jannaeus Overstrike." *Israel Numismatic Journal* 17: 37–38.

————2009/2010b. "Hasmonean Coin Chronologies: Two Notes." *Israel Numismatic Journal* 17: 34–38.

Hendin, D., and I. Shachar. 2008. "The Identity of YNTN on Hasmonean Overstruck Coins and the Chronology of the Alexander Jannaeus Types." *Israel Numismatic Research* 3: 87–94.

Hengel, M. 1974. *Judaism and Hellenism*. 2 vols. Philadelphia: Fortress.

Herman, D. 2006. "The Coins of the Itureans." *Israel Numismatic Research* 1: 58–60.

Hill, G. F. 1910. *Catalogue of the Greek Coins of Phoenicia*. London: Longmans.

Hirschfeld, Y., and D. T. Ariel. 2005. "A Coin Assemblage from the Reign of Alexander Jannaeus Found on the Shore of the Dead Sea." *Israel Exploration Journal* 55: 66–89.

Hjelm, I. 2005. "The Samaritans in Josephus' Jewish 'History'." Pages 27–39 in *Proceedings of the Fifth International Congress of the Société d'Études Samaritaines. Helsinki, August 1–4, 2000*. Edited by H. Shehadeh and H. Tawa with R. Pummer. Paris: P. Geuthner.

Hölbl, G. 2000. *History of Ptolemaic Egypt*. Trans. T. Saavedra. London: Routledge.

Hollander, W. den. 2014. *Josephus, the Emperors, and the city of Rome*. Leiden: Brill.

Holladay, C. R. 1989. *Fragments from Hellenistic Jewish Authors*. Vol. 2, *Poets*. Atlanta: Scholars Press.

Hölscher, G. 1904. *Die Quellen des Josephus für die Zeit vom Exil bis zum jüdischen Kriege.* Leipzig: Tuebner.

Hoover, O. D. 1994. "Striking a Pose: Seleucid Types and Mactpolitik on the Coins of John Hyrcanus I." *The Picus* 3: 40–57.

———2003. "The Seleucid Coinage of John Hyrcanus I: The Transformation of a Dynastic Symbol in Hellenistic Judaea." *American Journal of Numismatics* 15: 29–39.

———2005. "Dethroning Seleucus VII Philometor (Cybiosactes): Epigraphical Arguments Against a Late Seleucid Monarch." *Zeitschrift für Papyrologie und Epigraphik* 151: 95–99.

———2007a. "The Dated Coinage of Gaza in Historical Context (264/3 BC–AD 241/2)." *Schweizerische Numismatische Rundschau* 86: 63–90.

———2007b. "A Revised Chronology for the Late Seleucids at Antioch (121/120–64 BC)." *Historia: Zeitschrift für alte Geschichte* 56: 280–301.

———2008. "Ptolemaic Lead Coinage in Coele Syria (103–101 BCE)." *Israel Numismatic Research* 3: 81–85.

———2009. *Handbook of Syrian Coins.* London: Classical Numismatic Group.

Hoover, O. D., and R. Barkay. 2010. "Important Additions to the Corpus of Nabatean Coins Since 1990." Pages 197–212 in *Coinage of the Caravan Kingdoms.* Edited by M. Huth and P. G. Van Alfen. New York: American Numismatic Society.

Hoover, O. D., A. Houghton, and P. Vesely. 2008. "The Silver Mint of Damascus under Demetrius III and Antiochus XII (97/6 BC–83/2 BC)." *American Numismatic Society* 20: 305–36.

Houghton, A. 1983. *Coins of the Seleucid Empire from the Collection of Arthur Houghton.* New York: American Numismatic Society.

Houghton, A. 1989. "A Victory Coin and the Parthian Wars of Antiochus VII." Page 65 in *Proceedings of the 10th International Congress of Numismatics.* Edited by I. A. Carradice. London: International Association of Professional Numismatists.

Houghton, A. 1992. "The Revolt of Tryphon and the Accession of Antiochus VI at Apamea: The Mints and Chronology of Antiochus VI and Tryphon." *Revue Suisse de numismatique* 71: 119–41.

Houghton, A., C. Lorber, and O. Hoover. 2008. *Seleucid Coins: A Comprehensive Catalogue, Part II: Seleucus IV through Antiochus XIII.* Vol. 1. New York: American Numismatic Society.

Houghton, A., and A. Spaer. 1990. "New Silver Coins of Demetrius III and Antiochus XII at Damascus." *Schweizer Münzblätter* 157 (February): 1–5.

Houston, G. 2009. "Papyrological Evidence for Book Collections and Libraries in the Roman Empire." Pages 233–67 in *Ancient Literacies: The Culture of Reading in Greece and Rome.* Edited by W. A. Johnson and H. N. Parker. Oxford: Oxford University Press.

Hunt, A. 2006. *Missing Priests: The Zadokites in Tradition and History.* New York: T&T Clark International.

Huß, W. 2001, *Ägypten in hellenistischer Zeit 332–30 v. Chr.* Munich: C. H. Beck.

Ilan, T. 1987. "Greek Names of the Hasmoneans." *Jewish Quarterly Review* 78: 1–20.

———1993. "Queen Salamzion Alexandra and Judas Aristobulus I's Widow: Did Jannaeus Alexander Contract a Levirate Marriage?" *Journal for the Study of Judaism* 24: 181–90.

———1996. "Josephus and Nicolaus on Women." Pages 221–62 in vol. 1 of *Geschichte—Tradition—Reflexion.* Edited by H. Cancik, H. Lichtenberger, and P. Schäfer. Tübingen: Mohr Siebeck.

————2006. *Silencing the Queen*. Tübingen: Mohr Siebeck.

Jacobson, H. 2013. "Theodotus, 'On the Jews'." Pages 721–25 in vol. 1 of *Outside the Bible: Ancient Jewish Writings Related to Scripture*. Edited by L. H. Feldman, J. L. Kugel, and L. H. Schiffman. Philadelphia: Jewish Publication Society.

Johns, A. F. 1963. "The Military Strategy of Sabbath Attacks on the Jews." *Vetus Testamentum* 13: 482–86.

Jones, A. H. M. 1931. "The Urbanization of the Iturean Principality." *Journal of Roman Studies* 21: 265–75.

Jones, C. P. 2002. "Towards a Chronology of Josephus." *Scripta Classica Israelica* 21 (2002): 113–31.

Kaplan, Y. 1971. "The Yannai Line." Pages 201–5 in *Roman Frontier Studies 1967*. Edited by S. Applebaum. Tel Aviv: Students' Organization of Tel Aviv University.

Kapp, J., ed. 1772. *Iulii obsequentis quae supersunt ex libro De prodigiis*. Curiae Regnitianae: Vierling.

Kasher, A. 1988. *Jews, Idumaeans and Ancient Arabs*. Tübingen: J. C. B. Mohr.

————1990. *Jews and Hellenistic Cities in Eretz-Israel*. Tübingen: J. C. B. Mohr.

————2005. "'The Enclave of Cuthaeans'—A Factor in Jewish-Samaritan Relations in Antiquity." Pages 205–21 in *Proceedings of the Fifth International Congress of the Société d'Études Samaritaines. Helsinki, August 1–4, 2000*. Edited by H. Shehadeh and H. Tawa with R. Pummer. Paris: P. Geuthner.

Kashtan, N. 1988. "Akko-Ptolemais: A Maritime Metropolis in Hellenistic and Early Roman Times, 332 BCE–70 CE, as Seen through the Literary Sources." *Mediterranean Historical Review* 3: 37–57.

Keaveney, A. 2009. *Lucullus*. 2nd ed. Piscataway: Gorgias.

Keddie, G. A. 2013. "Solomon to His Friends: The Role of Epistolarity in Eupolemos." *Journal for the Study of the Pseudepigrapha* 22: 201–37.

Kindler, A. 1978. "Akko, A City of Many Names." *Bulletin of the American Schools of Oriental Research* 231: 51–55.

Klausner, J. 1972a. "The First Hasmonean Rulers: Jonathan and Simeon." Pages 183–207 in *The World History of the Jewish People VI: The Hellenistic Age*. Edited by A. Schalit. New Brunswick: Rutgers University Press.

————1972b. "John Hyrcanus I." Pages 211–21 in *The World History of the Jewish People VI: The Hellenistic Age*. Edited by A. Schalit. New Brunswick: Rutgers University Press.

————1972c. "Judah Aristobulus and Jannaeus Alexander I." Pages 222–41 in *The World History of the Jewish People VI: The Hellenistic Age*. Edited by A. Schalit. New Brunswick: Rutgers University Press.

Klawans, J. 2012. *Josephus and the Theologies of Ancient Judaism*. Oxford: Oxford University Press.

Klebs, E. 1929. "Aemilius." Pages 588–90 in vol. 1 of *Paulys Real-Encyclopädie der classischen Altertumswissenschaft*. Edited by G. Wissowa. Stuttgart: J. B. Metzlersche.

Klein, K. M. 2013. "Arabs." Pages 601–605 in *Encyclopedia of Ancient History*. Edited by R. Bagnall, K. Brodersen, C. Champion, A. Erskine, and S. Huebner. Oxford: Wiley Blackwell.

Kleiner, F. S. 1990. "The Arches of Vespasian in Rome." *Römische Mitteilungen* 97: 127–36.

Kloppenborg, J. S. 2005. "*Evocatio Deorum* and the Date of Mark." *Journal of Biblical Literature* 124: 419–50.

Koehler, L., and W. Baumgartner, J. J. Stamm, and B. Hartman. 2001. *The Hebrew and Aramaic Lexicon of the Old Testament*. Trans. M. E. J. Richardson. Leiden: Brill.

Kokkinos, N. 1998. *The Herodian Dynasty*. Sheffield: Sheffield Academic.

Kraus, C. S., and A. J. Woodman. 1997. *Latin Historians*. Oxford: Oxford University Press.

Krencker, D., and W. Zschietzschmann. 1938. *Römische Tempel in Syrien*. 2 vols. Berlin: de Gruyter.

Kropp, A. J. M. 2013. "Ituraea and Ituraeans." Page 3543 in *Encyclopedia of Ancient History*. Edited by R. Bagnall, K. Brodersen, C. Champion, A. Erskine, and S. Huebner. Oxford: Wiley Blackwell.

Kugel, J. 2007. "How Old is the *Aramaic Levi Document?*" *Dead Sea Discoveries* 14: 291–312.

Kuhn, A. 1891. *Beitrage zur geschichte der Seleukiden vom tode Antiochos' VII Sidetes vom tode Antiochus XIII. Asiatikos (129–64 V.C.)*. Altkirch: E. Masson.

Kushnir-Stein, A. 1995. "Gaza Coinage Dated LIC—A Reappraisal." *Schweizerische Numismatische Rundschau* 74: 49–55.

———2000. "Late Hellenistic Coins of Gaza and the Date of the Hasmonean Conquest of the City." *Schweizer Münzblätter* 198: 22–24.

———2000–2002. "Some Observations on Palestinian Coins with a Beveled Edge." *Israel Numismatic Journal* 14: 78–83.

Kushnir-Stein, A., and H. Gitler. 1992/93. "Numismatic Evidence from Tel Beer-Sheva and the Beginning of Nabatean Coinage." *Israel Exploration Journal* 12: 13–20.

Landau, T. 2006. *Out-Heroding Herod*. Leiden: Brill.

Landau, Y. H. 1961. "A Greek Inscription from Acre." *Israel Exploration Journal* 11: 118–26.

Laqueur, R. 1920. *Der jüdische Historiker Flavius Josephus*. Giessen: Münich Verlagsbuchhandlung.

Leach, J. 1978. *Pompey the Great*. London: Croom Helm.

Leibner, U. 2009. *Settlement and History in Hellenistic, Roman, and Byzantine Galilee*. Tübingen: Mohr Siebeck.

Leith, M. J. 2010. "Daliyeh, Wadi ed." Pages 507–509 in *Eerdmans Dictionary of Early Judaism*. Edited by J. J. Collins and D. C. Harlow. Grand Rapids: Eerdmans.

Levenson, D. B., and T. R. Martin. 2009. "Akairos or Eukairos? The Nickname of the Seleucid King Demetrius III in the Transmission of the Texts of Josephus' *War* and *Antiquities*." *Journal for the Study of Judaism* 40: 307–41.

Lichtenberger, A. 2003. *Kulte und Kultur der Dekapolis*. Wiesbaden: Harrassowitz.

Lichtenstein, H. 1931–32. "Die Fastenrolle." *Hebrew Union College Annual* 8–9: 257–351.

Liddell, H. G., R. Scott, H. S. Jones, and R. McKenzie. 1968. *A Greek–English Lexicon*. Rev. ed. Oxford: Clarendon.

Loginov, S. D., and A. B. Nikitin. 1996. "Parthian Coins from Margiana: Numismatics and History." *Bulletin of the Asia Institute* 10: 39–51.

Machiela, D. A. 2009. *The Dead Sea Genesis Apocryphon*. Leiden: Brill.

———2010. "A Brief History of the Second Temple Name 'John Hyrcanus'." *Journal of Jewish Studies* 61: 117–38.

Macurdy, G. H. 1932. *Hellenistic Queens*. Baltimore: The Johns Hopkins University Press.

Mader, G. 2000. *Josephus and the Politics of Historiography*. Leiden: Brill.

Magen, Y. 2008a. *Mount Gerizim Excavations*. Vol. 2. Jerusalem: Staff Officer of Archaeology—Civil Administration of Judea and Samaria Israel Antiquities Authority.

————2008b. *The Samaritans and the Good Samaritan*. Jerusalem: Staff Officer of Archaeology—Civil Administration of Judea and Samaria Israel Antiquities Authority.

————2010. "Bells, Pendants, Snakes and Stones: A Samaritan Temple to the Lord on Mt. Gerizim." *Biblical Archaeology Review* 36: 26–35, 70.

Magness, J. 2008. "The Arch of Titus at Rome and the Fate of the God of Israel." *Journal of Jewish Studies* 59: 201–17.

Manandyan, H. 2007. *Tigranes II and Rome*. Trans. G. A. Bournoutian. Costa Mesa: Mazda.

Marciak, M. 2011. "Seleucid–Parthian Adiabene in the Light of Ancient Geographical and Ethnographical Texts." *Anabasis: Studia Classica et Orientalia* 2: 179–208.

Marcus, R., trans. 1966. *Josephus: Jewish Antiquities, Books XII–XIV*. Cambridge, MA: Harvard University Press.

Marincola, J. 1997. *Authority and Tradition in Ancient Historiography*. Cambridge: Cambridge University Press.

Mason, S. 1991. *Flavius Josephus on the Pharisees*. Leiden: Brill.

————1997. "An Essay on Character: The Aim and Audience of Josephus's Vita." Pages 31–77 in *Internationales Josephus-Kolloquium Münster 1997*. Edited by J. U. Kalms. Münster: Lit.

————1998. "Should Any Wish to Enquire Further (*Ant.* 1.25): The Aim and Audience of Josephus's *Judean Antiquities/Life*." Pages 64–103 in *Understanding Josephus*. Edited by S. Mason. Sheffield: Sheffield Academic.

————2001. *Life of Josephus*. Leiden: Brill.

————2009. *Josephus, Judea, and Christian Origins*. Peabody, MA: Hendrickson.

————2011. "What is History? Using Josephus for Judaean-Roman War." Pages 155–240 in *The Jewish Revolt Against Rome*. Edited by M. Popović. Leiden: Brill.

McCarthy, C., ed. 2007. *Biblia Hebraica Quinta, Fascicle 5: Deuteronomy*. Stuttgart: Deutsche Bibelgesellschaft.

McLaren, J. S. 1991. *Power and Politics in Palestine*. Sheffield: JSOT.

————1998. *Turbulent Times?* Sheffield: Sheffield Academic.

Mendels, D. 1998. *Identity, Religion and Historiography*. Sheffield: Sheffield Academic.

Meshel, Z. 1998. "Questioning Masada Governments-in-Exile: The Judean Wilderness as the Last Bastion of Jewish Revolts." *Biblical Archaeology Review* 24: 46–53, 68.

Meshorer, Y. 1982. *Ancient Jewish Coinage*. Vol. 1. Dix Hills, NY: Amphora.

————2011. *A Treasury of Jewish Coins from the Persian Period to Bar Kokhba*. Nyack: Amphora.

Meyers, E. 1976. "Galilean Regionalism as a Factor in Historical Reconstruction." *Bulletin of the American Schools of Oriental Research* 221: 93–101.

Meyers, E. M., and M. A. Chancey. 2012. *Alexander to Constantine*. New Haven: Yale University Press.

Meyers, Eric, J. F. Strange, and C. L. Meyers, eds. 1981. *Excavations at Ancient Meiron, Upper Galilee, Israel 1971–72, 1974–75, 1977*. Cambridge: American Schools of Oriental Research.

Milgrom, J. 2001. *Leviticus 23–27*. New York: Doubleday.

Millar, F. 1993. *The Roman Near East 31 BC–AD 337*. Cambridge, MA: Harvard University Press.

Mine, H. 1981. "Coins of Alexander Yannai." *Journal of the Society for Ancient Numismatics* 12: 49–67.

Mitford, T. B. 1939. "Contributions to the Epigraphy of Cyprus: Some Hellenistic Inscriptions." *Archiv für Papyrusforschung und verwandte* 13: 34–36.

Mittmann, S. 1964. "Die römische Straße von Gerasa nach Adraa." *Zeitschrift des deutschen Palälstina Vereins* 80: 113–36.

———2006. "Die Hellenistische Mauerinschrift von Gadara (Umm Qēs) und die Seleukidisch Dynastische Toponoymie Palästinas." *Journal of Northwest Semitic Languages* 32: 25–54.

Moehring, H. R. 1975. "The *Acta pro Judaeis* in the *Antiquities* of Flavius Josephus." Pages 124–58 in vol. 3 of *Christianity, Judaism and other Greco-Roman Cults*. Edited by J. Neusner. Leiden: Brill.

Mommsen, T, ed. 1873. *Corpus Inscriptionum Latinarum*. Berlin: de Gruyter.

Mor, M. 1989. "Samaritan History: The Persian, Hellenistic and Hasmonean Period." Pages 1–18 in *The Samaritans*. Edited by A. D. Crown. Tübingen: J. C. B. Mohr.

Müller, J. 1711. *De Alexandra judaeorum regina tanquam specimine sapientis ex hacgente foeminae ad illustrandam historiam factionum judaicarum*. Altdorffi-Noricorum: Kohlesiano.

Muraoka, T. 2009. *A Greek–English Lexicon of the Septuagint*. Louvain: Peeters.

Myers, E. A. 2010. *The Ituraeans and the Roman Near East*. Cambridge: Cambridge University Press.

Nercessian, Y. T. 2000. "Tigranes the Great of Armenia and the Mint of Damascus." *Armenian Numismatic Studies* 9: 95–107 and plates 26–27.

Netzer, E. 2001. *The Palaces of the Hasmoneans and Herod the Great*. Jerusalem: Yad-Ben Zvi.

Neusner, J. 1965. *A History of the Jews in Babylonia*. Vol. 1. Leiden: Brill.

———1973. *From Politics to Piety*. Englewood Cliffs: Prentice-Hall.

Newell, E. T. 1939. *Late Seleucid Mints in Ake-Ptolemais and Damascus*. New York: American Numismatic Society.

Nicholls, M. C. 2011. "Galen and Libraries in the *Peri Alupias*." *Journal of Roman Studies* 101: 123–42.

Nickelsburg, G. W. E. 1984. "The Bible Rewritten and Expanded." Pages 89–156 in *Jewish Writings of the Second Temple Period*. Edited by M. E. Stone. Philadelphia: Fortress.

Niese, B., ed. 1892. *Flavii Iosephi Opera. Vol. III: Antiquitatum Iudaicarum Livri XI–XV*. Berlin, Weidman.

———1893. "Zur Chronologie des Josephus." *Hermes* 28: 194–229.

———ed. 1894. *Flavii Iosephi Opera. Vol. VI: De Bello Iudaico*. Berlin, Weidman.

Noam, V., ed. 2003. *Megillat Ta'anit: Versions, Interpretation, History with a Critical Edition*. Jerusalem: Yad Ben-Zvi (in Hebrew).

———2014. "The Story of King Jannaeus (*b. Qiddušin* 66a): A Pharisaic Reply to Sectarian Polemic." *Harvard Theological Review* 107: 31–58.

Olbrycht, M. J. 2010. "The Early Reign of Mithradates II the Great in Parthia." *Anabasis: Studia Classica et Orientalia* 1: 144–58.

Oren, E. D., and U. Rappaport. 1984. "The Necropolis of Maresha-Beth Govrin." *Israel Exploration Journal* 34: 114–53.

Overman, J. A. 2009. "Between Rome and Parthia: Galilee and the Implications of Empire." Pages 279–99 in *A Wandering Galilean*. Edited by Z. Rogers with M. Daly-Denton and A. F. McKinley. Leiden: Brill.

Pastor, J. 1997. *Land and Economy in Ancient Palestine*. New York: Routledge.

Pastor, J., P. Stern, and M. Mor, ed. 2011. *Flavius Josephus: Interpretation and History*. Leiden: Brill.

Pestman, P. W. 1967. *Chronologie égyptienne d'après les textes démotiques (332 av. J.-C.–453 ap. J. C.)*. Leiden: Brill.

Pfann, S. J. 2006. "Dated Bronze Coinage of the Sabbatical Years of Release and the First Jewish City Coin." *Bulletin of the Anglo-Israel Archaeological Society* 24: 101–13.

Pfanner, M. 1983. *Der Titusbogen*. Mainz am Rhein: P. von Zabern.

Piotrkowski, M. M. 2011. "When Did Alexander Jannai Capture Which Gadara?" *Jewish Studies Quarterly* 18: 266–76.

Plummer, R. 1982. "Genesis 34 in Jewish Writings of the Hellenistic and Roman Periods." *Harvard Theological Review* 75: 177–88.

————1989. "Samaritan Material Remains and Archaeology." Pages 135–77 in *The Samaritans*. Edited by A. D. Crown. Tübingen: Mohr.

————2009. *The Samaritans in Flavius Josephus*. Tübingen: Mohr Siebeck.

————2010. "Samaria." Pages 1081–84 in *Eerdmans Dictionary of Early Judaism*. Edited by J. J. Collins and D. C. Harlow. Grand Rapids: Eerdmans.

Popović, M. 2011. "The Jewish Revolt Against Rome: History, Sources and Perspectives." Pages 1–25 in *The Jewish Revolt Against Rome*. Edited by M. Popović. Leiden: Brill.

Price, J. J. 2001. "Josephus." Pages 219–43 in *The Oxford History of Historical Writing: Beginnings to AD 600*. Edited by A. Feldherr and G. Hardy. Oxford: Oxford University Press.

Pucci, M. B. Z. 2006. "Josephus' Ambiguities: His Comments on Cited Documents." *Journal of Jewish Studies* 57: 1–10.

Rajak, T. 1973. "Justus of Tiberius." *Classical Quarterly* 23: 345–68.

————1983. *Josephus*. London: Duckworth.

————2001. *The Jewish Dialogue with Greece and Rome*. Leiden: Brill.

Rappaport, U. 1994. "Where Was Josephus Lying?—In His Life or in the War?" Pages 279–89 in *Josephus and the History of the Greco-Roman Period*. Edited by F. Parente and J. Sievers. Leiden: Brill.

————2012. "Review of *The Hasmoneans and their State: A Study in History, Ideology, and the Institutions* (Kraków: Jagiellonian University Press, 2010)." *Journal for the Study of Judaism* 43: 392–94.

Rasp, H. 1924. "Flavius Josephus und die jüdischen Religionsparteien." *Zeitschrift für die neuetestamentliche Wissenschaft* 23: 27–47.

Rawson, E. 1994. "Caesar: Civil War and Dictatorship." Pages 421–67 in *The Cambridge Ancient History Volume IX: The Last Age of the Roman Republic, 146–43 B.C.E.* Edited by J. A. Crook, A. Lintott, and E. Rawson. Cambridge: Cambridge University Press.

Raynor, J., and Y. Meshorer. 1988. *The Coins of Ancient Meiron*. Winona Lake: Eisenbrauns.

Reed, J. L. 2000. *Archaeology and the Galilean Jesus*. Harrisburg, PA: Trinity Press International.

Regev, E. 2013. *The Hasmoneans*. Göttingen: Vandenhoeck & Ruprecht.

Reisner, G., A. Clarence, S. Fisher, and D. G. Lyon. 1924. *Harvard Excavations at Samaria, 1908–1910*. 2 vols. Cambridge, MA: Harvard University Press.

Restö, J. 2003. *The Arabs in Antiquity*. New York: RoutledgeCurzon.

Richards, G. C. 1939. "The Composition of Josephus' *Antiquities*." *Classical Quarterly* 33: 36–40.

Richardson, P. 1996. *Herod*. Columbia: University of South Carolina Press.

Ritmeyer, L. 1992. "Locating the Original Temple Mount." *Biblical Archaeology Review* 18: 24–29.

Rives, J. 2005. "Flavian Religious Policy and the Destruction of the Jerusalem Temple." Pages 145–66 in *Flavius and Flavian Rome*. Edited by J. Edmondson, S, Mason, and J. Rivers. Oxford: Oxford University Press.

Rodgers, Z. 2006a. "Justice for Justus: A Re-Examination of Justus of Tiberius' Role in Josephus' *Autobiography*." Pages 169–92 in *Biographical Limits in the Ancient World*. Edited by B. McGing and J. Mossman. Swansea: Classical Press of Wales.

Rodgers, Z., ed. 2006b. *Making History: Josephus and Historical Method*. Leiden: Brill.

————2009. "Monarchy vs. Priesthood: Josephus, Justus of Tiberius, and Agrippa II." Pages 173–84 in *A Wandering Galilean*. Edited by Z. Rogers with M. Daly-Denton and A. F. McKinley. Leiden: Brill.

Rooke, D. W. 2000. *Zadok's Heirs*. Oxford: Oxford University Press.

Roschinski, H. P. 1980. "Geschichte der Nabatäer." *Bonner Jahrbücher* 180: 141–44.

Rothschild, C. K., and T. W. Thompson. 2011. "Galen: On the Avoidance of Grief." *Early Christianity* 2: 110–29.

Rubenstein, J. L. 1995. *History of Sukkot in the Second Temple and Rabbinic Periods*. Atlanta: Scholars Press.

Runesson, A., D. D. Binder, and B. Olsson, eds. 2008. *The Ancient Synagogue from Its Origins to 200 C.E.* Leiden: Brill.

Sachs, A., and H. Hunger, ed. 1996. *Astronomical Diaries and Related Texts from Babylonia*. Vol. 3, *Diaries from 164 B.C. to 61 B.C. 161*. Vienna: Verlag der Osterreichischen Akademie der Wissenschaften.

Sarte, M. 1979. "Rome et les Nabateens a la fin de la republique (65–30 a.v. J.C.)." *Revue des etudes anciennes* 81: 37–53.

Sarte, M. 2005. *The Middle East Under Rome*. Trans. C. Porter and E. Rawlings with J. Routier-Pucci. Cambridge, MA: Harvard University Press.

Savalli-Lestrade, I. 1998. *Les "Philoi" royaux dans l'Asie hell énistique*. Geneva: Droz.

Schenker, A. 2008. "Le Seigneur choisir-t-il le lieu de son nom ou l'a-t-il choisi? L'apport de la Bible Grecque ancienne à l'histoire de texte samaritain et massorétique." Pages 339–51 in *Scripture in Tradition*. Edited by A. Voitila and J. Jokiranta. Leiden: Brill.

Schöene, A., ed. 1999. *Eusebi Chronicorum canonum quae supersunt*. 3rd ed. 2 vols. Zurich: Weidmann.

Schofield, A., and J. C. VanderKam. 2005. "Were the Hasmoneans Zadokites?" *Journal of Biblical Literature* 214: 73–87.

Schorch, S. 2005. "The Reading(s) of the Tora in Qumran." Pages 105–14 in *Proceedings of the Fifth International Congress of the Société d'Études Samaritaines. Helsinki, August 1–4, 2000*. Edited by H. Shehadeh and H. Tawa with R. Pummer. Paris: P. Geuthner.

Schuller, E. M. 2006. "Prayers and Psalms from the Pre-Maccabean Period." *Dead Sea Discoveries* 13: 306–18.

Schuller, E., and M. Bernstein. 2001. "371–373. 4QNarrative and Poetic Composition[a-c]." Pages 153–204 in *Qumran Cave 4.XXVIII: Miscellanea, Part 2*. Edited by M. Bernstein, M. Brady, J. Charlesworth, P. Flint, H. Misgav, S. Pfann, E. Schuller, E. J. C. Tigchelaar, and J. VanderKam. Oxford: Clarendon.

Schürer, E., G. Vermes, F. Millar, and M. Black, eds. 1973–87. *The History of the Jewish People in the Age of Jesus Christ (175 B.C.–A.D.135*. 3 vols. Rev. ed. Edinburgh: T. & T. Clark.

Schwartz, D. R. 1983. "Josephus and Nicolaus on the Pharisees." *Journal for the Study of Judaism* 14: 157–71.

———2000. "Aemilius Scaurus, Marcus." Pages 9–10 in vol. 1 of *Encyclopedia of the Dead Sea Scrolls*. Edited by L. H. Schiffman and J. C. VanderKam. Oxford: Oxford University Press.

———2005. "Herodians and *Ioudaioi* in Flavian Rome." Pages 63–78 in *Flavius Josephus and Flavian Rome*. Edited by J. Edmondson, S. Mason, and J. Rivers. Oxford: Oxford University Press.

———2011a. "Josephus, Catullus, Divine Providence, and the Date of the *Judean War*." Pages 331–52 in *Flavius Josephus: Interpretation and History*. Edited by J. Pastor, P. Stern, and M. Mor. Leiden: Brill.

———2011b. "Yannai and Pella, Josephus and Circumcision." *Dead Sea Discoveries* 18: 339–59.

———2013. *Reading the First Century*. Tübingen: Mohr Siebeck.

Schwartz, S. 1990a. "Georgius Syncellus's Account of Ancient Jewish History." *Proceedings of the Tenth World Congress of Jewish Studies* 8: 1–8.

———1990b. *Josephus and Judaean Politics*. Leiden: Brill.

———2001. *Imperialism and Jewish Society, 200 B.C.E. to 640 C.E.* Princeton: Princeton University Press.

Scolnic, B, E. 2010. "Mattathias and the Jewish Man of Modein." *Journal of Biblical Literature* 129: 463–83.

Seager, R. 1979. *Pompey*. Berkeley: University of California Press.

Seeman, C. 2013. *Rome and Judea in Transition*. New York: Peter Lang.

Seger, J. D. 1977. "The Search for Maccabean Gezer." Pages 389–95 in *Proceedings of the Sixth World Congress of Jewish Studies Held at the Hebrew University of Jerusalem, 13–19 August 1973 Under the Auspices of the Israel Academy of Sciences and Humanities*. Edited by A. Shin'an. Jerusalem: World Union of Jewish Studies.

Seager, R. 1979. *Pompey*. Berkeley: University of California Press.

Seyrig, H. 1950. *Notes on Syrian Coins*. New York: American Numismatic Society.

———1958. "Monnaies Grecques des fouilles de Doura et d'Antioche." *Revue Numismatique* 1: 177–81.

Shachar, I. 2004. "The Historical and Numismatic Significance of Alexander Jannaeus's Later Coinage as Found in Archaeological Excavations." *Palestine Exploration Quarterly* 136: 5–33.

Shahar, Y. 2004. *Josephus Geographicus*. Tübingen: Mohr Siebeck.

Shatzman, I. 1991. *The Armies of the Hasmonaeans and Herod*. Tübingen: Mohr Siebeck.

———1995. "Stone-Balls from Tel Dor and the Artillery of the Hellenistic World." *Scripta Classica Israelica* 14: 52–72.

———1999. "The Integration of Judaea into the Roman Empire." *Scripta classica Israelica* 18: 49–84.

———2007. "Jews and Gentiles from Judas Maccabaeus to John Hyrcanus According to Contemporary Jewish Sources." Pages 237–70 in *Studies in Josephus and Varieties of Ancient Judaism*. Edited by S. J. D. Cohen and J. J. Schwartz. Leiden: Brill.

Sherwin-White, A. N. 1994. "Lucullus, Pompey and the East." Pages 229–73 in *The Cambridge Ancient History Volume IX: The Last Age of the Roman Republic, 146–43 B.C.E.* Edited by J. A. Crook, A. Lintott, and E. Rawson. 2nd ed. Cambridge: Cambridge University Press.

Shutt, R. J. H. 1961. *Studies in Josephus*. London: SPCK.

Siegert, F., H. Schreckenberg, and M. Vogel. 2001. *Aus meinem Leben (Vita)*. Tübingen: Mohr Siebeck.

Sievers, J. 1990. *The Hasmoneans and Their Supporters*. Atlanta: Scholars Press.

———2001a. "Josephus, First Maccabees, Sparta, the Three *haireseis* and Cicero." *Journal for the Study of Judaism* 32: 241–51.

———2001b. "What's in a Name? Antiochus in Josephus' *Bellum Judaicum*." *Journal of Jewish Studies* 34–47.

Sievers, J. 2007. "The Ancient Lists of Contents of Josephus' Antiquities." Pages 271–91 in *Studies in Josephus and the Varieties of Ancient Judaism*. Edited by S. J. D. Cohen and J. J. Schwartz. Leiden: Brill.

———2013. "Josephus' Rendering of Latin Terminology in Greek." *Journal of Jewish Studies* 64: 1–18.

Sinclair, T. 1994–95. "The Site of Tigranocerta. I." *Revue des Études Arméniennes* 25: 183–253.

———1996–97. "The Site of Tigranocerta (II)." *Revue des Études Arméniennes* 26: 51–117.

Sivan, R., and G. Solar. 1994. "Excavations in the Jerusalem Citadel, 1980–1988." Pages 168–76 in *Ancient Jerusalem Revealed*. Edited by H. Geva. Jerusalem: Israel Exploration Society.

Smallwood, E. M. 1981. *The Jews Under Roman Rule*. Leiden: Brill.

Smallwood, E. M., and T. Rajak. 2012. "Josephus (Flavius Josephus)." Pages 798–99 in *Oxford Classical Dictionary*. Edited by S. Hornblower, A. Spawforth, and E. Eidinow. 4th ed. Oxford: Oxford University Press.

Smith, M. 1956. "Palestinian Judaism in the First Century." Pages 67–81 in *Israel: Its Role in Civilization*. Edited by M. Davis. New York: Harper & Row.

———1966. *Studies in The Cult of Yahweh*. Leiden: Brill.

Smith, P. 1997. "The Human Skeletal Remains from the Abba Cave." *Israel Exploration Journal* 27: 121–24.

Steiner, R. C. 1999. "Incomplete Circumcision in Egypt and Edom: Jeremiah (9:24–25) in the Light of Josephus and Jonckheere." *Journal of Biblical Literature* 118: 497–505.

Sterling, G. E. 1992. *Historiography and Self-Definition*. Leiden: Brill.

———2000. "Explaining Defeat: Polybius and Josephus on the Wars with Rome." Pages 135–51 in *Internationales Josephus-Kolloquium Aarhus 1999*. Edited by J. U. Kalms. Münster: Lit.

Stern, E., and Y. Magen. 2002. "Archaeological Evidence for the First Stage of the Samaritan Temple on Mount Gerizim." *Israel Exploration Journal* 52: 49–57.

Stern, M. 1961. "The Relations Between Judea and Rome During the Reign of John Hyrcanus." *Zion* 26: 3–19 (in Hebrew).

Stern, M., ed. 1974–80. *Greek and Latin Authors on Jews and Judaism*. 2 vols. Jerusalem: Israel Academy of Sciences.

Stern, P. 2010. "*Life of Josephus:* The Autobiography of Flavius Josephus." *Journal for the Study of Judaism* 41: 63–93.

Steudel, A. 2000. "Testimonia." Pages 937–38 in vol. 2 of *Encyclopedia of the Dead Sea Scrolls*. Edited by L. H. Schiffman and J. C. VanderKam. Oxford: Oxford University Press

Stiebel, G. D. 2004. "A Hellenistic *Gladius* from Jericho." Pages 229–32 in *Hasmonean and Herodian Palaces at Jericho*. Vol. 2, *Final Reports of the 1973–1987 Excavations*. Edited by E. Netzer. Jerusalem: Israel Exploration Society.

Syon, D. 1992/93. "The Coins from Gamala: Interim Report." *Israel Numismatic Journal* 12: 34–55.

———2004. "Tyre and Gamla." PhD diss., Hebrew University, Jerusalem.

———2006. "Numismatic Evidence of Jewish Presence in Galilee Before the Hasmonean Annexation?" *Israel Numismatic Research* 1: 21–24.

———2008. "The Bronze Coinage of Tyre: The First Years of Autonomy." *American Journal of Numismatics* 20: 295–304.

Tcherikover, V. 1959. *Hellenistic Civilization and the Jews*. New York: Jewish Publication Society of America.

Tessaro, T. 1995. "Hellenistic and Roman Ceramic Cooking Ware from Bethsaida." Pages 127–39 in *Bethsaida*. Edited by R. Arav and R. A. Freund. Kirksville, MO: Truman State University Press.

Thackeray, H. St. J., trans. 1927. *Josephus: The Jewish War, Books I–III*. Cambridge, MA: Harvard University Press.

———1929. *Josephus, the Man and the Historian*. New York: Jewish Institute of Religion.

Thoma, C. 1994. "John Hyrcanus I as Seen by Josephus and Other Early Jewish Sources." Pages 127–40 in *Josephus and the History of the Greco-Roman Period*. Edited by F. Parente and J. Sievers. Leiden: Brill.

Tov, E. 2010. *Revised Lists of the Texts from the Judaean Desert*. Leiden: Brill.

Tushingham, A. D. 1972. "A Hellenistic Inscription from Samaria-Sebaste." *Palestine Exploration Quarterly* 114: 59–63.

Tuval, M. 2011. "A Jewish Priest in Rome." Pages 397–411 in *Flavius Josephus: Interpretation and History*. Edited by M. Mohr, P. Stern, and J. Pastor. Leiden: Brill.

Van Berchem, D. 1983. "Une inscription flavienne du Musée d'Antioche." *Museum Helveticum* 40: 187–89.

Van der Spek, R. J. 1997–98. "New Evidence from the Babylonian Astronomical Diaries Concerning Seleucid and Arsacid History." *Archiv für Orientforschung* 44/45: 167–75.

Van Ooteghem, J. 1954. *Pompée le grand: bâtisseur d'empire*. Brussels: Palais des Académies.

Van 'T Dack, E. 1981. "Le conflict judéo-syro-égyptien de 103/102 av. J.-C." Pages 303–12 in *Proceedings of the Sixteenth International Congress of Papyrology*. Edited by R. S. Bagnall et al. Chico: Scholars Press.

Van 'T Dack, E., W. Clarysse, G. Cohen, J. Quaegebeur, and J. K. Winnicki, ed. 1989. *The Judean Syrian–Egyptian Conflict of 103–101 B.C.: A Multingual Dosier Concerning a "War of Sceptres"*. Brussels: Publikatie van het Comité Klassieke Studies, Subcomité Hellenisme Koninklijke Academie voor Wetenschappen, Letterèn en Schone Kunsten van België.

VanderKam, J. C. 2004. *From Joshua to Caiaphas*. Minneapolis: Fortress.

Varneda, P. V. I. 1986. *The Historical Method of Flavius Josephus*. Leiden: Brill.

Vermes, G. 2007. "Historiographical Elements in the Qumran Writings: A Synopsis of the Textual Evidence." *Journal of Jewish Studies* 58: 121–39.

Wacholder, B. Z. 1962. *Nicolaus of Damascus*. Berkeley: University of California Press.

———1973. "The Calendar of Sabbatical Cycles During the Second Temple and the Early Rabbinic Period." *Hebrew Union College Annual* 44: 153–96.

———1974. *Eupolemus*. Cincinnati: Hebrew Union College Jewish Institute of Religion.

———1983. "The Calendar of Sabbath Years During the Second Temple Era: A Response." *Hebrew Union College Annual* 54: 123–33.

Walbank, F. W. 1972. *Polybius*. Berkeley: University of California Press.

———1993. *The Hellenistic World*. Rev. ed. Cambridge, MA: Harvard University Press.

Weber, W. 1973. *Josephus und Vespasian*. Hildesheim: Olms.

Weiss, H. 1998. "The Sabbath in the Writings of Josephus." *Journal for the Study of Judaism* 29: 363–90.

Werman, C. 2006. "Epochs and End-Time: The 490-Year Scheme in Second Temple Literature." *Dead Sea Discoveries* 13: 229–55.

Werner, C. 1877. *Johann Hyrkan*. Wernigerode: A. Angerstein.

Wheaton, G. 2012. "The Festival of Hanukkah in 2 Maccabees; Its Meaning and Function." *Catholic Biblical Quarterly* 74: 247–62.

Whitehorne, J. E. G. 1994. *Cleopatras*. London: Routledge.

Wilker, J. 2011. "Josephus, The Herodians, and the Jewish War." Pages 271–89 in *The Jewish Revolt Against Rome*. Edited by M. Popović. Leiden: Brill.

Will, E. 1983. "Un vieux problème de la topographie de la Beqa' antique: Chalcis de Liban." *Zeitschrift des deutschen Palälstina-Vereins* 99: 141–46.

Wise, M. O. 1994. *Thunder in Gemini*. Sheffield: Sheffield Academic.

———1997. "To Know the Times and the Seasons: A Study of the Aramaic Chronograph 4Q559." *Journal for the Study of the Pseudepigrapha* 15: 3–51.

———2003. "Dating the Teacher of Righteousness and the Flourit of His Movement." *Journal of Biblical Literature* 122: 53–87.

———2005. "4Q245 (PSDAN^c AR) and the High Priesthood of Judas Maccabaeus." *Dead Sea Discoveries* 12: 313–62.

Wright, G. G. 1957. "The Second Campaign at Tell Balâtah (Shechem)." *Bulletin of the American Schools of Oriental Research* 148: 11–28.

Wright, N. L. 2010. "A Late Seleukid Bronze Hoard, c. 1988 (*CH* 10, 349)." Pages 245–64 in *Coin Hoards*. Vol. 10. Edited by O. Hoover, A. Meadows, and U. Wartenberg. New York: American Numismatic Society.

———2011a. "The Iconography of Succession Under the Late Seleukids." Pages 41–46 in *Coins from Asia Minor and the East*. Edited by N. L. Wright. Sydney: Australian Centre for Ancient Numismatic Studies.

———2011b. "The Last Days of a Seleucid City: Jebel Khalid on the Euphrates and Its Temple." Pages 117–32 in K. Erickson and G. R. Ramsey. Wiesbaden: Harrassowitz.

Yardley, J. C., and R. Develin, trans. 1997. *Justin: Epitome of the Philippic History of Pompeius Trogus*. Oxford: Clarendon.

Yarrow, L. M. 2006. *Historiography at the End of the Republic*. Oxford: Oxford University Press.

Zangenberg, J. K. 2013. "Pure Stone: Archaeological Evidence for Jewish Purity Practices in Late Second Temple Judaism (Miqwa'ot and Stone Vessels)." Pages 537–72 in *Purity and the Forming of Religious Traditions in the Ancient Mediterranean World and Ancient Judaism*. Edited by C. Frevel and C. Nihan. Leiden: Brill.

Zeev, M. P. B. 1998. *Jewish Rights in the Roman World*. Tübingen: J. C. B. Mohr.

———2010. "Jews Among Greeks and Romans." Pages 237–55 in *Eerdmans Dictionary of Early Judaism*. Edited by J. J. Collins and D. C. Harlow. Grand Rapids: Eerdmans.

Zeitlin, S. 1918. "When Did Jerusalem Surrender to Antiochus Antiochus VII Sidetes?" *Publications of the American Jewish Historical Society* 26: 165–71.

———1922. *Megillat Ta'anit as a Source for Jewish Chronology and History in the Hellenistic and Roman Periods*. Philadelphia: Dropsie College.

Zollschan, L. T. 2004. "The Earliest Embassy to the Romans: 2 Macc. 4:11?" *Journal for the Study of Judaism* 55: 37–44.

———2012. "A Bronze Tablet from the Church of San Basilio in Rome." *Classica et Mediaevalia* 63: 217–45.

INDEX OF REFERENCES

INDEX OF AUTHORS